# SUSTAINING PREACHERS
# AND PREACHING

# SUSTAINING PREACHERS AND PREACHING

# A PRACTICAL GUIDE

George Lovell
and
Neil Richardson

t&t clark

**Published by T&T Clark International**
*A Continuum Imprint*
The Tower Building, 11 York Road, London SE1 7NX
80 Maiden Lane, Suite 704, New York, NY 10038

www.continuumbooks.com

All rights reserved. No part of this publication may be reproduced or transmitted in any form or by any means, electronic or mechanical, including photocopying, recording or any information storage or retrieval system, without permission in writing from the publishers.

© George Lovell and Neil Richardson, 2011

George Lovell and Neil Richardson have asserted their right under the Copyright, Designs and Patents Act, 1988, to be identified as the Author of this work.

British Library Cataloguing-in-Publication Data
A catalogue record for this book is available from the British Library

ISBN13 :   978-0-567-18141-1 (Hardback)
           978-0-567-50785-3 (Paperback)

Typeset by Fakenham Photosetting Ltd, Fakenham, Norfolk
Printed and bound in India by Replika Press Pvt Ltd

To the preachers of the Leeds North-East
Methodist Circuit, 2000 to 2010
With whom we have been priviliged to work and minister

# CONTENTS

**Introduction** ix
**Acknowledgements** xiii

**Part One: Preachers and Preaching** 1

Chapter 1: The Debate About Preaching: a Challenge for all the Churches 2
Chapter 2: Steps Towards Sustainable, Effective Preaching 21

**Part Two: Working Dynamics and Relationships** 33

Introduction 33
Chapter 3: The Private and Public Vocational Life Cycles of a Preacher 35
Chapter 4: The Preaching Circle 53
Chapter 5: Preachers and the Nature of Congregations 71

**Part Three: Making a Sermon** 83

Introduction 83
Chapter 6: Pressures on Preachers Today 84
Chapter 7: Using the Bible in Preaching 103
Chapter 8: Constructing a Sermon 120

**Part Four: Sustaining Developmental Support Cultures, Services and Networks** 135

Introduction 135
Chapter 9: Sustaining Personal and Interpersonal Support 137
Chapter 10: Facilitating Local Developmental Programmes and Interpersonal Support 157

| | | |
|---|---|---|
| Chapter 11: | An Ongoing Local Development Programme | 173 |
| **Part Five:** | **Sustaining Preachers in a Fast Changing World** | **197** |
| Chapter 12: | For Such a Time as This: Continuity and Change in Preaching | 198 |
| Chapter 13: | The Renewal of Preaching | 212 |
| Appendix I: | Commitment, Challenge & Faith | 228 |
| Appendix II: | What Jesus Wanted Most for his Church | 234 |

| | |
|---|---|
| **Index of Subjects** | 239 |
| **Index of Subjects** | 245 |
| **Biblical References** | 247 |

# *INTRODUCTION*

Two convictions lie behind the writing of this book: first, Christian preaching matters profoundly, and second, preaching today is at a critical juncture of challenge and opportunity. Preaching matters because it is an activity vital to the health of the Church and to the spread of the gospel in and beyond the Church. But in the view of many it has been made obsolete in our post-modern world by new, technologically-based forms of communication, and by far-reaching social, cultural and theological changes. Such changes present new challenges for preachers: how are they to communicate the faith in this post-modern, globalized world, and how are they to address the complex issues of modern life? Maintaining high standards of preaching in this demanding context is not easy.

For these reasons, this book focuses upon contemporary preaching as a discipline in its own right. Generally speaking, preaching is an integral part of acts of Christian worship with which it has an important symbiotic relationship. Preaching of the kind described in this book can make vital contributions to worship as, indeed, it can to all aspects of Christian life. However, it would require another book to examine the complex and somewhat mystic relationship between preaching and liturgical praxis.

Christian preaching as understood in this book is a world away from authoritarian, stentorian monologues. Rather, it is seen as an exercise in engagement that draws upon conversations with people in the church and in the world, which stimulates reflective thought and dialogue between people of all faiths and none. Such preaching, grounded in the scriptures and prayer and inspired by the Holy Spirit, increases the faith, renews the hope, and replenishes the love of those who hear it. While this is a highly personal activity, it is enhanced by collaborative preparation and mutual support.

The book originated from practical experience: not only the authors' own experience of preaching, but also their involvement in a local in-service training programme for preachers. It is intended to be a textbook useful to preachers, ordained and lay, of all Christian traditions, at all stages of their ministry. It addresses directly the urgent question of how to equip and sustain preachers today, covering four crucially important areas:

- *The present context.* Chapter 1 examines current challenges to preaching, restating its biblical and theological foundations; Chapter 6 looks at how preachers can live and work creatively under contemporary pressures, while Chapters 12 and 13 explore continuity and change in preaching in a fast-changing world, and the question of how preaching might be renewed.
- *Practical guidance.* Chapters 2 and 9 seek to map out the preacher's basic resources, including the resource of other people. Subsequent chapters (7 and 8) offer practical advice on the use of the Bible and on sermon construction.
- *The preacher's vocational life and its settings.* Chapters 3 and 4 set out the working dynamics and relationships of a preacher's vocational life, and how to negotiate and live with them constructively. Chapter 5 deals with the nature of congregations, and the interactions of preachers with their congregations.
- *In-service training and support.* This is a vital but long-neglected area. Preachers have been left too much to their own devices and, humanly speaking, their own resources, vital as they are. Chapters 9, 10 and 11 provide information and advice about the use and provision of in-service training and interpersonal support, with details of a still-continuing ten-year local programme of such training.

The book reflects our conviction that women and men are called to preach, and accordingly, where possible, we have tried to use inclusive language.

We believe the book offers a rationale for preaching and has a number of distinctive features. They derive not only from its origin in the locally-based training programme, but also from our combined expertise and experience of using different disciplines to train and support clergy and laity of several denominations. So biblical and theological insights are brought together with methods and processes from the behavioural sciences widely used in church, community and consultancy work.

Throughout, we have presented the range of interdisciplinary tools in ways that preachers, who would not claim to be professionals in any of the fields, can use to good effect to develop their own vocations and to promote and provide interdisciplinary in-service training and interpersonal support.

These support services, rarely available to preachers, need to be made available to them throughout their ministry, in ways similar to in-service training in other walks of life. Pre- and in-service support should be all of a piece, the one following directly and naturally from the other. Preachers in training should be inducted into using such means of support, just as they are taught the importance of life-long study. We believe them to be increasingly necessary if preachers are to achieve and maintain the all-round quality of preaching currently needed today.

Whether it should be compulsory is a difficult question. Any form of training is most effective when participants enter into it willingly. Sadly, experience shows that many of those most in need of in-service training will not use it if it is voluntary and are unlikely to benefit from it if it is obligatory. However, although there are strong arguments for making it compulsory to maintain standards, they need to be resisted. Instead, a new culture is needed in which in-service training and support are accepted as normative: one which acquires authority simply by virtue of its results. We believe that this will, as implied in the double entendre in the book title, sustain preachers and help them in their preaching to be more effective in sustaining members of their congregations and the mission of the Church.

An American theologian, John Cobb, wrote that there will be no renewal of the Church without the renewal of preaching. We share that conviction, recognizing that both can happen only with the help of the Holy Spirit, and offer this book as a contribution to that end.

George Lovell and Neil Richardson.
April 2010

# ACKNOWLEDGEMENTS

This book, like the preaching it advocates, grew out of many conversations and much discussion. Its origins lie in an extensive in-service training programme in which we were involved with the lay and ordained preachers of the Leeds North-East Methodist Circuit. Sharing in the exciting and memorable conferences, preaching projects, and self-programming groups was a great privilege. We are indebted to all the preachers who participated in this project for all that we learned from working with them. We are particularly grateful to Catherine Frieze and Anne Vautrey who were co-facilitators of the project for some seven years and to John Summerwill who set up and edited the website, a resource additional to this book. It is not possible to name everyone else who made significant contributions, but we record our gratitude here.

Convinced of the value of the work done and its importance to a wider ecumenical constituency of preachers, some of those involved encouraged us to write up the project, particularly Peter Harper, Peter Howdle, David Laycock and John Summerwill. We gratefully acknowledge these promptings, which reinforced our own feelings that there was a need for such a book. We are thankful for all the help, encouragement and support we received during its preparation and writing. We are especially grateful to Colin Lake, Val Ogden, Stanley Pearson, Steve Phillipson, Adam Sanders, John Summerwill, Adrian Williams and Catherine Widdicombe, who read various chapters in draft and made many helpful suggestions; to Mary Patchett, who computerized the diagrams; and to Pat Brooke, Val Faint, Anne Millett, Susan Philo, Hazel Rayner and Sheila Ryder for their help with typing. We are grateful to Peter Howdle and to Stanley Pearson, respectively, for permission to include a diagram and to quote from an e-mail.

We are also grateful to Thomas Kraft, the associate Publisher for Theology, for believing in the value of the book when it was only at the stage of being a 'proposal' and for his continuing enthusiasm and practical guidance. We are grateful too, to Kim Storry and David Defew of Fakenham Photosetting for being so helpful and professional throughout the proof reading stage. Last but not least, our profound gratitude goes to Molly and Rhiannon, our wives, for their moral support and much practical help.

George Lovell and Neil Richardson.
April 2010

# Part 1

# PREACHERS AND PREACHING

## Chapter 1

# THE DEBATE ABOUT PREACHING: A CHALLENGE FOR ALL THE CHURCHES

All is not well with Christian preaching today. Many churchgoers find sermons at best mediocre and at worst decidedly thin, simplistic or downright irrelevant to life as they know it. Very busy preachers, especially ordained ministers, sometimes wonder whether hours spent preparing a sermon is the best use of their time. So it is not surprising that, in many places, the sermon is being replaced – increasingly, it seems – by PowerPoint presentations, drama, short addresses and the like.

We do not under-estimate the potential of new forms of worship. But this book is written in the conviction that preaching matters. People may joke about sermons, or heave a sigh of relief when a sermon ends sooner than they expected. Overworked ministers may be glad of a week when they do not have to write a sermon. But if preaching is a core activity of the Church – and this chapter will argue that it is – a lack of good preaching will lead to a Church which is seriously deficient. Similarly, preaching which is anaemic will result in an anaemic Church. There is unlikely to be a renewal of the churches without a renewal of preaching.

But we should not focus solely on the Church. The fragile state of the world poses the question: if there is supposed to be a world-saving quality about the Church's message, can there be a more urgent task than communicating it? The central questions here are all to do with God: God's reality, God's nature and God's purpose for humankind and the world. Is there a Creator who is extraordinarily committed to his creation, and who passionately wills it to flourish?

Another set of questions arises naturally from these questions about God: what kind of people are human beings meant to be; what is the best way to live and what really matters in life? Is there a life-enhancing wisdom which can save the world from self-destruction? If, indeed, the Christian gospel addresses questions as crucial as these, then people outside as well as inside the Church need to know. The world needs to know if there is a Creator who cares that his world survives and flourishes, rather than self-destructively implodes. This also is why preaching matters.

Although this book is written primarily for preachers whose preaching is likely to be solely, or largely, within the four walls of a church, it is important to recall how, in times of revival and renewal, preaching has broken out of this ecclesiastical confinement. It needs to do so again, even though it is likely to be in new ways that we cannot at present foresee.

On the face of it, the less than healthy state of preaching today is a puzzle: it is a core activity of the Church, and the world desperately needs a world-saving Gospel, yet a crisis seems to hover over preaching in the so-called 'developed' world. Practitioners of preaching seem unsure of what they are doing, unconvinced that it is worthwhile, or perhaps unsure of what they are supposed to be saying. If that is so, we need to address the problems behind what we may call – without undue exaggeration – a crisis in contemporary preaching.

One dimension of the problem is the pressure on many preachers. Ordained ministers of all Christian traditions find themselves with far more to do than can be fitted comfortably into a six-day, or even a seven-day week. They do not easily find or make adequate time to prepare a sermon that ideally will help the congregation to understand more fully the difficult Bible passages which crop up with annoying frequency in the lectionary. As if that were not enough, the events of the previous week – an earthquake or headlines about our 'broken society' – may call out for informed Christian comment from the pulpit.

But even if they are able to make the time to prepare a sermon, not all will be convinced that that will be the most important thing to be done. There are other pressing claims on their time: visiting a person critically ill in hospital, supporting a colleague suffering from stress, dealing with the countless practical details of church life, because there are not enough people to whom such responsibilities can be delegated, and so on. But in spite of all these pressures, if preaching is as important as we are suggesting, a sermon merits far more time than a couple of hours on Saturday evening.

It is, of course, not only ordained preachers who are busy. Lay preachers are under similar pressure. It is a tall order to make time, after getting home from a demanding day at work, to prepare the sermon to be preached next Sunday. They, too, find it hard to give preaching the attention it deserves, and to wrestle with the challenges of Christian belief and living today; we return to this question in Chapter 6.

Quite apart from pressures of time, preachers may well ponder sometimes the strangeness of what they are doing. Speaking at public meetings is no longer a common phenomenon in modern life. In education many teachers and lecturers will offer something which is either interactive in its style, or supported by texts and pictures on PowerPoint. By contrast, the traditional sermon appears old-fashioned, even counter-cultural.

There are other powerful factors at work today which sap the confidence of preachers in what they are doing: far-reaching changes in society, phenomenal advances in science and technology and continuing theological ferment are just three of these factors, and we shall need to keep returning to them in this book. We also note how profoundly these influences are affecting not only preachers, but also the congregations to which they preach.

So in this first chapter, against a background of uncertainty about – if not crisis in – preaching, we shall look at some fundamental questions. First, are there some widespread misconceptions about preaching which need to be cleared away (if that is possible), in order to give us a clearer idea of what preaching is supposed to be? But even if we dispel such misunderstandings, that does not dispose of the question which these days is never far away: 'Has preaching had its day?' While certain kinds of preaching probably are, or should be, a thing of the past, we shall argue that through all the changes of our time, the ministry of preaching remains, and must remain, central to the Church's life and mission.

But the sheer rate of change today poses a further set of questions: how different will be the preaching of the future? Do fundamental assumptions need to be examined? Should familiar working practices be revised? The extent and, it seems, accelerating rate of change have contributed to make preaching today a particularly difficult and challenging task. What will be needed to sustain effective preaching?

I Misunderstandings About Preaching:

Preaching is not simply preachers doing their own thing from the pulpit or – as happens more often these days – from the lectern, or somewhere else at the front of the church. No one would dream of saying something like that about the service of Holy Communion: it's just the celebrant doing their own thing. Admittedly, preaching and communion do not seem to be parallel activities: one has a liturgy, with words prescribed, the other does not. Yet just as Scripture and Christian tradition have invested the Eucharist, and Christian worship in general, with a particular shape and content, so the sermon is not something preachers make up as they go along.

It is not difficult to see how such misunderstandings about preaching arise. Some preaching is idiosyncratic, if not downright eccentric. The writer recalls a sermon he heard as a boy on an obscure text from the Old Testament:

> Jehoshaphat made ships of Tharshish to go to Ophir for gold: but they went not; for the ships were broken at Eziongeber.
>
> (1 Kgs. 22.48)

In fact that particular sermon was anything but eccentric, as the preacher on that occasion was gifted and experienced. The unusual text became the focus of a powerful sermon about coping with disappointed hopes and tragedy.

Preaching is a very personal form of communication. That is part of its uniqueness. But there is a world of difference between a personal communication based on Scripture and tradition, and an offering which owes more to the whim or eccentricity of the preacher than to anything else. It will help our discussion if we can clarify the source and nature of the preacher's authority.

*The Preacher's Authority*

This authority can be misunderstood by preacher and congregation alike. The preacher may sincerely believe that God told him what to say from the pulpit. That does not mean he is correct in that view. But such a conviction may make him particularly sensitive, if not impervious, to criticism. From their side, members of the congregation may well register, even if unconsciously, reservations, doubts and disagreements about the sermon. At the same time, they may feel that they should not be criticizing or questioning in this way. The old idea that the preacher is 'six feet above contradiction' dies hard.

There are two sources of the preacher's authority, both of which are important. They are 'called' to preach. Such a call, in churches which use lay preachers, may not be connected to a sense of vocation to ordained ministry. Sometimes the call to preach does precede the call to ordination, but however or whenever it comes, personal conviction is important: preachers preach because they feel this is what they must do.

Another source of the preacher's authority is the Church. In most churches a person stands in the pulpit because they have been authorized or permitted to do so. The Church does not normally invite anyone who feels called to do so to have a go. It is true that there has been a place since earliest times for spontaneous contributions in Christian meetings for worship (e.g. 1 Cor. 14.26), but the Church has also found it wise and helpful to regulate such utterances in public gatherings, (as this early letter of Paul shows – v. 40).

Yet, important as those two sources of authority are – the personal call and the Church's authorization – there is a deeper level still to which we must go, if we are to arrive at an understanding of the authority of preaching which is soundly biblical and theological.

'Soundly biblical' may be an oppressive idea to many. A cursory reading of the Bible, and particularly the Old Testament, could suggest that the normal style of the preacher is a thunderous imitation of the prophetic message: 'Thus says the Lord'. Yet a closer inspection of Scripture shows that God's preferred way of communicating with us is not as megaphonic as first appears. Almost from the beginning of the biblical story, God is portrayed as engaged in the search for conversation partners and covenant partners. In this quest, with all its tortuous twists and turns, dialogue is common. So too are questions – puzzled, angry, protesting questions – from God's (mostly failed) human partners. So a fundamentalist approach to the Bible, which tends to exclude discussion, question and protest, obscures the real nature of biblical revelation, and is a travesty of the Bible's authority. That authority is to be construed differently – and that will help us grasp the true authority of preaching as well.

In his book *Voices of Authority*, the Roman Catholic theologian, Nicholas Lash, suggests that authority is fundamentally a source of life, truth and growth. Such an understanding of authority seems to fit the conclusion in Matthew's Gospel to the Sermon on the Mount:

> Now when Jesus had finished saying these things, the crowds were astonished at his teaching, for he taught them as one having authority, and not as their scribes
>
> (Mt. 7.28–9).

We must avoid caricaturing the scribes, about whom we know little. But if we may imaginatively paraphrase the crowd's reaction to Jesus' preaching in modern English, they will have said something like 'This sounds authentic; this is real; this is about life'.

*The Aim and Character of Preaching*

This understanding of authority goes to the heart of what preaching is supposed to achieve: it is meant to enlighten, liberate and give life. The enlightenment given through authentic preaching is not a matter of learning that St Paul may not, after all, have written Ephesians. Rather, it consists of seeing life in clearer focus than before; seeing our neighbour without the distorting lens of prejudice, suspicion or fear; seeing ourselves as the children of God we are created to be, and, underlying and enabling all these things, seeing more clearly the God revealed in Jesus Christ. (See also the 'Aims and Outcomes' of preaching in Chapter 6).

Similarly, true preaching liberates – for example, liberates people from the burdens God does not want them to carry, part of the meaning of what the Christian gospel calls 'sin'. And preaching aims to fulfil the intention of Jesus to give life (Jn. 10.10). As the late Bishop John Taylor wrote, 'God is not so much interested in making us religious, as in making us alive'. In more explicitly Christian language, the authority of a good sermon will be experienced by the way in which it increases the faith, renews the hope and replenishes the love of those who hear it.

So preaching can never be preaching *at* a congregation. A sermon in which the preacher unwisely decides to have a go at his congregation will not only be counter-productive; it will also be barely recognizable as Christian preaching. Even a properly critical and challenging sermon will, if it has authority, still enlighten, liberate and help people grow. But such authority in preaching is not easily come by. It will come from somewhere deep inside preachers: the fruit of prayer, faithful discipleship, thoughtful reflection and genuine love for the people to whom they preach.

Of course, in exploring the nature and source of the preacher's authority, we should not ignore some basic practicalities. If a preacher's trend of thought is difficult to follow, or if he/she is simply inaudible, it is difficult to see how people will experience his preaching in the life-giving way envisaged here. Yet, if this discussion is on the right lines, it will be clear that authority in preaching is not to be measured primarily by the volume of sound, the quality of the rhetoric, or the dogmatic style of the preacher. It is something altogether deeper and more spiritual.

*What Kind of Communication is Preaching?*

Alongside misunderstandings about the authority and purpose of preaching, there may also be some imbalance in contemporary views about the aim of communication. The communications revolution of the last few decades might lead us to suppose that its aim is the sharing of information. One of the great inventions of our time, the internet, disseminates information on an unprecedented scale. Yet the younger generation in particular knows another important purpose of communication: to establish and maintain relationships, by mobile phones, texting, Facebook and so on. The personal character of preaching, arising from the personal nature of Christian faith, means that relationships are an important test of preaching: for example, has the sermon refreshed people in a way that makes them more ready to greet each other than perhaps they were when they arrived at church? A congregation may, indeed, learn from a sermon something they did not know before, but that is not its main purpose.

Apart from an undue emphasis on the imparting of information, the mass media today may distort our perceptions of preaching in another way. Is the Sunday sermon simply the preacher's 'party political broadcast'? Is it his or her opportunity to put their 'spin' on current affairs, or to urge the faithful to still greater efforts in raising money for the church restoration fund? In our discussion of the authority of preaching, we have suggested that something altogether deeper is, or should be, going on.

There are different theories of communication. At first sight, preaching seems to resemble what has been called 'the basic cybernetic model':

Sender — message — receiver[1]

This might be an appropriate model for preaching if its basic aim is to communicate information. But it is not. There is far more going on in preaching – or there should be:

> The preacher must not be restricted to the active role of the sender, nor the hearer to the passive role of the receiver ...[2]

Other theories of communication recognize that communication is a two-way process. A congregation listening passively (it would seem) to

---

[1] Achim Hartner & Holger Eschmann, *Learning To Preach today. A Guide for Communicators and Listeners* (Calver, Sheffield: Cliff College Publishing, 2004) pp. 167–8).

[2] *Idem*, p. 170.

a sermon might suggest otherwise. But a sermon is really an extract from a broader dialogue between preacher and congregation. As we noted earlier, the authority of preaching is to be measured by whether the preaching is the source of life, truth and growth. So it follows that the relationship between the preacher and the congregation in their communication with each other is crucially important. Even if the preacher is a visitor to a church, that will still be true. Does the preacher want the best, Christianly understood, for the congregation? And does the congregation trust the preacher sufficiently to be open to receive it?

Important though the relationship between preacher and congregation is, still more is involved in the communication which takes place in church. Everyone comes to church with their own particular history: their entire life and, more immediately, what they have experienced in the past week. A pastorally sensitive preacher will have thought – and prayed – about this. The congregation, too, will see the preacher, whether they know him or not, in all his particularity. He or she stands before the congregation as one human being before another. That is the essence of the task.

So we are suggesting that far more is involved in preaching than sharing information, even though it must include teaching the Christian faith. Preaching and teaching, of course, are closely related, and have been so from the Church's earliest days. They may overlap, but they differ in intention and in the hoped-for outcomes. Teachers intend their hearers to know and understand, and that will be the outcome they want most. The preacher's intention is deeper and wider. A person preaches, not so much because they know and understand what they are preaching, like a geography teacher teaching geography; preachers preach because they believe, and wish to create or nurture the same faith in their hearers. And faith embraces the whole person, not just the mind.

So preaching cannot be readily equated with other forms of communication. Above all, its business is a message about God – the Christian Gospel. This, and the context of worship within which it normally happens, makes preaching a unique form of communication. This is why the perception of a sermon as a monologue is not the whole picture – a theme to which we return in the next chapter. But before we come to that, there are other challenging questions about preaching to be faced.

## II Has Preaching Had Its Day?

### *What Has Happened?*

Newcomers to church, especially young newcomers, are likely to find preaching a strange activity. There may be a screen in church on which the preacher's main themes are projected, but that is unlikely, so for the duration of the sermon the preacher is the focus of attention. By contrast, even a party political broadcast these days is unlikely to stretch the tolerance of viewers by zooming in on the speaker for more than five minutes at a time.

Does our newcomer's educational background give them any clues about how they should respond during the sermon? Is it permissible to interrupt with a question or comment, in the way that they might at school or college when the teacher or lecturer is using an interactive whiteboard? Does the preacher take questions in mid-sermon? Are you allowed to register disagreement? Is there no equivalent in church of Prime Minister's Question Time?

We may be overstating the case, but it must be conceded that preaching these days is a counter-cultural activity for these – and other – reasons. How long is the average person's attention span? Television researchers tell us it is no more than three or four minutes. Makers of children's television programmes work on the principle that attention-winning events need to occur every thirty seconds if they are not to lose their viewers to a rival channel.

So there is bound to be a question mark over preaching today. If we cast our eye back over Christian history, the sermon seems to have had an unchallenged place from earliest times. But few, until now, had doubted that preaching had a rightful, central place in the Church's life and mission. Has that time now come? Jonathan Hustler addresses this question in the final chapter of his book on the shape of the sermon through Christian history.[3] By the 1970s, he argues, there was a lack of confidence in preaching in many parts of the western Church. There were several reasons for this: the rapid decline (in Britain, at least) in church attendance; a growing sense that 'old certainties were no longer to be trusted', and from the 1960s onwards, far-reaching changes in social attitudes and communications, which put the preacher under greater pressure. These changes also had a subtle effect on language: 'words did not only become

---

[3] Jonathan Hustler, *Making the Words Acceptable. The Shape of the Sermon in Christian History* (London: Epworth, 2009). (Quotations from pp. 167 and 170).

cheap ... they became untrustworthy'. In the light of all this, how is the Church to respond?

*What is Preaching?*

'Preaching', unfortunately, is a limiting word. To seasoned church-goers, it suggests churches, pulpits and three-point monologues lasting fifteen or twenty minutes, or even longer. The very word 'sermon' invites jokes about being bored and nodding off to sleep. It is worth observing that the New Testament has a much richer vocabulary to denote the activity we call 'preaching'. The word which perhaps comes nearest to our word preach is the word 'proclaim' (in Greek *kerussein*), but other verbs used in the New Testament suggest that the fundamental task of 'proclaiming' the Kingdom of God, or Jesus as the Christ, also involved teaching, encouraging, explaining, discussing.

The locations in which this variegated activity we call preaching took place varied enormously as well, since there were no church buildings then. Jesus began by preaching in a synagogue, according to St Luke (Lk. 4.16–31), but most of his time was spent in the open air. Similarly, Paul preached and taught both indoors and out of doors, the Mediterranean climate being more congenial for such an activity than more northern climes. And while, according to Luke, he usually started at the local synagogue, he didn't necessarily continue his preaching there, (Acts 19.8–10).

So, for the moment at least, we need to release preaching from its contemporary ecclesiastical straitjacket, and ask the fundamental question, 'What is it?' We must not define it too narrowly as a fifteen or twenty minute monologue – usually with three points – delivered in church from the pulpit. Earlier in the chapter I suggested that the aims and intended outcomes of preaching are wider and deeper than those of teaching: 'preaching is an operation from faith to faith'.[4] Preaching at its best is an *event* – an existential event that, however imperceptibly or partially, is meant to transform the existence of those who hear. This is the fundamental reason why it is irreplaceable.

*'Truth Through Personality'*

One definition of preaching which has commanded widespread assent since it was first published is that offered by the nineteenth century American preacher, Phillips Brooks. For him, preaching is

---

[4] John Stacey, *Preaching Re-assessed*, (London: Epworth, 1980), p. 19.

the communication of 'truth through personality'. We shall need to discuss each of these important words.

'Truth' both underlines the contemporary problem with preaching, and at the same time shows why the Church cannot abandon it. Ours is a suspicious age. People have grown suspicious of claims and sales propaganda – of anyone, in fact, with an 'agenda'. It is tempting to go with the post-modern flow and simply encourage people to have an experience, embark on their own personal journey, get in touch with their inmost selves, and so on. All these aims may be laudable, but much depends on the nature of the experience, the direction of the journey, and what we find deep inside ourselves. None of these approaches, however, is to do with truth 'outside' or beyond ourselves. Indeed, many today would deny that such truth exists at all: there is only what is 'true for you' and 'true for me'. In any case, the strident claims of modern religious fundamentalisms suggest to many that any claim to absolute truth is bound to be oppressive and constraining.

Christian faith quietly but insistently equates 'truth' with Christ. In this it follows the claim found on the lips of Jesus in John's Gospel (Jn 14.6). But the same Gospel makes another claim about 'truth': it 'will make you free' (Jn 8.32). This is not the place to explore that claim in depth. But if we are to see authentic Christian preaching for what it is, we need to consider not only the source of truth, according to Christian faith, but also the nature of that source.

According to Christianity the source of truth is God, and the nature of God is love. So *this* truth is not so much a dogmatic claim as a life-giving experience; it is a truth which, in some deep, mysterious sense, makes people free. Human beings are never more truly themselves than when they love. The seventeenth century poet and priest, Thomas Traherne, speaks for the whole Christian tradition in his claim that:

> By loving [a soul] attains itself. Love also being the end of Souls... They were made to love, and are dark and vain and comfortless till they do it.

Unless this understanding and experience of truth and love inform both preaching and the preacher from start to finish, truth claims are likely to be oppressive and destructively divisive. But this is the theological basis for insisting that preaching is an event.

The communication of truth might still suggest a message which is absolute and non-negotiable. This might seem to rule out the second word in Phillips Brooks' definition of preaching: 'personality'. Yet more needs to be said. St Paul's own definition of preaching will help us grasp the essentials of Christian preaching, and what Phillips Brooks meant by 'truth through personality'. In his second letter to the Corinthians, Paul wrote,

> For we do not proclaim ourselves; we proclaim Jesus Christ as Lord and ourselves as your slaves for Jesus' sake
>
> (2 Cor. 4.5).

The twofold 'ourselves' highlights the paradox of preaching. In some churches it is the normal practice, before a service, for a leading layperson to pray with the preacher before they go into the church itself. On one occasion, one such person offered the following prayer: 'Lord, bless Thy servant who will preach Thy word today, and, as he enters Thy house, blot him out'. The last part of this prayer illustrates rather dramatically what Paul meant by 'we preach not ourselves'. Preaching can never be an opportunity for self-display or self-promotion. It is a profoundly self-effacing activity.

Yet '... we proclaim ... ourselves as your slaves for Jesus' sake'. Preaching, even though self-effacing, remains a very personal form of communication. This personal character of preaching, according to Paul, is inseparable from its content, i.e. Jesus Christ. There are two essential aspects to this. First, the Christian faith celebrates the mystery of a Creator who shared our human life in Jesus, and, second, the deeply human character of Christianity is confirmed and filled out by its central theological tenet and moral imperatives: God is love, and humans are called to love God and to love their neighbour as themselves.

This means that, in the Christian view of things, relations with other people are as important as our relationship with God. We cannot relate to God in love without relating to our fellow human beings in a similar way. A church at its best embodies this truly human ideal. Of course, the Church as a whole falls a long way short, but it cannot escape its fundamental requirement: 'Love one another'. In this essentially personal tradition, preachers stand in the pulpit (or elsewhere) *in the service of those to whom they speak.*

All of this is crucial to a proper understanding of preaching, and why it must remain central to the Church's life. It is a deeply personal form of communication. One human being stands before other human beings and speaks from the heart about all that matters most: life, love, justice, peace and God. In doing so, preachers really have nowhere to hide. In practice, they may do all sorts of things — give a slide show on the Holy Land, talk about their hopes for a new church organ, and so on – for all of which there may well be a proper place. But real preaching honours the central place of what has been called 'the human face of God' in the Christian revelation, the Christian faith, and therefore the Christian Church.

So preaching is 'truth through personality' – inescapably human. But there is a second aspect to the humanness of preaching. In an earlier letter to Corinth, the apostle described his first visit to them:

> I came to you in weakness and in fear and in much trembling
>
> (1 Cor. 2.3).

'Weakness' here carries a particular meaning. Earlier in the same letter Paul had written about the weakness of God revealed in the crucified Christ (1.18–25). So the apostle's weakness on his first visit was not so much his natural limitations – though it included those – but rather a weakness which he *voluntarily assumed* for the sake of the Corinthians, the same 'weakness' he had perceived in the cross of Christ (1 Cor. 1.25).

A late twentieth century description of one man's evangelism in a remote part of Africa conveys well this weakness of preaching. In *Christianity Re-discovered*, Vincent Donovan, a Catholic priest, described his first visits to the Masai people:

> Here I was at last, face to face with an adult pagan people, with nothing between me and them but the gospel of Jesus Christ ... Each day in that brisk, early morning hour, still unheated by the equatorial sun, there in the Masai highlands ... As I stood waiting for them to gather, I was conscious of the knot in my stomach, wondering if this were the day it would all blow up in my face ...[5]

Donovan was describing a particular experience in a particular country. But the fundamental humanness is the same wherever someone authentically preaches the gospel of Jesus: the same risk, the same vulnerability: 'nothing between me and them but the gospel of Jesus Christ'.

This also is part of what it means to say that the communication of Christian truth can only be through 'personality'. It explains, too, why the authority of Christian preaching is a world away from authoritarian, stentorian monologues. Proof of its genuineness lies in its outcome: does it communicate life, truth and growth?

This is why preaching is both a deeply self-effacing activity and

---

[5] Vincent J. Donovan, *Christianity Rediscovered* (SCM, 1982), p. 24.

also a very personal means of communication. Such preaching – we note the poverty of English once more – need not be in the form of a traditional sermon; it need not be delivered from a pulpit, nor even in a church, although a church service of worship remains its natural home. But whenever or however preaching occurs, its integrity will be seen in its content, its humanness and its outcomes. The nature of the Christian gospel means that its natural means of communication will always be from person to person.

## III Preaching in a Fast-changing World

So far in this introductory chapter we have reviewed some widespread misunderstandings of preaching, and tried to respond to the suspicion that preaching has had its day. We have argued that at its best it reflects the heart of Christian faith, and therefore also the Christian Church at its best: a person-to-person communication, enhancing life, sharing truth, and enabling growth in the basic building blocks of Christian living, namely faith, hope and love.

But there is another dimension to the challenge which the Church faces today. If preaching is to be sustained and engaged in effectively, we need to look long and hard at the vastly changed situation in which we now find ourselves. The theme of change is one to which we shall keep returning (especially in Chapters 6 and 12). Here we build on the observations of Hustler, noted in the previous section, and take a preliminary look at some of those changes which have a direct bearing on the preacher and the preacher's task. Although this discussion comes from a British context, there are parallels, or partial parallels in other countries, particularly in western Europe.

### *The End of Christendom*

Social scientists and others still debate what the word 'secular' means, and therefore what a secular society really is. Beyond dispute, however, is the dramatically changed position of the churches in western Europe and, perhaps increasingly, parts of eastern Europe. We mention Europe in particular because for well over a millennium it was dominated by the Church and by rulers who professed to be Christian, and often imposed the faith on their subjects. So villages and towns grew up round the parish church or cathedral; the Christian 'writ' ran everywhere. By contrast, in new communities today the churches find it hard to establish and maintain a visible presence of any kind; Christian voices and influences increasingly struggle to be heard and felt. In this vastly changed context, the preacher is as marginal as the Church. As we shall have occasion to note in subsequent chapters, how we preach and what we preach are bound to be affected by this vastly different situation.

*Sundays*

The growth of Sunday trading in western Europe illustrates this development in a particularly sharp way. For the most part, the churches have been slow to respond to the changed pattern of Sunday. But it would perhaps be fairer to say that we have not known how to respond. Should churches change the times of their services? But the prevalence of sport on Sunday mornings, the widespread demise of evening services, and the general busyness of almost everyone do not suggest that alternative times for worship would be any more popular. There have been successful experiments with short informal services in the late afternoon in some places, but these are few and far between. There has also been an increase in the number of services held during the week, though churches would be unwise to discard the special place of Sunday in the Christian tradition.

Sunday trading, however, is only the tip of a much bigger iceberg. Working hours are different, with more people working on Sundays. Above all, Sunday has become a family day, as families who no longer live as near to each other as they once did take the opportunity to visit. It is also relevant to note that many people are so busy during the week, and on Saturdays too, with the result that there is more pressure to make Sunday, if possible, 'time for me' or 'time for us'.

The very nature of Sunday inevitably impacts on the approach of preachers to their task. They might consider, for example, how many other things members of the congregation could be doing instead of coming to church. As one preacher has written, 'Love your people just for being there in church on Sunday!'[6]

*Other Cultural Changes*

Many other cultural changes have a bearing on the task of preaching. The slow tortuous progression towards greater equality between women and men has, not surprisingly, affected the churches. A careful reading of the New Testament should have persuaded the Church that it should anyway have been leading the way in this development, rather than struggling to catch up. New Testament scholars

---

[6] Brad R. Braxton, *Preaching Paul* (Nashville: Abingdon, 2004), p. 41.

have observed that the long list of names cited by St Paul in Romans 16 includes a number of women in positions of leadership. Even one of the two people called 'apostles' in v. 7 has turned out to be a woman called Junia, not, as older translations have it, a man called Junias.[7]

So it is natural for women to take their place alongside men in the Church's preaching ministry. We are still exploring the often subtle ways in which women and men differ, apart from the obvious physical differences. It is sometimes suggested that women, more than men, value working in teams. However that may be, one of the major themes of this book is that preachers have worked for too long in not-so-splendid isolation, and so the advent of women into the ordained ministry of some Churches in the late twentieth century may be one of the ways in which, under the providence of God, a richer ministry of preaching might be discovered. We return to this theme in the next chapter.

*Christian Tradition and Language in the Post-Modern Era*

But now we need to look more closely at what has been happening within the churches. It would be unwise to make sweeping generalizations, and yet there have been clear signs of what we might call the fragmentation of the tradition. We look first at what has been happening to language.

'Words mean what I want them to mean'. These words from Lewis Carroll's *Alice Through the Looking Glass* have always been true up to a point, but we may have become more aware of this than previous generations. After all, if language has always changed and developed, it should not surprise us if, in a fast-changing world, it changes at an even faster rate. New words come into being, and even old ones change their meaning; on the lips of younger people in particular 'awesome', 'wicked' and 'cool' have acquired quite new meanings.

---

[7] There are other verses in Paul where the apostle seems a long way from acknowledging what has been called 'equality of regard' for women and men (e.g. 'Wives obey your husbands', Col. 3.18). Such verses need to be understood against their social and cultural background. If such wives were the only Christian in their home – and even if they were not – it would have caused scandal, and, above all, in an honour-based culture, brought shame on their husbands if they disobeyed. More difficult is 1 Cor. 14.34, where Paul appears to say 'Let wives (women? The Greek could mean either) be silent in the churches (literally, 'assemblies'). The words are probably addressed to a specific, local problem in Corinth, the precise nature of which we can't now identify. But it is clear that women at Corinth prophesied (1 Cor. 11.5).

More important for the preacher are old words which lose their resonance and purchase. Words with a long biblical and Christian pedigree become problematical or more enigmatic than they used to be. 'Sin' and 'salvation' are two words among many which could be mentioned. But the problem for the preacher does not stop there. A few years ago a member of my congregation in Leeds observed that preachers use words which, for them, have a particular meaning, but they may not realize that the congregation understands those words quite differently – or else doesn't understand them at all. The word 'orthodox', for example, means different things to different people, and so, perhaps, does the word 'God'. So the message intended may not be the message received, and preachers face the challenge of minting new words and images to express the Christian gospel today.

Today, however, we are facing the fragmentation of the Christian tradition in western Europe – and, increasingly perhaps, north America too. There are many complex reasons for this. One contributory factor, however, over many decades now, is a diminishing familiarity with the Bible. Church life in Britain was dominated for three centuries and more by one English translation of the Bible, the Authorized Version. Now its stately language sounds dated, and people hearing it for the first time would struggle to make sense of most passages. In its place have come many different translations and paraphrases, so it is harder for the average churchgoer to remember much of the Bible by heart; they hear too many different versions for that to be possible. Alongside this development, the recitation and memorization of passages from literature, including the Bible, play a less significant role at all levels of education in many countries. Not least, the Bible seems to be read less often even by regular churchgoers. All of this adds to the challenge facing the Christian preacher today.

There is yet another strand to what we are calling the fragmentation of the Christian tradition in our time. New Christian hymns and songs have proliferated; the words of the best of them are uplifting, and the music of the best of them often beautiful. But the end result is often unseemly arguments about competing theologies and worship styles, with a preacher perhaps struggling, like an ecclesiastical restaurateur, to cater for all tastes.

*Congregations of Great Diversity*

Words change their meaning, versions of the Bible vary, contemporary hymns and songs vary even more. Are congregations too more varied? Admittedly, the age profile of many congregations is worryingly high, but there is still a remarkable variety. Because many people travel more widely and enjoy more leisure, the range of experience of many congregations is often astonishing. A third of the congregation has been abroad in the last year, the different jobs done by those in full-time work is fascinatingly varied, and so on.

There are likely to be other kinds of variety, which, if not visible, are increasingly acknowledged. Church congregations include people who have been divorced, or who have divorced and re-married or who live with a same or opposite sex partner. There will be others whose families have been affected by divorce. Although church congregations may not entirely reflect changing family and other social patterns, these patterns will still be there.

There is a third way in which members of a congregation may differ from many congregations in the past. We live in an age which is not only suspicious of authority and cynical about claims to truth, but one beset by questions and doubts. Sadly, the Church is not always comfortable in such an environment. A long-standing church member recently asked his minister whether there was room in the church for people like him with questions and doubts. He came away with what he felt was a very ambivalent response.

Many other factors help to make the preacher's task today a particularly challenging one. We cannot easily measure the effect on us all of our exposure day by day to newspapers, television, radio and advertising. Much of what we absorb through these channels – often without realizing it – is a thorough mixture of the good, the bad and the indifferent. But it means that a preacher will normally be faced in church by a congregation which has spent more time exposed to the mixed values of the wider world than to the influence of the Bible. We return to the challenge of preaching to diverse congregations coping with a formidably complex world in Chapter 6.

The rate and extent of change over the last few decades have been enormous. We have touched briefly on only a few of those changes as they affect the life of the churches, and especially the task of the preacher. Whatever the roots of such change, whatever future changes there might be, the conclusion is unavoidable: the task of the preacher today is a daunting one.

CONCLUSION:

The character of the Christian faith and of the Christian Church, rooted in eternity, yet down to earth, human and vulnerable, makes Christian preaching unique. This is why the truest test of its authenticity is whether it enables growth in faith, freedom and love. It is also the theological foundation of Philipps Brooks' definition of preaching as the communication of truth through personality.

So preaching cannot be an optional extra in the life of the Church. Nor can it ever be a means of communication left behind in the wake of the electronic revolution in communication in our time. Its currency is not information, nor even opinions and values – not even 'Kingdom values' – but the life-giving truth whose source Christians believe to be the Creator God. In seeking to share this truth, all preachers, from the beginning to the end of their ministry, are dependent on the Spirit of God, present in all their endeavours, and all their relationships. That is a dependence which underlies everything written in the chapters which follow.

So the challenge for the Church is this: if it is to find renewal in the years to come, its preaching needs to be renewed. The renewal of preaching may not be the sole requirement or condition for the renewal of the churches, but it is surely fundamental. Yet, as this chapter has tried to show, the context in which the preacher works today, is as demanding as it has ever been. This is why congregations and preachers alike need to ask with some urgency: how may preaching and preachers be sustained today?

## Chapter 2

## *STEPS TOWARDS SUSTAINABLE, EFFECTIVE PREACHING*

In Chapter 1 we argued that if the Church today is to experience renewal, its preaching will need to be renewed. Preaching is a core activity of the Church, however unfashionable or ineffective it may sometimes be. It takes both its content and its character from Jesus, so its authority is of the kind which the gospels attribute to Jesus: it promotes life, truth and growth. It is 'the communication of truth through personality', (Phillips Brooks' definition). This means that authentic preaching is both a deeply human form of communication, and at the same time an event rooted deeply and mysteriously in God.

Yet even when we have established the unique, irreplaceable character of preaching, a fragmented, fast-changing world poses an immense challenge to the preacher as we saw in Chapter 1. So we turn in this chapter to the practical question of how a preaching ministry can be sustained today. As everyone who preaches regularly knows only too well, Sundays come round with remarkable speed; there are only six days between each one!

Resourcing preachers is not a new problem, although this challenge confronts us today with greater sharpness and fresh urgency. In the past it was assumed that preachers usually found their own resources. Ordained ministers may have been less busy, or at least had more time to think and read in an era when the pace of life was markedly slower. What has changed? Books are still a valuable resource for preachers, if the books are available, and preachers can afford to buy and find time to read them. Yet people learn in different ways, and not all preachers turn naturally or easily to books. In any case, the traditional picture of a preacher toiling away in splendid isolation, (whether accurate or not), needs to be questioned. It is a very widespread model which, we shall suggest, does not have a strong biblical foundation.

I RESOURCING RELATIONSHIPS

It should be said at once that preachers need a measure of solitude. Even if some can mentally prepare a sermon whilst engaged in other tasks, preparing *themselves* requires some disengagement for reflection and prayer. But that is not all. The preacher, in a sense, is a 'separated' person. That does not mean they stand aloof or apart from others – quite the contrary. But their friendships in the churches where they preach, and their attachment or involvement in church groups, require an awareness that no allegiances or relationships can be allowed to impair their ministry to the whole congregation. But, when we have acknowledged that preachers need reflection, and their 'separateness', are preachers as solitary as they are often supposed, or should they be?

The pictures of leading figures in the Bible seem to support the traditional view of a preacher toiling away in solitude to prepare for their task. Moses goes up the mountain to communicate with God, and returns with the ten commandments (Exod. 19.20 and 19.25); the Spirit drives Jesus into the wilderness before he embarks on his preaching ministry (Mk 1.12–15); St Paul went to Arabia (Gal. 1.17), supposedly to prepare for his future apostolic work. In this instance, however, 'Arabia' may simply mean the area where he first preached the gospel.[1]

But there is another side to this biblical picture. The Old Testament gives us examples of prophets living in solidarity with the people, (e.g. Ezek. 1.1 and 8.1). Jesus, on occasion at least, seems to have treated his disciples, particularly Peter, James and John, as colleagues in the work of the Kingdom (e.g. Lk. 9.1–6, and 28–36). St Paul, however, offers the clearest example in Scripture of someone working as a member of a team, or rather of several teams. Barnabas was a close colleague until the two had a row about John Mark, (e.g. 1 Cor. 9.6); Timothy and Titus were valued colleagues (e.g. 1 Cor. 4.17, 2 Cor. 2.13 and 7.6) and even though it may be difficult for us to imagine this, Paul co-wrote some of his letters with others – 1 Thessalonians, for example, with Silvanus and Timothy, (1 Thess. 1.1).

---

[1] Although we tend to associate Arabia with desert, the area Paul calls 'Arabia' may have been far more populous, and neither Galatians nor Acts refers to a 'retreat' preparatory to Paul's ministry.

Does the ministry of Paul illustrate the point we are making here, of *the preacher as preacher* working with others? Direct evidence is lacking. But if we imagine daily life in the first century Mediterranean world, including the kind of accommodation an itinerant apostle would have had, (no private rooms for the likes of Paul!), privacy and solitude would have been hard to come by. Countless conversations – in many contexts – would have contributed to Paul's preaching over the years.

So a one-sided reading of the Bible may have contributed to the widespread picture of a preacher working primarily and normally in isolation. The internal architecture of many churches down the centuries – at least in Western Europe – has probably strengthened this image: the pulpit was often so high that the preacher could not fail to preach, literally, six feet above contradiction.

We are not questioning the preacher's need for reflection and prayer, but the perspective needs to be adjusted, especially for those who are ordained. The preacher, whether ordained or lay, is a member of the *laos* of God. *Laos* is the Greek word in the New Testament meaning 'people'; so all Christians, by virtue of their faith and baptism, are members of God's *laos*. Such solidarity in faith and baptism of all God's people precedes and outweighs any ordained/lay distinction. In saying this, we do not detract for one moment from the distinctive ministries of both lay and ordained. Both belong together in the Body of Christ. It is often wrongly supposed that a 'high' doctrine of ordained ministry must entail a 'low' doctrine of the laity, and *vice versa*. In fact the opposite is true: a 'high' view of lay ministries, properly understood, includes a correspondingly 'high' view of ordained ministry as well. We use the word 'high' in this context meaning 'important' – important before God and before the Church – and not with reference to churchmanship.

The argument that the preacher is 'one of the people' does not mean that pulpits should now be abandoned. Preachers have been called; they have been given a word to speak to the congregation and so, at the point of preaching, they stand apart. There is also a practical point. Whereas in offering intercessions, intercessors often stand among the congregation as they pray – even if ordained – preachers must be clearly seen and heard. But in a very real sense preachers belong with, and stand with, their people. That is the truth behind the observation that preachers always preach to themselves, as well as to congregations.

Where preachers stand to preach is not a vitally important issue, as long as they are visible and audible. Much more important are their relationships with the people to whom they preach and – as a more rounded understanding of the Bible suggests – their working relationships with fellow-preachers. Yet many pressures today make it difficult for the ordained person to be one of the people in the way we have outlined here, and to spend time with them. This is true in many other professions. For example, social workers in some parts of the world find themselves spending more than three-quarters of their time in front of their computers, rather than in face-to-face work with their clients. In a similar way, ordained ministers can easily become full-time managers of churches, or a dispersed civil service for central Church bureaucracies. Even preparing Sunday services, in some parts of the world today, is a far more complicated task than it used to be. In the face of these contemporary pressures, we need to affirm what the Church has traditionally said: the ministry of preaching involves a pastoral relationship with the congregation. Not everyone is called to both a preaching and a pastoral ministry; our emphasis here is on relationships. Most people who preach are likely to preach more effectively if they know and understand, with insight and compassion, what is going on in their people's lives and in their hearts.

So we need radically to revise our inherited picture of a preacher working primarily in isolation. It is a far cry from the biblical picture, and it is a long way from the Church's own self-understanding: 'we are members one of another' (Romans 12.5). This is an important first step in discovering the road to sustainable, effective preaching for the future.

## II Preachers and Congregations in Dialogue

We are taking a risk in giving the next section of this chapter such a title. It naturally suggests two people engaged in a conversation in church, each one perhaps standing at a lectern at the front. There is a place for such dialogues: preachers may question members of the congregation about how their faith shapes their approach to their job, or explore with, let us say a scientist, how his understanding of science has deepened his understanding of the doctrine of creation.

But here we have something else in mind. A major reason why preaching has fallen into disfavour in some quarters arises from the isolation – perceived or actual – of the preacher. A sermon is usually perceived or heard as a monologue: the preacher stands up, gives the message he believes he has been given for that particular Sunday, and proceeds, usually, without interruptions from the congregation (except, in some traditions and cultures, for murmurs of agreement, or, more loudly, a heartfelt 'Amen!). But again we must ask, how biblical is the perception of the sermon as a monologue?

At first sight, it seems to be correct: the Sermon on the Mount (Mt. 5–7), Peter on the day of Pentecost (Acts 2.14–36), Paul on Mars' Hill at Athens (Acts 17.22–31) seem obvious examples. But are they? Most scholars take the view that the Sermon on the Mount is a compilation of the teaching of Jesus, probably put together by the writer of the gospel. We know from many other passages in the gospels that Jesus proclaimed and taught people about the Kingdom of God in different ways. Of course, it is more than likely that people listened in rapt attention to Jesus for long periods of time as well. But the gospels also show that much of his preaching and teaching took place in more conversational and dialogical contexts; Jesus often responded to questions people asked him (e.g. Lk. 10.25–37).

The same was true of the apostles in the early Christian communities, and also in the homes and streets in which they lived, walked and worked. The sermons of Peter and Paul to which we referred earlier are what we might call edited summaries of early Christian preaching. But when we look more closely at the narrative of Acts, it is clear that something else was going on. Paul, in particular, engaged in many conversations, both out of doors (e.g. Acts 17.16) and indoors (e.g. Acts 19.8–10). (The Greek word used in both these passages, *dialegomai*, is the word from which the English word 'dialogue' derives.) They are the more public manifestations of many informal dialogues.

So, just as the preacher turns out to be not such an isolated figure in the Bible as we may have thought, so the sermon, or, rather, examples of preaching in Scripture turn out to contain fewer examples of monologues than we might have previously imagined. My argument is not a simple invitation to vary the form of the sermon and way of preaching, though that may be advisable as we easily get into predictable, boring patterns in our preaching. The implications of this biblical picture go deeper and further. Whilst most sermons will be *delivered* in the form of a monologue, the question is whether they emerge from all kinds of conversations and relationships in which the preacher has engaged. Such conversations and relationships are a vital part of resourcing and sustaining preaching today.

So, too, is the imaginative exploration of the lives of others. We turn to some examples.

*Studying the Bible Readings with Others*

The Gospel of Matthew includes a saying of Jesus not found in any of the other gospels:

> For where two or three meet together in my name, I am there among them.
>
> (Mt. 18.20)

There is a similar saying in Jewish rabbinic literature:

> If two sit together and the word of the Law (is spoken) between them, the divine Presence rests between them.[2]

Both sayings illustrate what many Christians know from personal experience: the value of studying the Bible with others and finding that light and truth have been shed on the passages. This points to a much-neglected resource for the preacher, that of studying with others the Bible passage, or passages, from which they hope to preach. Those others will preferably be a fellow-preacher, or members of the congregation to whom they will preach. It is especially helpful to know, or at the very least to anticipate, the preconceived ideas or questions which the congregation may bring to those Bible readings.

Perhaps even more important will be their objections. Some readers may find difficult, or even offensive, the idea that we might object to Scripture. They have a point. As an attendant in the National Gallery in London once remarked to a visitor who said he didn't think much to the pictures, 'It is not the pictures, sir, which are on trial'. But even when we have acknowledged that we are not in church to sit in judgement on the Bible, it is unrealistic to imagine that people will have no difficulty with many biblical passages today: Paul's apparently unquestioning acceptance of slavery, his command to wives to obey their husbands, and the sharp language of John's gospel about 'the Jews', not to mention the violence of the Old Testament, are just a few of many examples which could be given.

So preachers should try to anticipate the resistance of the congregation to some biblical passages. They need to imagine the questions, doubts, objections which may arise in their minds as they listen to a difficult reading. This is not to go looking for trouble, or to meet trouble halfway, but prayerfully and sensitively to place themselves

---

[2] Quoted by David Hill in *The Gospel of Matthew* (London: Oliphants, 1978), p. 276.

where congregational members might be. What are they to make, for example, of the call of Jesus in Luke's Gospel,

> Whoever comes to me and does not hate father and mother, wife and children, yes, and even life itself, cannot be my disciple. (Lk. 14.26)[3]

There is a further reason for studying the Bible with members of the congregation. Just over a hundred years ago, P. T. Forsyth, the distinguished Scottish preacher and theologian, had this to say:

> ... I will go so far as to confess that one of the chief miscalculations I have made in the course of my own ministerial career has been to speak to congregations as if they did know and use the Bible. I was bred where it was well known and loved, and I have spent my ministerial life where it is less so. And it has taken me so long to realize the fact that I still find it difficult to adjust myself to it.[4]

Of course, it would be quite wrong to assume that only preachers know the Bible well. But, whatever levels of knowledge of Scripture there are in congregations, it is still a challenging, searching task to engage in shared Bible study. It takes time. But we are suggesting that here is a vital way to sustain preaching. The shared questions, explorations and insights are a hugely under-valued and under-used resource.

*Other Conversations with Members of the Congregation*

Shared study of the Scriptures is not the only conversation or dialogue which will be a valuable resource to the preacher. To use a modern colloquial expression, the preacher needs to know where his/her congregation is coming from. Chapter 1 pointed out how easily a preacher may use a word or phrase quite oblivious that what the words mean to him/her may not be what the congregation understands by them. This is why we cannot remind ourselves too often of the wise observation that 'the Gospel has not really been preached until it has been heard'.[5] So sharing the lives of the congregation, being a fellow-believer alongside them, is vital, but not to be taken for granted.

Some conversations may be especially valuable. First, the more preachers can understand the doubts and questions which jostle

---

[3] The same saying in a slightly different form in another gospel indicates the meaning of the difficult verse in Luke: 'Whoever loves his father or mother *more than* me is not worthy of me' (Mt. 10.37).

[4] P. T. Forsyth, *Positive Preaching and the Modern Mind*, (London: Hodder & Stoughton, 1907), p. 34.

[5] A. Outler, *Evangelism in the Wesleyan Spirit*, (Nashville: Tidings, 1971), pp. 96–104. Outler went on to say that 'the world hears the Gospel when it sees it' (p. 104), a point which underlines the importance of the preacher's life, discussed below.

alongside Christian faith and beliefs in the minds of the congregation, the more effectively they will be able to respond to them. And it would be difficult to exaggerate the sheer diversity of many congregations in this respect. Second, the world of work is often left out of preaching. That is not surprising, since it is not easy for a preacher, even one who knows the congregation well, to be acquainted with all the challenges to Christian faith and conduct which a person's employment may throw at them. So again, the more a preacher can learn through such conversations, the better. A third area which is often neglected in contemporary preaching – at least, in many pulpits of Western Europe – is the significance of the Gospel for the world at large. Preachers turn more naturally and easily to the personal, spiritual relevance of the Scriptures for their congregation. But that may mean that preacher and congregation alike are, in effect, colluding in excluding a whole range of difficult questions which need to be faced if preaching is to engage with the 'real world', as it surely must. Bible study is critically important to Christian preachers, but so is that of the contemporary world and events. We return to this subject in Chapter 6.

So, as well as trying to anticipate the congregation's responses to the Bible readings, the preacher will find it valuable to ponder other questions as well. For example, how has the congregation responded to, or what do they think about, the national and international events of the past week? Have those events challenged, or even threatened their faith? Can they be helped to see those events in the light of their Christian faith? And of the twenty, thirty, fifty people who will be sitting before them in church on Sunday, how many will be firm believers, how many less sure about their faith, how many in church, perhaps, reluctantly there because their partner or other members of the family wanted to go? And, for those in paid employment, what kinds of challenges await them on Monday mornings?

The questions can be multiplied. Where preachers have no opportunity to meet the congregation to whom they will preach, they must think through such questions as prayerfully and sensitively as they can. Or they will think about conversations they have shared or overheard during the past week which will shed light on these questions. But whether they know their congregation well, a little, or not at all, such conversations or dialogues will be an invaluable resource to them as they prepare for Sunday.

## III The Life and Prayers of the Preacher

So far in this chapter we have attempted to correct what we believe to be an over-individualized picture of both the preacher and preaching. In particular, the ordained preacher has been perceived as one who works primarily in a mysteriously holy isolation, preparing the monologue which he will deliver from on high on Sunday. But as we have seen, we have tried to show that the Bible offers us a more rounded picture: the preacher as one of a team, and the sermon as the outcome of many conversations and dialogues. In this section we look at the preacher's own life. This, too, is immensely important as a resource for preaching, provided that his or her life is rooted and lived in Christ.

A preacher who does not pray is a contradiction in terms. Preachers who neglect their prayers become something else: charlatans, propagandists, moralists, self-advertisers ... anything but those who, by the grace of God, communicate life, truth and growth in the life of Christ to those to whom they speak. As long as God is pleased to use preachers in the service of His Kingdom, it will remain true: no-one can preach who does not pray.

Of course, preachers who arrive at Saturday evening without the remotest idea of what they are going to preach about the next day will be likely to pray some very desperate prayers. But where such a crisis has been unavoidable, and especially if it is due to the preacher's own faithfulness to what God was asking of him that week – in response, perhaps, to a family crisis, or a crisis in the church or at work – God, we believe, responds generously to such *cris de coeur* from preachers.

### *'Laborare est Orare – to work is to pray'*

The preacher's prayer life must not rise and fall according to whether there is a sermon crisis or not. Like all Christians, preachers will seek to make their life their prayer, and their prayer their life. The more they do so, the more they will find that life itself begins to resource and sustain their preaching. Or, to be precise, God's grace, working through their daily life, will resource their ministry.

A great Christian teacher of the seventeenth century, Jean-Pierre de Caussade, expressed very well this unseen hinterland of the Christian preacher's life. He never tired of expounding how every moment of our lives has the potential to be a sacrament, a means of grace:

> 'The present moment is always full of infinite treasure, it contains far more than you have the capacity to hold. Faith is the measure; what you find in the present moment will be according to the measure of your faith. Love is also the measure; the more your heart loves, the more it desires, and the more it desires the more it finds'.[6]

Central to de Caussade's vision of the Christian life was his understanding of God's providence, to which we are called to abandon ourselves day-by-day, and even moment-by-moment. Another great Christian – of the twentieth century this time – has also expressed very well a vision of the Christian life in which life and prayer are coterminous:

> This is what I mean by worldliness – taking life in one's stride, with all its duties and problems, it successes and failures, its experiences and helplessness. It is in such a life that we throw ourselves utterly into the arms of God and participate in his sufferings in the world and watch with Christ in Gethsemane.[7]

## Listening to God

So the preacher's own journey with God is a vital resource; no-one can hope to sustain a preaching ministry without this largely unseen hinterland. One discipline, however, is especially important: the discipline of listening to God. A major strand of the Bible tells us that there will be no renewal of preaching unless we listen – listen prayerfully and patiently for what the prophets called 'a word from the Lord'. The prophets, especially, remind us that the most profound and creative word comes not from ourselves, but from the Ultimate Mystery, above, beneath, beyond, within us, whom we call God.

Christians talk about this in different ways. But it may be helpful to quote here the striking words of the writer Naomi Mitchison. Speaking of the source of a writer's inspiration, she said, 'It comes from so deep inside yourself, it might almost be from somewhere else'. There is not always a clear dividing line between what we have thought of (or so it seems), and what we have been given. But Naomi Mitchison's words are a reminder to go deep – and that means listening hard and long.

Of course, people can be mistaken in claiming 'God told me ...'; every preacher needs to be keenly aware of the danger of self-

---

[6] J-P de Caussade, *Self-Abandonment to Divine Providence* (Glasgow: W. Collins, Fontana Library of Theology and Philosophy 1971, this translation first published by Burns and Oates in 1933), p. 56.

[7] D. Bonhoeffer, *Letters and Papers from Prison*, (London: SCM, 1953, Fontana, 1959, p. 125.

delusion. As with the fruits of preaching, we might well say, 'The proof of the pudding ...'. In more theological language, do we recognize in this alleged 'word from the Lord' the God and Father of our Lord Jesus Christ? We are less likely to be deluded in our listening if our listening to God is combined with listening to our fellow-Christians. The person 'who can no longer listen to his brother (*sic*) will soon no longer be listening to God either'.[8]

There is an important place for listening to God in solitude, but with disciplined practice we can listen and hear wherever we are able to pray – and that need not be in solitude at all. We can engage in such listening whenever we hold the congregation in our thoughts and prayers as we think about the sermon. At such times, questions such as 'What do they need to hear from me?' or 'What transforming word from God may I be given for them?' come naturally to the preacher's mind. The preacher's own Christian experience will deepen, shape and inform his preaching. How often preachers should refer in their sermons to their own experience is an important question. Are they justified in using themselves as examples or illustrations in their own sermons? The scope for self-deception here is great. But there is a simple rule of thumb. Will a reference to myself in my sermon serve the Gospel? We return to this question in Chapter 8.

There is another vital theme to touch on here. The preacher's own spirituality is fundamentally important: life and prayer permeate each other. But none of these words – life, prayer, spirituality – are explicitly Christian. So we end this section by recalling the Christ-centred nature of the preacher's life, calling and ministry. Preachers are called to their task by Christ: their vocation is to preach Christ, and their life-journey is to live in Christ. P. T. Forsyth, in his characteristically trenchant way, expresses it well:

> Your charter as preachers is not contained in what the world says to your earnest thought but in what the Word says to your sinful conscience. And the question is not 'What do you think of Christ" but, "How do you treat Him?" It is not what is He *to* you. It is more even than what is He *for* you. And still more it is what is He *in* you. And are you in Him? That last is in some ways the most crucial question of all.[9]

Yet even such an emphasis as this has its dangers – a point we address in the conclusion to this chapter.

---

[8] D. Bonhoeffer, *Life Together,* (London: SCM, 1954), p. 88.
[9] Forsyth, *Positive Preaching*, p. 249.

## Conclusion: A Journey With God and With Others.

We have been concerned in this chapter to explore what we believe to be important first steps towards sustainable, effective preaching. In order for this to happen, we need a different, more rounded model of both the preacher and of preaching. It is not an exaggeration to say we need a new culture of preaching. The perceived isolation of the preacher needs to be corrected; it is only half the biblical picture. The perception or experience of a sermon as a monologue also needs correction. A sermon grows out of many conversations and dialogues, including the study of the Bible with colleagues and, when possible, with those to whom we preach. Those were the basic arguments of sections I and II of this chapter.

In section III we turned to a more familiar theme: the preacher's own life of prayer. It has been, and always will be, utterly essential to a preaching ministry. But our spirituality must not become a self-isolating kind of piety. Such piety is probably one of the most widespread distortions of the Christian life. It is a distortion which goes back to New Testament times. Two letters – 1 Corinthians and 1 John – reminded the addressees that love is the most important measure of spirituality (1 Cor. 13), and that the claim to know and to love God is empty if there is no love for other people (1 Jn 2.4; 2.9 and 4.20). So we return to one of the main themes of this book.

The preacher's call to preach is an intensely personal experience. Similarly, the preacher's own ministry may be punctuated from time to time by the conviction, 'This I *must* say', or 'This is the word God has given me to speak'. Such a conviction may well be right, though again, great discernment is needed. Not least, the preacher's entire life and ministry has to be seen in a broader context. 'We are members one of another' (Rom. 12.5), and often we shall find that God sends resources to sustain a lifelong preaching ministry in the form of other people. That will be explored further in Parts 2 and 4 of this book.

## Part Two

# WORKING DYNAMICS AND RELATIONSHIPS

INTRODUCTION

Innumerable lay and ordained people in all the Christian denominations are extensively involved in preaching week by week. Most ordained ministers in the Christian Church exercise a preaching ministry although the importance attached to it by them and their congregations varies considerably. Some denominations place great emphasis on preaching and require its ordained and lay preachers to have a call to preach from God. For priests and ministers it is an integral part of their ministry. Lay preachers in secular employment pursue their preaching ministry side by side with their job or profession.

Consequently the ministry of preaching operates continuously in a wide variety of ways and settings and has done so throughout the universal Church worldwide over a long period of history. It is a discipline in its own right, a proper field of study, with its own professional identity, bodies of knowledge, praxis and spirituality. Many facets of this discipline have been exhaustively researched, studied and documented including: the theory and practice of preaching; composing liturgies and conducting public worship; the Bible and theology; and contemporary secular and religious issues that impact upon faith and preaching. Parts I, II and III address these aspects. Here we turn to less well-documented facets of the discipline. They are the nature, phases, dynamics, rhythms, and cycles and relational aspects of preachers' working lives, which are *common fundamentals to any one and all of the ways* of exercising a preaching ministry. They involve engaging creatively in private and public activities and in personal and interpersonal relationships, which are intricately interconnected, intellectually and spiritually demanding, and emotionally charged.

Against this background, Part Two examines the characteristics and implications of the following aspects of the working life of a preacher: the vocational life cycle; private and public domains; the preaching circle; and preachers and their congregations.

## Chapter 3

# *THE PRIVATE AND PUBLIC VOCATIONAL LIFE CYCLES OF A PREACHER*

Exercising a preaching ministry is not simply an occupation; it is a way of life with its own cyclical processes. This chapter examines how the vocational life cycle of a preacher functions and malfunctions, and the private and public domains of a preacher's working life. Conceptualizing them helps preachers to live and work within them more creatively, to endure and survive the psychologically and spiritually rough passages, and to prevent them from dominating the preacher's life. Chapters 9 and 10 describe how preachers can develop their abilities to engage with these aspects of their ministry.

I. THE VOCATIONAL LIFE CYCLE OF A PREACHER

'Stages of life' and 'a cycle of life' are two concepts widely used to overview the development and decline of people and institutions and to distinguish the different phases of their existence. Aristotle, for instance, used the idea of three stages of human life, youth and young adulthood, prime time and old age. Jean Piaget developed ideas about the stages of psychological development, Lawrence Kohlberg of moral development and James Fowler of faith development. Martin F. Saarinen and others developed models of congregational life cycles.[1] Applying these conceptual tools to the life

---

[1] See, for instance: Nathan Isaacs, *The Growth of Understanding in the Young Child: A Brief Introduction to Piaget's Work* (Norwich: Ward Lock Educational Company Ltd., 6th edition, 1961); Lawrence Kohlberg's work on the cycles of moral development are discussed in relation to Piaget's in *Introduction to Moral Education* by John Wilson et al. (A Pelican Original, 1966); James W. Fowler et al. analyse faith development in *Stages of Faith and Religious Development. Implications for Church, Education and Society* (London:

cycle of a preacher, five phases can be identified: latent; inaugural; preaching ministry; retirement; and death and resurrection. Each phase is described as a prelude to modelling the cycle.

*Phase 1: The Latent Phase*

During this phase potential preachers experience a call to preach or a vocation to ministry or priesthood. This can happen gradually over a long period of time, or dramatically and suddenly. Much heart-searching and feelings of unworthiness and inadequacy normally accompany receiving and responding to such a call; certainly this was Jeremiah's experience in the Old Testament. However it occurs, it is a formative process during which vocational foundations are laid for lay preaching ministry or for preaching as a function of ordained ministry or priesthood.

In some denominations an established call to preach from God is required of all candidates for lay or ordained ministry. Raymond Brown says that, 'A compelling sense of vocation is one of the most important factors in the spirituality of a Christian preacher.'[2] Thorough testing of the validity of the call to preaching or priesthood during this phase is essential for the good of the person concerned and the church. Much is at stake. To proceed without a genuine call or with a doubtful one could lead to vocational dissonance and frustration and worse. A genuine call is a defining event in a person's life and vital to the rigours of pursuing a preaching vocation: it is the spiritual mandate to the preaching ministry, which becomes deeply embedded in a preacher's psyche, burnt into their soul. It suffuses all that follows. 'I am called', is an ever-present part of the preacher's consciousness, shaping their self and public identities, career and destiny. It acts as a fulcrum and variously assures, challenges and guides preachers, holds them to their vocations and sustains them in good times and bad.

Exploring and facing up to the vocational and relational implications of a call can be exciting and daunting. Deciding how to respond can be difficult, especially if it involves far reaching life changes for those who are called and their families. If those closely involved, such as spouses, are disturbed about the implications for them, much

---

SCM Press, 1992); Martin F. Saarinen examines congregational development in *The Life Cycle of a Congregation* (The Alban Institute, Special Papers and Research Reports, 1986).

[2] Gordon S. Wakefield (ed.) *A Dictionary of Christian Spirituality* (London: SCM Press Ltd, 1983) p. 319

sensitive discussion and give and take is required. Most people need moral and spiritual support and guidance as they seek to understand, interpret and pursue what is happening to them.

*Phase 2: The Inaugural Phase: testing, training and qualifying*

The inaugural phase opens when would-be preachers offer themselves, and are accepted, as candidates for lay ministry of the word or for ordained ministry. It closes when those who qualify are commissioned as lay preachers or ordained as deacons, ministers or priests. What happens to candidates between these two important junctures in their vocational lives, as they undergo the testing and assessing procedures and participate in the training programmes required by their denomination, varies enormously. Essentially it is a period of initial vocational formation. Our purposes are most appropriately served not by generalizing about these processes, but by considering two transforming transitions made by candidates during this phase and what might be involved in making them, that is, by concentrating on the candidates rather than on what the churches require of them. The first of these, the transition from being a member of the church to being a preacher in training, provides entry into this inaugural phase. The other, the transition from being a preacher in training to being a qualified and accredited or commissioned preacher or ordained minister of the word, concludes this phase and provides entry into the next. Recognizing the significance of these transitions is a key to understanding the personal, relational and vocational dynamics of this phase and the emotional, intellectual and faith demands and challenges that candidates can encounter, and to proffering appropriate help and support.

To inaugurate the first of these transitions, those who previously have been cherishing and pondering inner promptings towards a preaching ministry and privately sounding out their ideas with soul friends, have to take their courage into both hands and submit themselves and what they believe to be God's call to the critical scrutiny of the church through its appointed officers. It is their function to come to an initial judgement about the validity of the religious experience and whether they consider that the candidate has the abilities, gifts and graces required to exercise an effective preaching ministry. If they decide in the affirmative on all counts, candidates continue to be rigorously tested through a study and training programme. If they decline, candidates may need much pastoral help and support to re-interpret their call and to find their vocation. Some churches now offer this along with pre-candidating vocational guidance.

Candidates are now in an intermediate temporary stage in their vocational life with a status akin to that of an apprentice or an undergraduate: they are neither simply a church member nor a qualified preacher. They are students involved in three interrelated core activities: learning and practising the craft of preaching; ongoing reflection on and discernment of their vocation personally and with the church; and critical scholarly study of the Bible, the Christian faith and theology. As students they are likely to spend more time studying than preaching. On the whole they will have some, if not extensive, knowledge of the subjects to be studied. Most certainly, as members of congregations, they will have experienced many different preaching styles; they may well be connoisseurs of the art! Undoubtedly they will have distinctive views about what constitutes good preaching and how they are going to preach. Now, however, they approach preaching, not as recipient observers but as preachers, who prepare and deliver sermons, very different positions and perspectives!

The personal experience of doing these things in structured, disciplined ways varies considerably from one student preacher to another. Several factors influence the emotional, intellectual and spiritual impact of these reflective studies upon full- or part-time students including their age, intelligence, personality, spirituality, circumstances, previous education and training and occupation, the strength of their call, faith and vocation and how congenial they find the process. Academic study of itself can pose problems for various groups of students including those who are older, or consider themselves to be practical, rather than academic or intellectual, or who have never previously done academic studies at all or not for a considerable time. Again, they may have been schooled in quite different disciplines, such as the physical sciences, or have demanding jobs, and so are studying in their leisure time. For many, if not for most, systematic guided study and reflection on their vocation and on the praxis of preaching is liberating, rewarding and exciting. For them it opens up new ways of understanding the faith and generates new insights and ideas. But for others studying theology and encountering for the first time critical analyses of their preaching, the Bible and traditional beliefs is disturbing, and can raise questions about their faith and vocation which they find difficult to resolve. Consequently, for them this phase can be an emotional, spiritual and intellectual rollercoaster with much soul-searching. But whether students find this training period congenial or not, the outcome, if all goes well, will be that they learn to preach, and at the same time grow in their own faith and understanding of their vocation. In short, they will be formed holistically as preachers.

The second transition, the result of candidates or students successfully negotiating the first, and the training that follows it, occurs at the end of this phase and inaugurates the next one, the preaching ministry phase. For some this transition is from being a lay member of the church to becoming a lay preacher; for others it is from being a lay member of the church to becoming an ordained minister or deacon. As they make this transition they are endowed with the official status of preachers in the Christian church and its congregations. This gives them an established and honoured role, function and position in institutional Christianity and a distinctive public profile. They become Christian religious role models, mandated representatives of Christianity, primary reference points on matters of faith, and those whose counsel and opinions people seek. Cloistered congregational membership with its comparative anonymity gives way to exposed public life in church and community. One of the many things that they may have to work at in order to pursue *their* ministry is to guard against stereotypes of preachers, and to continue to be in empathic touch with the congregations and communities they seek to serve. Comparing these changes in status with those between a patient and a doctor, or a student and lecturer, illuminates the measure and extent of the transition from congregational member to preacher, even though they are not direct parallels.

Another important thing that happens as a consequence of this transition is that preachers become fully-fledged members of communities or colleges of lay and/or ordained preachers. These communities can be challenging and even inspiring, as well as providing opportunities for mutual help (see Chapter 9). They help preachers to develop broad-based perspectives on the preaching ministry as they explore it through their own experience and that of others. Belonging to preaching communities can be one of the great privileges of being a preacher. It is an important safeguard against the isolation into which many preachers easily fall, as noted in Chapter 2.

*Phase 3: The Preaching Ministry Phase: practising, maturing and declining*
During this phase preachers live out the life of a preacher and work out their preaching vocation through the formal and informal

opportunities presented to them and their private preparation. As they do so, they encounter the ups and downs of their preaching ministry, but hopefully, as they gain experience, they mature as preachers and as Christians. During this phase preachers need to be involved in two main streams of activity. First there is forming a bedrock to their ministry as a whole by living what they preach and through studying relevant biblical and theological subjects, keeping up their general reading, taking a diligent interest in current affairs and seeking to understand significant contemporary events as they occur in the light of their faith. (See Chapters 1, 6 and 12 on the importance of preachers engaging with the various contexts in which they live.)

It is important that this foundational layer is maintained and developed by preachers throughout their ministry. Those who neglect this task are prone to become stale or superficial and even hypocritical. Conscientious, long-term study generates insights and helps preachers to build up their worldview, acquire authority, respect and self-confidence. It also resources the second stream of activity: the preachers' actual preaching assignments. In relation to each assignment preachers engage in an interactive sequence of preparation, preaching, feedback, and reflection. These sequences are referred to here as a 'preaching circle' (not to be confused with the 'vocational life cycle of a preacher'). They are represented in Figure 3:1 by loops, slightly tilted to indicate they are completed over variable lengths of time. This circle is discussed in detail in Chapter 4. The frequency of these assignments varies from preacher to preacher. Some lay preachers will preach every few weeks whereas some ministers and priests will do so weekly or even more often. For them, working their way round the preaching cycle is a part of their weekly routine. Others work their way round it over longer periods, but it can be more complex than this. Preachers can be working through more than one cycle at the same time. A major, demanding or difficult preaching appointment, for instance, can be at the back of a preacher's mind for a prolonged period during which she/he can have preached several other sermons, some of which may serve as a 'trial run' for a big event.

So two streams of activity form the character of the ministry of preachers: a continuing commitment to living their faith, and equipping themselves for their vocation, and the actual experience of preaching. We continue to explore both throughout this book.

There are subtle but important differences for preachers between preaching to congregations for which they have pastoral responsibilities in churches of which they are the appointed minister or priest, and preaching to congregations for which they have no such responsibilities. For instance, preachers, lay or ordained, with executive and pastoral responsibilities for churches and who know members of congregations, have to take especial care not to use their privileged position and sermons to make allusions to confidential pastoral matters or to score points in ongoing discussions or arguments about controversial policy issues when people are unable to reply publicly. Avoiding such pitfalls can be difficult; people can take offence when none is intended. Preachers preaching to congregations they do not know are freed from all this!

During the latter part of this phase, there is a period of variable duration when ministers and priests have retired from full time ministry and lay preachers have retired from secular employment but still continue to preach. Often this means they have more time and energy to dedicate to preaching, either to take more appointments or to study and/or to spend more time preparing fewer sermons. Either way, this can be a rich period of mature and more relaxed preaching ministry, frequently prolonged in these days when early retirement and longevity are increasingly common. In terms of preaching, ministers and priests can become more like lay preachers in their relationships with congregations when they move to new churches without pastoral charge.

*Phase 4: The Retirement Phase*

Retirement from preaching appointments is not necessarily the end of a preacher's ministry: these two things should not be confused or equated. At retirement the public aspects of ministry cease, but preachers do not cease to be preachers: they are not divested of their carefully formed persona; they can continue to feel and to be seen as preachers. Much that is intrinsic to a preaching ministry continues during this final and important phase for preachers and their lives. Retirement mirrors in reverse the transition from the latent to the inaugural stage and it is as radical, requiring considerable psychological and spiritual adjustment, which can be difficult and costly. This is especially so when it is not possible to respond to a persistent and unrelenting sense of vocation because of other responsibilities and physical decline. Equally this phase can be freeing and a benediction on preachers and their ministry.[3]

This is a much-neglected phase for several possible reasons: it is in the private domain, largely hidden from public view; retired preachers are no longer in the spotlight; attention is understandably and rightly focused on the earlier phases; the issues and difficulties of retirement are either unrecognised or underestimated; it is commonly and wrongly assumed that retirement is the end of a preaching ministry. Consequently, preachers are often left to their own resources to come to terms with their retirement and to resolve any difficulties themselves at a time when they may be in serious need of pastoral care and help. Short courses on retirement from preaching could be enormously helpful for lay and ordained preachers.

*Phase 5: Death and Resurrection*

This brings the vocational life cycle to an end, but not necessarily its influence, which can continue indefinitely in the providence of God. Paul reassures all Christians who work for the Kingdom of God, in a text that is particularly appropriate to those who are faithful preachers of the word: 'Therefore my friends, stand firm and immovable and work for the Lord always, without limit, since you know that in the Lord your labour cannot be lost.' (1 Cor. 15:58, REB) The context of these words, which come at the end of a great chapter about the resurrection of the dead, suggests to me the redemption and resurrection of the work associated with and the outcome of our preaching. It will not die a death; it cannot be lost. Or, to quote Isaiah, '... my word ... will not return to me empty without accomplishing my purpose and succeeding in the task for which I sent it.' (Isa. 55: 11 REB) The life cycle of any preacher can be seen as one of countless rounds of witness and work subsumed in the full circle of God's saving activity. Our ministry is caught up in and completed in that of Christ.

---

[3] A structured way of thinking about retirement is on the website, http://www.preacherdevelopment.uk7.net. It can help preachers to understand, interpret and negotiate their retirement, treat it as an integral part of their vocational life, and live with it more happily and creatively. It presents ways of reflecting on two aspects of retired life. *What might continue into retirement*: gratitude; the abiding reality of the call to preach; opportunities to live out the implications of their vocation and converse about the faith; membership of the fraternity of preachers; yearning to preach; reflecting on and evaluating your preaching ministry. *What might be new in retirement*: changes in the rhythm and pattern of life; downsizing; sense of identity.

## II MODELLING THE PHASES AND DYNAMICS OF THE LIFE CYCLE

This section presents a general diagrammatical model of the phases of the life cycle in Figure 3:1 and draws out its characteristics and discusses its dynamics.

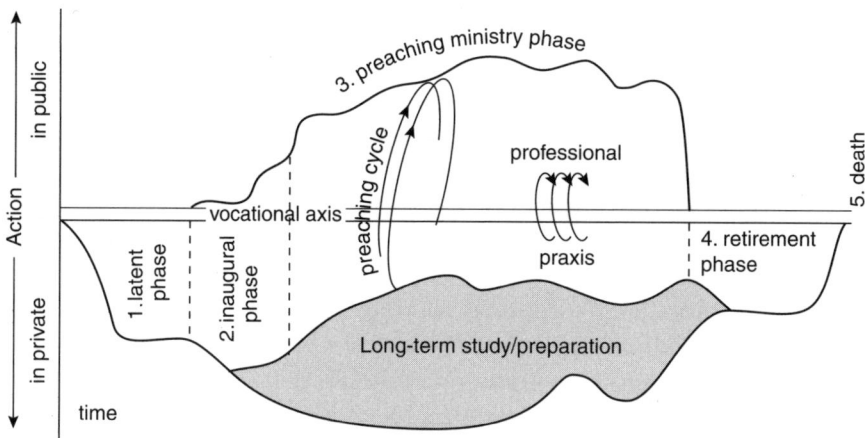

**Figure 3:1** Phases and Dynamics of a Vocational Life Cycle of a Preacher: an unscalable general model

*Private and Public Activities*

The upper contour on the model represents levels of a preacher's public preaching activity; the first lower contour represents her/his preparation for specific preaching appointments; the area between the two lower contours represents her/his long-term preparation. The undulation of the public contour indicates variations in the number of preaching engagements. There are no appointments represented in the latent and retirement phases, although there may be some, and comparatively few in the inaugural phase where the emphasis is on study and training. The undulations of the private contour quite deliberately do not follow those of the public one, indicating that the length of time it takes to prepare a sermon defies prediction; it is not an exact science! Some sermons come in a moment of inspiration; others take enormous amounts of time, energy and periods of heart-breaking depression and despair. And, to complicate life further, it is simply not always possible to discern in advance within which of these categories the preparation of a sermon is going to fall. The model brings to the fore the fact that preachers are required to perform well in private and public domains, two very different but equally necessary working contexts. The preacher's interior life is common to all phases and to private and public activities.

*The Vocational Axis and Professional Praxis*

Central and key to both the private and public activities is vocational life brought into being by God and activated by the preacher's faithful response. Preaching activity without this relationship is hollow, regardless of the preacher's gifts, graces, knowledge and oratorical abilities. It is the axis of the vocational life-cycle, sustained and developed by God through the spiritual and pastoral life of the preacher. This axis, about which the life-cycle rotates, is God's mandate for the preaching ministry, which endows the preacher with authority and credibility. Formative processes are generated within the hearts and minds of preachers and in their preaching through this deep vocational rooting. However, the importance of these personal and private activities does not necessarily mean that preachers should be solitary practitioners left entirely to their own devices in preparing themselves, for instance, to respond to the contemporary challenges to faith or to tackle the kind of complex socio-religious issues discussed in Chapter 2. Throughout, this book argues for and demonstrates that collaboration between preachers and others, in these and other tasks, is a contemporary imperative and describes ways in which this can be done without eclipsing the vocational integrity of preachers. (See especially Chapters 2, 4 and 9.)

Of itself, however, a sense of vocation, essential as it is, does not equip a preacher for ministry. It must be accompanied by appropriate professional abilities. Taking seriously the following complementary characteristics of vocation and professionalism helps to establish and maintain a creative relationship between them:

- Vocation is the *why* of a preaching ministry, professionalism the *how*.
- Vocation provides the rationale, the moral and spiritual basis for professionalism; professionalism facilitates the exercise and fulfillment of vocation.
- Professionalism is the praxis of vocation; vocation is given; professional abilities are acquired through serious study, thoroughgoing critical reflective practice and experience.

Professionalism is not to be confused with careerism characterized by self-fulfillment and naked ambition: careerism is anathema to and destructive of vocational professionalism. Figure 3:2, which depicts four possible relationships between vocation and professionalism, enables preachers to position and appraise themselves in relation to them and to read off any implications that emerge. *Preachers are most likely to be fulfilled and their preaching to be effective when their professional praxis revolves around their vocational axis and is driven by it, rather than the other way round.*

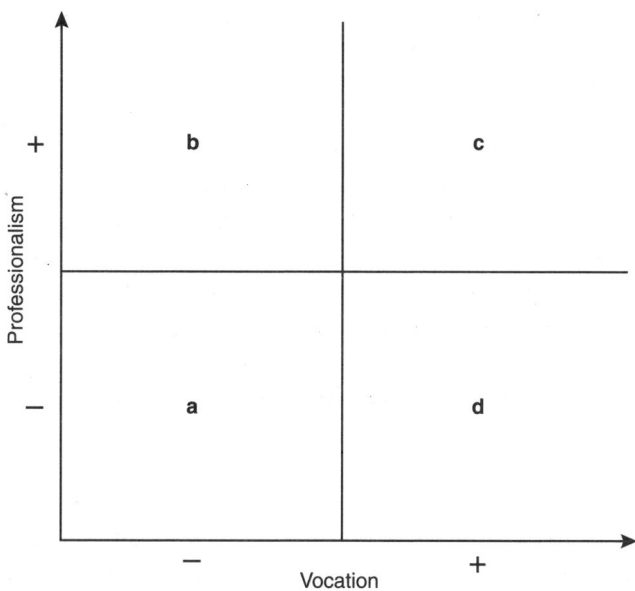

a: the preacher's sense of vocation and professional abilities are weak or absent

b: the preachers have professional ability but, as their sense of vocation is weak or absent they lack purposeful vocational thrust.

c: preachers have both a sense of vocation and professional ability.

d: preachers have a sense of vocation but lack professional ability.

**Figure 3:2** A Four-Quadrant Model of Vocation and Professionalism[4]

*Phases 1 to 4*

As preachers work their way through successive 'preaching circles', their vocational life-cycles evolve phase by phase and take on their particular nature and shape. Normally, vocational life cycles run their natural term but, sadly, they can be prematurely terminated by various causes, such as the preacher's loss of call or by illness.

---

[4] Professor Peter D. Howdle drew this diagram during private discussions about vocation and professionalism in medicine and ministry in 2003.

### Junctures Between the Phases

Junctures between the phases are significant, and dramatic points of transition. In Figure 3:1 they appear as instantaneous to represent the moment when they actually occur. Privately and inwardly, however, they are most likely to be anticipated, prepared and planned for (and in some cases agonized over) by preachers and their associates over varying lengths of time. Consequently, transitions are normally preceded and followed by periods of adjustment – what might be called 'run-in' time.

### Effects and Abilities

The cycle is about phases of a preaching ministry, not the effect it can have, which can outlive the preacher. Unlike the diagrams of some life-cycles, this one does not represent the growth and decline of the preacher's ability and effectiveness, which are likely to undulate. Generally speaking, effectiveness rises and falls from one preaching appointment to another. For instance, it is possible for preachers to be at their spiritual height when their physical vigour is at its lowest ebb or *vice versa*.

### Quality

The quality of the public preaching ministry is closely related to the quality of the input from the interior life of the preacher and the use he/she makes of his/her gifts and graces, opportunities to study and the support offered.

### Vocational Flow

From this general description of the vocational lives of preachers, it could be assumed that they flow in an orderly, smooth and progressive manner. Such a view could be confirmed by observing effective preachers in action. But all the preachers I have known and read about experience periods of inner turbulence, as will become apparent as we proceed.

### Possible Uses of the Vocational Life Cycle Concept

Preachers can use this pictorial outline of the overall dimensions of their vocational life as a template to:

- position themselves
- construct life cycle diagrams representative of their own preaching life as an aid to evaluative reflection

*The Private and Public Vocational Life Cycles of a Preacher* 47

- describe the positive and negative characteristics of each of the phases as they experience them
- reflect on and review the past, assess the present situation, and determine the implications for them of their future preaching ministry and any adjustments they need to make. For instance this could include discerning changing patterns in the mode of preaching and variations in the substance.
- consider their preaching life cycle in relation to their other professional and personal life cycles and read off any implications indicated by their findings.

Doing these things, demanding as they might be, can keep preachers on their providential vocational track, renew their commitment to professional praxis, give direction and thrust to their ministry, and induce quiet confidence and spiritual poise.

## II Private and Public Domains of a Preacher's Working Life[5]

Figure 3:1 shows that to pursue their ministry preachers have to work in both private and in public. Using another model, this section examines what is involved in working in and moving between these two domains. Basic preparation for preaching is done in the private work domain, out of the pulpit, by preachers on their own or in collaboration with other preachers, and with church officials such as organists or choirmasters. Leading worship, preaching, relating to congregations formally and individual members informally are done in the public work domain, the pulpit, a very different experience from that of the privacy of the study or the study group. These are represented diagrammatically in Figure 3:3. This static diagram indicates the complexity of the systems within which preachers work, but it does not do them justice because they are dynamic: even lines with arrows to indicate interaction and movement do not make this clear. Diagrams of a similar kind can, of course, be drawn for every participant in this collective activity. Constructing and connecting up one or two such diagrams quickly reveals the complexity of these corporate activities. But here we are focusing on preachers' perspectives and the systems in which they operate.

---

[5] cf George Lovell, *Analysis and Design: A Handbook for Practitioners and Consultants in Church and Community Work* (Tunbridge Wells: Burns and Oates, 1994) pp. 193–196 and in *Consultancy Ministry and Mission: A Handbook for Practitioners and Work Consultants in Christian Organizations* (London: Burns and Oates, 2000) p 22.

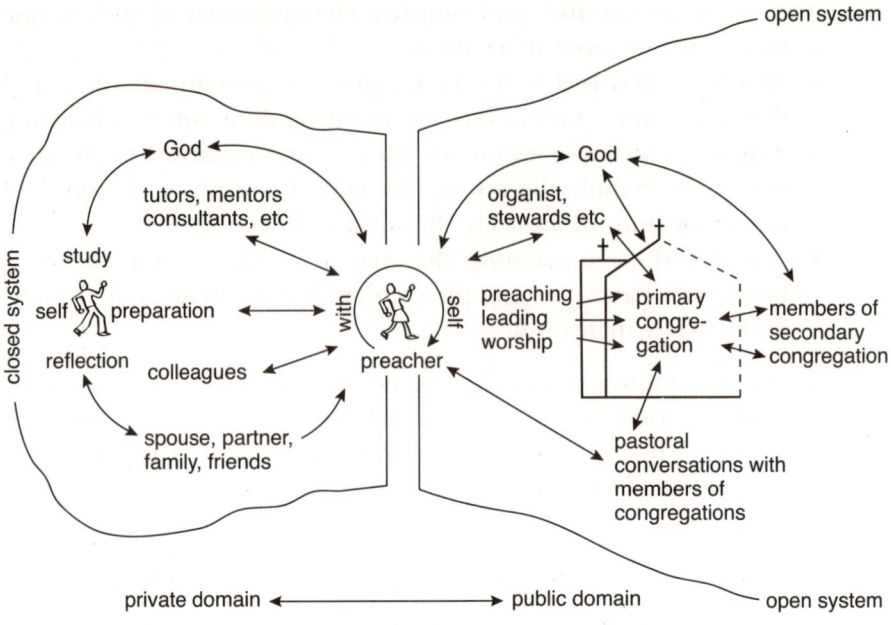

**Figure 3:3** Private and Public Domains of a Preacher's Working Life

Private domains are closed, safe systems, predominantly controlled by preachers themselves through the boundaries of confidentiality and privacy which they establish and maintain. Public domains, on the other hand, are open, risky systems through which, as we will see later, preaching can reverberate well beyond the confines of congregations in all kinds of ways and directions that preachers cannot possibly foresee or control.

Preachers criss-cross the domains continuously, physically, imaginatively and emotionally. What happens in the public domain, for instance, is rehearsed and relived in private, joyfully and painfully. In fact the domains in this diagram are profoundly interactive and interdependent. As preachers pray about preaching appointments and plan and write sermons, they bring congregations to mind. A telephone call raising tricky issues on the very thing the preacher is working on but not ready to discuss can break into a period of private preparation. As they preach, empowered and inspired by the Holy Spirit, preachers translate the sermon notes drafted and rehearsed in private into preached sermons in the public domain. Clearly, the experience in one domain critically affects that of the other, positively or negatively.

## The Private and Public Vocational Life Cycles of a Preacher 49

Preachers are pivotal figures to both domains: they integrate them and inwardly process the transactions between them. They embody within themselves their experiences of both domains which intersect and interact within them. The circular arrow around the figure in the diagram representing the preacher is meant to indicate that thoughts, ideas and feelings are ever with them, pulsating through their hearts and minds in both private and in public. Some people refer to this as the 'inner dialogue' or 'self-talk'. I prefer to call it 'interior personal work' to emphasize that preachers have to work at it in order to make their best contributions, and this can be quite demanding intellectually and emotionally. For instance, they have to sweat over and work hard at deeply embedded painful memories of preaching experiences, negative and positive comments about their preaching and their doubts and insecurities.

Inner experiences can affect preachers quite dramatically, positively or negatively, even though they are not always a realistic or reliable guide to the value of their abilities or performances in preparation, preaching and worship: private perspectives can idealize or distort. (See the section on feedback in Chapter 4). All this is inevitable, but there are compensatory joys and satisfactions, which support, energize and make preachers humbly thankful. These inner experiences interact somewhat unpredictably with the preacher's outer experiences; preachers can be acutely aware of their inner world in public and of the public world in private. The respective dominance of the domains rises and falls in their consciousness, sometimes through deliberate choice of focus; at other times, changes in focus are unbidden and unwanted. At best, the tension between the private and public dimensions in their preaching ministry can be creative and enriching even when it causes anxiety and pain. In such circumstance it generates personal energy within and finely tunes both preaching performances and preachers. At its worst, however, tension can debilitate preachers by sapping and squandering their energy, undermining their confidence and generally impairing their performance.

Movement between private and public domains and their different atmospheres involves crossing various physical, environmental, psychological and spiritual boundaries. In turn this involves adjusting from one way of behaving, conceptualizing, experiencing and thinking about things to another. Some of the ways in which this occurs have already been discussed. Display 3:1 sets out some of the attributes and abilities preachers require to practise well in private and public.

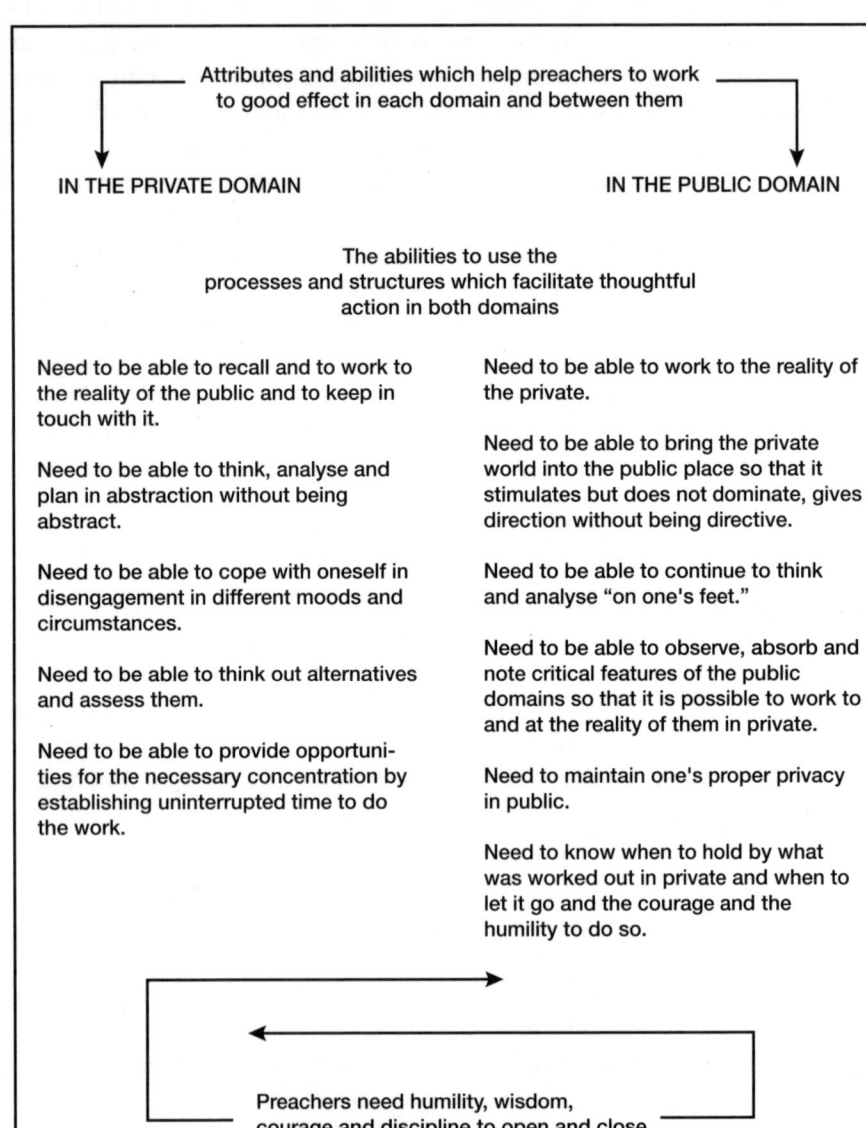

**Display 3:1** Attributes and Abilities Preachers Require to Practise in the Private and Public Aspects of Their Ministry

This section has focused on preachers and what they do in private and public to pursue their preaching ministries, so at the centre of Figure 3:3 is 'the preacher' but importantly, as the diagram shows, the preacher lives and operates in various relational settings. In the public domain the central relationship is with congregations. (This is considered in Chapter 5.) Working relationships with organists and others help to facilitate this side of this relationship with congregations. Then there are the relationships with individual members of congregations initiated by sermons and built up through conversations on things they are interested in and concerned about. There are several clusters of relationships in the private domain. One is with spouses, family members and soul friends. These can be extremely important, offering preachers loving encouragement, support and criticism. Another cluster – tutors, mentors, consultants and colleagues – can offer professional, technical and spiritual support of the kinds discussed in Chapter 9. Together these clusters of relationships can provide preachers with a secure base from which to go out to preach and to which they can return to share the joy of successful preaching, or alternatively to lick their wounds and find solace and support. All in all, the clusters of relationships in the private domain are an inestimable resource for public ministry; they counterbalance its demands. And of course throughout, in both domains and in between them, there is the preacher's spiritual relationship with God, which is foundational to the preacher's life and vocation. So preachers need to be self- differentiated team players who can work well on their own.

So while acts of preaching are personal solo activities in public, they are set in a network of facilitating relationships. This book argues and demonstrates that in addition to these relationships, new forms of collaboration are required to meet current challenges (see Chapters 2, 9 and 11). In the wider and deeper picture, individual preaching vocations contribute to the collective vocation of all preachers and of the Church, and therefore to Christ's ministry. (Chapter 11 describes how a group of preachers discovered and worked at both their individual and collective vocations in relation to the churches in which they preached.)

Focusing on working contexts and dynamics – as this chapter does – directs attention to the abilities preachers require and the personal attributes and skills they need to be effective in both private and public domains. Most people are not equally comfortable and competent in both domains: for instance, introverts may find public domains intimidating while extroverts may experience difficulties in giving themselves to reflection and the discipline of study and preparation. However, motivated and driven by vocation and professionalism, most preachers put a lot of effort into becoming as competent as possible in both domains. Even so, some preachers are more consummate and inspirational performers in the pulpit than others, some are more profound, and a few are equally competent in both domains. Consequently, it is difficult and possibly unwise to try to formulate a 'fit all' preacher personality profile. History shows that God calls, equips and uses people with a wide range of personalities and abilities to preach – with sometimes surprising results.

## Chapter 4

# *THE PREACHING CIRCLE*

Preachers work their way through four basic sequences in relation to each preaching appointment: preparation – preaching – feedback – reflection. This chapter examines these private and public sequences, which we refer to here as a *preaching circle*[1] rather than a cycle, to avoid confusion with the 'vocational life cycle of a preacher'. It is represented diagrammatically in Figure 4:1.

Preachers for the most part work through the sequences themselves, whereas in politics and the media a team of researchers, scriptwriters and producers share a process not unlike this. This comparison helps to put what preachers do into a wider perspective, as well as indicating the sheer complexity of their work. While we are focusing on the preacher's perspective and experience of this circle, we recognize that as preachers work their way through the circle, others accompany them. Sometimes they will do so in a quite personal way, as they contribute their own perspectives and experiences of the sequences. And, of course, congregations are essential co-participants in the preaching sequence.

The aim of this chapter is to help preachers to work their way through these circles more effectively. Understanding the nuances of the sequences helps preachers to engage with them more effectively, to rise above them, and to carry forward what is learnt from working through one circle to the next. This continuous learning process, consolidated in the reflection sequence, helps preachers to improve and develop stage by stage. Part 4 describes how preachers can be

---

[1] It is based on the concept of the 'pastoral cycle.' For further information about this cycle see: Joe Holland and Peter Henriot, *Social Analysis: Linking Faith and Justice* (Victoria, Australia: Orbis Books, 1980) particularly p. 8; Laurie Green, *Let's Do Theology: a pastoral cycle resource book* (London: Mowbray, 1990).

further helped with these sequences through in-service training programmes and various forms of interpersonal support such as coaching, consultancy and spiritual direction.

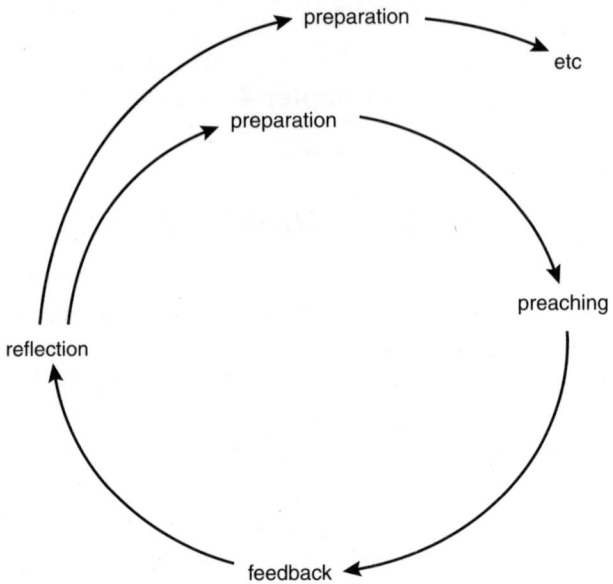

**Figure 4:1** The Preaching Circle

THE PREPARATION SEQUENCE

This part of the circle is about the research and preparation directly related to specific preaching events, which, of course, draw upon the preacher's devotional and spiritual life and long-term preparation. Sermons are forged through prayer, spiritual preparation and private study of biblical, religious and secular material, and through conversations and studies with others of the kind described in Chapters 2, 7 and 8. (See also the discussions about hermeneutics in Chapters 7 and 11.)

Chapters 6, 7 and 8 look in some detail at the task of preparing a sermon. Here we concentrate on the dynamics of preparation and particularly on its affective aspects, which can vary a great deal as helpful and unhelpful feelings arise spontaneously at the most unlikely moments. At one end of the spectrum of these emotional ups and downs are spiritually electric moments. These occur, for instance, when new, exciting insights come in a flash, seemingly from nowhere, along with the inner conviction to preach on them and the opportunity to do so. A range of feelings can be associated with such events: awe, euphoria, intellectual and spiritual animation. In such circumstances sermons may be drafted quite quickly in a flow of inspiration, with a sense of being used by God. Anticipating preaching is exciting. Such humbling and fulfilling experiences confirm vocations and re-energize preachers.

At the other end of the spectrum are the occasions when preachers simply do not know what to preach about, even though they have lots of sermons and commentaries. Preparation is laborious, mechanical, uninspired and blighted by sermon writer's block. Feelings engendered by these experiences are the antithesis of those associated with the first kind. Then there is a variety of experiences and feelings that fall between these extremes: when, for instance, one or other of the components – insight, inner prompting, and preaching opportunity – is disconcertingly absent. There is also the added complication of the time factor: working against the clock can focus the mind or induce panic; on the other hand, preparation can take all the time available and more, expanding into time that should be given to other things and creating guilt feelings.

The emergence of these different scenarios is unpredictable: we cannot of our own volition engineer or create the good ones, nor avoid or prevent the bad ones; they just happen unexpectedly. While we cannot foresee, engineer or prevent them, we must expect them in their unexpectedness, accept them as part and parcel of the way things actually work out in our unfolding ministry, be patient with ourselves when they occur, and discover ways of coping with the different emotional conditions they engender. Quite simply, we have to learn to live with them in mature and contained ways. Somehow, through prayer and reflection, we have to keep on trying to cultivate and nurture deep inner poise and a philosophical approach to the fluctuating emotional states. This can be very difficult, but the points made below about handling feedback will, we hope, be helpful, as well as the suggestions of support described in Chapter 9. Internalizing the essence of the following three statements can also help us to be more effective and composed both when preparation flows excitedly, and when it is painful and we are experiencing sermon writer's block.

*Emotional highs and lows do not necessarily indicate that we are either good or bad preachers.*

My own personality may make me prone to various emotions and affect their degree and intensity, but highs and lows do not unfailingly represent the quality of my preparation or performance with any accuracy nor do they indicate or determine my true worth as a preacher nor the effectiveness of the outcome: sermons which have a difficult birth can have a powerful life. Many of the sermons I have struggled with and agonized over are among the most rewarding that I have ever preached, but some of them are the worst! Unpredictably, what are considered to be 'good' sermons go badly wrong when preached in one church and extremely well in another.

*Feelings about preaching ministry are the effects of some things and also the cause of others.*

Feelings are facts of life to be taken seriously. They can be reactions to disappointment over a preaching performance or to criticism of a sermon. But they may be displaced from unrelated occurrences such as a family argument. Whatever their source, once stirred, they can have a life of their own and become causal agents. For instance, as already noted, they have the power to distort one's self-image and lead preachers to underestimate or over estimate themselves, and to become depressed or conceited. Preachers can help themselves to interpret and cope with these experiences by asking questions such as: What caused the feelings? What is sustaining them? What effects are they having on my preaching and me? What can *I* do about them?

*Respecting and trusting our personal and idiosyncratic human and spiritual creative systems helps them to perform their functions*

At times when I am preparing and drafting sermons, I find that a lot of thoughts and ideas are buzzing around in my head, but no matter how hard I work at them, I simply cannot get them into a pattern or find a structure that holds them together thematically. Attempts to commit them to paper end in a collage of disparate thoughts. From experience, I know that left to its own devices my unconscious mind will, in its own time, bring them into some order – frequently in the middle of the night! But I have often persisted in working at them doggedly long after I should, because I want to finish the sermon and get on with something else. The result is an impasse: I tire myself out and deepen my despair. Sermons of quality cannot be produced mechanically to order; they are conceived within us and, after their proper period of gestation, we give birth to them. For most of the time, however, I do work more sensibly to the rhythms of my creative processes, and then I find the Holy Spirit is better able to work *with* and *through* me at different levels of my consciousness. That is a wonderful and humbling experience of prevenient grace. A basic general principle of sermon construction and preparation, therefore, is that preachers need to understand their own creative processes, to trust, respect and nurture them and to work *with* and *through* their moods, rhythms and time cycles; they must not try to mimic those of others. When preachers collaborate with themselves in these ways, God seems to be able to collaborate with them more naturally and effectively; the Holy Spirit appears to enter the processes as a cooperative partner and to infuse them with divine inspiration. Such holy/human partnerships are at the heart of a preacher's true vocational life.

Another important aspect of this sequence is the psychological and spiritual preparation for preaching appointments. Getting into a good frame of mind and heart is clearly desirable but it can be quite difficult. Some feelings of unworthiness and inadequacy are natural; they are a healthy and proper response to the awesome responsibility of preaching the word of God. These feelings can induce creative tension and humility, but they also generate emotional and spiritual energy in preachers, leading them to reach out to the Holy Spirit for help and inspiration. They are conditions necessary both for effective preaching and for the preacher's spiritual well-being. Preachers have the privilege and thrill of experiencing these creative moments again and again. Unhealthy feelings can, however, become confused with these healthy ones and undermine them. This can be unnerving and disabling. For instance, overfamiliarity with their material can mislead preachers into feeling that their sermon ideas are elementary or mundane or lacklustre when they are not. Confidence ebbs away, despair and even panic can set in. Gradually, as they come to understand and expect the emotional ups and downs of these processes and the patterns they take, they can establish at the centre of their being, beneath the emotional flux, a quiet confidence and assurance. This has a stabilizing effect, sustains their morale, and enables them to pursue their vocation and each preaching task with a measure of equanimity.

So preaching means living with emotional cycles, including the build up of tension and its creative release. The nature and intensity of these will differ from one preacher to another and from one appointment to another, as will the ways in which they cope with them. Some will simply endure them stoically. But a more positive response is to accept them as part of what is involved in pursuing their calling, offering these fluctuating feelings to God, along with themselves and their sermon preparation. The following circumstances, which can impede the healthy build up of tension and its creative release, indicate that preachers need to take a careful look at their emotions, their effects and the ways in which they are trying to live with and control them. When, for instance, preachers

- feel the affective aspects of their preaching life and their ways of coping with them are unsatisfactory and having undesirable effects upon their preaching and their family and friends
- are having to steel or 'psych themselves up' for preaching appointments to compensate for a lack of inspiration, excitement and spiritual anticipation, commonly associated with the work of the Holy Spirit
- feel the emotional cost to them and others is simply too high
- find that the preaching tension is being released in damaging ways
- are unhealthily depressed and emotionally drained
- find it difficult to regain their energy, equanimity and equilibrium after preaching, or that it takes an inordinate length of time to do so.

Reactions like these can be associated with dysfunctional emotional dissonance and stress. It is not possible to offer advice here to anyone who has such symptoms, other than to suggest that they admit to themselves that they are experiencing them and possibly seek advice and help. One of the ways of getting support set out in Chapter 9 may be helpful.

THE PREACHING SEQUENCE

The description of this sequence is shorter than the others, even though the act of preaching is our central theme. But then, the whole book could be folded into this section because every part of it is designed to raise the quality and effectiveness of preaching. Here, however, the focus is on some of the emotional cycles commonly experienced by preachers during this sequence. The next chapter explores the relationships and interaction between preachers and congregations, which are vital to this sequence.

Preaching takes place in a world far removed from that of private preparation. The luxury of drafting, revising and editing has been left behind in the study for the actual delivery of the sermon. What happens now cannot be edited, no matter how much preachers would like to, except in their minds. Instead, preachers are faced with a congregation and with responsibility for preaching the gospel, and perhaps also leading worship. They are caught up in an event, preaching to a heterogeneous group of people with diverse feelings and expectations. Now they are using quite different skills from those used in preparation in order to relate and communicate with the congregation in the presence of God. But as they do so, preachers may have a range of emotional experiences not dissimilar to those they have both in preparation and in the aftermath of preaching. On some occasions they know and feel that they are attuned to themselves, in rapport with God and the congregation and communicating effectively. These are uplifting experiences. On other occasions, their experience is the very opposite.

Strangely, bad experiences in preparation can lead to bad or good experiences in preaching; similarly, good experiences in preparation can lead to good or bad experiences in preaching. It is not possible to predict the sequence, even though it is natural to expect that a good experience in preparation will be followed by a good one in preaching, not least because the preacher is more likely to approach the event with confidence. But that does not always happen. On the other hand, preachers may find that a good preaching experience follows on from a bad time in preparation. In the one case, preachers have to cope with a crushing crash of expectations; in the other, they are lifted by a dramatic rise in feelings.

This bewildering variety of experiences arises from a diversity of causes, many of which will remain hidden in the mysteries of human and divine encounters in preaching. In evaluating them we need to remember what has already been said about preachers' feelings. Some of them arise from the difficulties preachers face in making reliable assessments of their preparation, the material they produce and the feelings they have about it. For instance, as already noted, over-familiarity with their material can lead them to feel that it is commonplace or pedestrian and lose confidence in it. On the other hand, growing awareness of the complexities they are addressing may lead them to feel they are being simplistic – with a similar emotional response. Or again, they may overvalue their sermon ideas out of ignorance, and have misplaced confidence. Yet again, preachers may feel at the top of their form whilst preparing, full of energy and inspiration, and out of form when they come to preach, or *vice versa*.

The truth of the matter is that preaching is an existential event in which preachers are only one of the participants. Much depends on what members of congregations bring to the experience and contribute to it: their knowledge, expectation, need, and ability to listen and engage with the preacher. All this will condition the performance of preachers, affecting what both they and members of congregations get out of it. In turn, that will depend upon the mood in which members approach the preacher and the preaching and the positive or negative atmosphere generated.

This brief commentary on the variable human factors in preaching and their effects does not take into account the activity of God in the event, in preachers and congregations, and in the interaction between them. For example, the Holy Spirit may achieve things in the preaching event which could not possibly have been anticipated in the preparation. Because of this unpredictable interaction between God, preachers and congregations, we simply cannot know all that is going on in preaching, still less assess the impact it has. But true though that is, it still does not exonerate preachers from trying to discover as much as possible about the underlying causes of their feelings, successes and difficulties in order to develop their abilities, their sense of equanimity, and their capacity to serve their congregations.

## THE FEEDBACK SEQUENCE[2]

Feedback is important to preachers because it can profoundly affect them, positively and negatively. They need congregational feedback from their preaching: the absence of it is unnerving. Naturally, whether they deserve it or not, they want complimentary feedback. Appreciation encourages and makes all the hard work seem worthwhile. But both genuine and insincere feedback can be a dangerous, heady commodity with undesirable side effects. For instance, it can be misleading; it can make preachers conceited or complacent or depressed. The desire for complimentary responses can become addictive, and seeking it can lead preachers to compromise their integrity and deflect them from their vocational aims. Digesting the feedback as they receive it is obviously important; it enables them to assess their preaching ministry as it evolves. Definitive evaluation of preaching, of course, is impossible: significant results can be delayed, displaced and hidden from preachers; only God can know the full impact of preaching. Consequently all human assessments

---

[2] cf George Lovell, *Consultancy Ministry and Mission: A handbook for practitioners and work consultants in Christian organizations* (Tunbridge Wells: Burns and Oates, 2000) pp 342-344.

of preaching are partial; but they are still critically important if they are based on reliable data and, at the same time, treated as interim and incomplete. Preachers need to bear this in mind. Then, by approaching positive and negative feedback in the ways described below, they can contribute to their own development, tackling difficulties purposefully, and making good responses to the ups and downs of their ministry. A proper understanding of what is going on can also help preachers to neutralize any tendency they might have towards preoccupation with feedback. Processing feedback creatively also enables preachers to get a better understanding of themselves and their preaching as they really are, and to make any necessary changes in their attitude to and practice of preaching. To do this, preachers need to assess both positive and negative feedback critically and imaginatively:

- in relation to their vocational beliefs, purposes, self-image of themselves as preachers and their resources
- with respect to their feelings, the given realities of their abilities, current circumstances and resources and the status of the data
- in the light of their intuitions, instinctive assessments and hunches.

Such an approach means preachers are earthed in a healthy self-knowledge, and orientated to the aims of their calling. But, rewarding as it might be, handling feedback in this way can be demanding: it calls for discipline and courage; it may involve acquiring new skills and learning how to be more objective. It has the potential to correct casual, emotive and irrational ways of dealing with feedback. We turn now to ways of doing this with four kinds of feedback, which can be positive or negative.

*Self-feedback*

This is the inner, automatic and intuitive response preachers experience in private and in public that indicates to them how *they* think and feel things are going. Such responses can affect preachers profoundly, for good or ill, in many different ways. For instance they can galvanize and freeze them, confirm, confound, liberate and embarrass them; they can be variously pleasing, painful, insightful, misleading and damaging; they can engender thankful satisfaction, euphoria, relief, a sense of humiliation or failure. As they affect mood, composure and energy levels, they can affect the ability to think and act for better or worse. Some of the most acute experiences of negative feedback come when least expected, and consequently are difficult to deal with.

Taking both positive and negative experiences of self-feedback seriously can be difficult, but doing so is essential. Poise, well-being and performance depend upon being able to handle creatively, both in public and in private, all the forms it takes. However, although it can be persistent and clamorous, it is not always a reliable – and never an infallible – guide to the effectiveness of the preacher's performance. Nonetheless, it is a valuable personal indicator when it is interpreted carefully and the implications read off circumspectly. The left hand column of Display 4:1 suggests some ways of doing these things.

*Unsolicited feedback from others*

Preachers frequently receive this after a service. Mostly it is offered as an accepted social courtesy, generally it is complimentary, and occasionally it is critical or patronizing. Its potential depends upon the motives, insights and sincerity of those offering it. For instance, it can be an expression of genuine gratitude or a caring challenge; it can be an attempt to support and encourage, or to curry favour. All too easily preachers can make distorted assessments of the impact of their preaching for instance, by embracing the complimentary comments they wish to hear and eschewing or nullifying those they do not want to hear, or alternatively, by allowing crushing remarks to eclipse or negate genuinely appreciative ones. Such responses can reinforce or challenge the substantive image they have built up of themselves as good, bad or indifferent preachers and what their congregations say to them. Even those considered to be poor preachers can have extraordinary effects upon some people when God has completed his work in and through their preaching.

In order to make appropriate responses preachers need first to be able to identify and act upon anything that they need to take seriously; second, to accept critical comments, handle them constructively and cope with any associated pain, and thirdly, to sift out that which is inconsequential and neutralize it graciously. The right hand column of Display 4:2 suggests some ways of doing these things.

*Casually solicited feedback*

Preachers are inclined to seek this kind of feedback when they do not receive any response whatsoever to their preaching, or when they feel a sermon has not gone very well, or when they feel a little disap

### Personal experience and feedback

Some questions help to prepare to receive and work on feedback that comes in all ways:

- What kind of good and bad inner responses and reactions do you customarily make when you receive feedback that is positive/negative?
- What responses do those with whom you work often make and what effects do they have upon you?
- What would you have to do in order to improve the way in which you process and use feedback?
- What kind(s) of feedback do you need from whom or from what?
- Why do you need it?
- Are there any dangers in trying to get it?
- How can you get and receive it

### Guidelines to processing feedback

Remain critically open to negative and positive feedback; don't dismiss or quench it by denigrating the sources. In relation to feedback, however, the source may be wrong and you may be right. Several things can help:

- Make it usable and manageable by:
  - collating and condensing it to avoid the problems of feedback overload;
  - try to depersonalise and objectify it possibly by writing it down, or talking to someone else about it. Look at it from different perspectives. Feelings are facts but try to avoid being preoccupied with them. Delay reaction when possible.

- Determine quite specifically to what the feedback properly relates: To you? Your preaching? Your beliefs/purposes? Your behaviour? Your church? Or is it a projection of a problem that others have?

- Decide whether or not anything can be done about it and whether it is worthy of serious attention.

- Try to keep things in proportion by counter balancing but not balancing positive with negative feedback and *vice versa*.

- Avoid confusing qualitative with quantitative feedback: one person may be right and the rest wrong and vice versa; the person who makes the most noise may or may not be right!

- Evaluate feedback, determine its implications in relation to beliefs, purposes, needs, resources and your personal performance (not only in relation to yourself), and in relation to what you know of its source.

- Whenever possible seek help and support, not just one or the other.

**Display 4:1** Some Guidelines for Reflecting on and Processing Feedback[3]

---

[3] cf George Lovell, *Consultancy*, pp. 343.

pointed or uncomfortable. Fishing for feedback and especially for compliments is an unhealthy and dangerous occupation. It can leave preachers feeling that they have demeaned or ingratiated themselves, and that can adversely affect their self-image and their relationships with those from whom they have sought such feedback. Loaded rather than unloaded questions come most naturally to the lips of preachers as they reach out for reassurance: 'That sermon was all right, wasn't it?' rather than, 'How do you honestly feel that went? I would very much like to know.' Giving an honest answer to the first of these questions is more difficult than to the second, because the implied request is for uncritical affirmation, not a realistic assessment. While there are good reasons to veer away from casually solicited feedback, it is easier said than done when sermons leave you dejected, flat and ill at ease. On such occasions it takes a lot of personal confidence and self-restraint to keep one's own counsel. If preachers must seek feedback in such circumstances, it is best to approach soul friends forthrightly.

*Carefully solicited feedback*

Feedback can be obtained formally and informally, through serious structured and unstructured interactive discussions or interviews. (Unstructured interviews and discussions are free flowing; structured ones have set questions to be tackled in a given sequence.) Many of these are initiated and led by preachers themselves and some by others, as is the case of formal assessments. Another way is for someone to solicit and to collect feedback on behalf of preachers and report back to them. When it is done well, this method has some uses, but it can leave preachers uneasy about what has been said in their absence. Generally speaking, first- rather than second-hand feedback is to be preferred, as it is normally easier for preachers to cope with. The following factors are key to preachers getting feedback without compromising themselves and their relationships:

*The preacher's disposition*: Preachers must want to know what others really think. To discover this they must be open, receptive and undefensive. Then they need to be able to consider the feedback critically and objectively in private, and in some cases with those from whom they seek it.

*The disposition of those offering feedback*: They need to be genuinely interested in helping preachers to fulfil their potential and respectful of their autonomy. Ideally they will be forthright, gracious, understanding, non-judgemental and non-directive.

*Understanding between those offering feedback and preachers:* There needs to be an understanding, tacit or contracted, between them, that preachers will consider the feedback seriously and do what seems right to them, but that it will not be imposed upon them in a way that compromises their autonomy.

*Questions:* As already demonstrated, unloaded questions are basic tools in getting and exploring feedback; they facilitate qualitative exchanges between preachers and their informants which enables them to think together.[4]

Further help towards getting reliable independent feedback may be found in some – but not all – denominational assessment and appraisal schemes for ministers and preachers and through inter-personal support (see Chapter 9). Preachers are likely to experience all four kinds of feedback: self and unsolicited and casually solicited feedback and possibly carefully solicited feedback. Whilst these forms of feedback can be differentiated, they do not form nice tidy patterns; they combine and interact in a preacher's consciousness to form emotive systems of reflective thought, which can be messy. Figure 4:2 illustrates the systemic nature of feedback and the different forms that can operate separately and in different combinations at any given point of time. Self-feedback, for instance, which can be experienced independently, is also generated by feedback from others. Sometimes different kinds of feedback clash and confound. A good response to such experiences is emotionally-controlled thought that leads to constructive action; a bad one is to dismiss out of hand anything that is uncongenial. At other times, the sources are in unison. When all forms of feedback are overwhelmingly positive, preachers have to avoid becoming conceited or complacent and continue to work humbly for improvement. When they are negative and strident, preachers may have to cope with depression and loss of self-worth and find the courage and resources to assess the implications, and respond creatively to them. All forms and combinations of feedback have good or bad potential.

Receiving and obtaining feedback is one thing; processing it creatively through the human psyche is quite a different matter. Finding ways of doing so is enormously important to preachers. It is the quality of the ways in which they process feedback through

---

[4] cf George Lovell, *Analysis and Design: A handbook for practitioners and consultants in church and community work* (Tunbridge Wells: Burns and Oates, 1994) e.g. pp. 184–188 for information about different kinds of questions and their uses.

their system, not the nature nor the quality of the feedback, that ultimately determines the long- and short-term impact it has upon them, their preaching, and their relationships with family, friends and congregations.

Several things that help preachers have already been noted: self-knowledge and acceptance of themselves; understanding their inner mental processes and the ups and downs of their feelings; confidence to trust themselves; the ability and resources to think clearly under pressure and to access appropriate bodies of knowledge; the ability to bond with people emotionally at levels and depths appropriate to the nature of their working relationships; and lastly the ability to respond constructively to challenging preaching events. Further guidelines about processing feedback are suggested in the right hand column of Display 4:1. Again, the ideas for support in Chapter 9 could help preachers to handle feedback. Overall, a key to being objective and realistic about any kind of feedback and to making good assessments of it, is for preachers to evaluate it in relation to its quality and their beliefs, purposes and intentions, and not simply by how bad or good it might make them feel, important as feelings and their effects can be. (See the penultimate suggestion in Display 4:1).

Developing the ability to handle any and all forms of feedback creatively is especially important at a time when evaluation, assessment and accountability are being stressed in preaching and other circles. Awareness and understanding of the vital importance of doing so can motivate preachers to work at evaluative, reflective learning processes even when to do so makes heavy demands upon their intellect, emotions, and spiritual resources.

The Reflection Sequence

Throughout the sequences of the preaching circle, preachers reflect, pray, think and do theology about things in private and public. But a discrete reflection sequence, strategically placed between one preaching appointment and the preparation for the next, provides preachers with valuable formal and informal opportunities to: reflect; catch up with themselves; determine the implications of the feedback from the previous appointment; explore biblical passages that have 'spoken' to them; examine and research their thoughts and feelings about spiritual and secular events. Firming up their conclusions from these reflections consolidates the evaluative learning processes and informs the preparation for the next and subsequent appointments

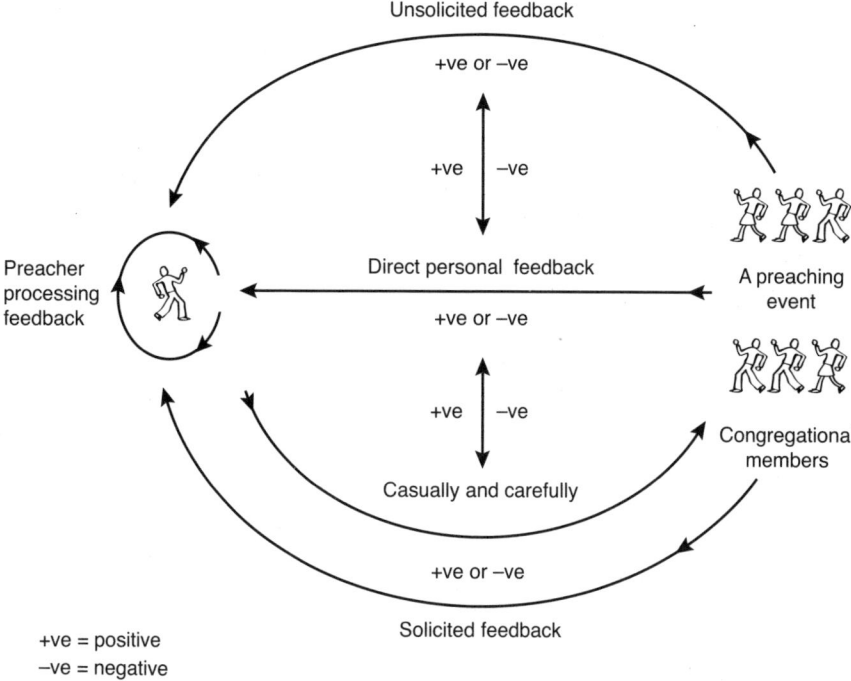

**Figure 4:2** Elements in the Systemic Pattern of Feedback

There are various approaches to mental and spiritual reflection, each of which has its own characteristics moods and modes. However, because they have features in common, boundaries between them can become blurred. Here the features that differentiate them are described briefly as an aid to understanding and using them more effectively.[5]

*Thinking things through* involves different but complementary activities. *Analysing situations and subject matter and designing and constructing sermons* use the active mood and mode of thoughtful being and doing. This kind of thinking involves the disciplined application of mind and heart to the job of exploring, questioning and working things out systematically. It is carried out in various ways through logical thought informed by intuitions and hunches; by forming and testing hypotheses; by submitting the product of the imagination to critical scrutiny.

*Meditating and reflecting* are in quite different moods and modes, relaxed rather than active. They involve concentrating and waiting upon things expectantly, mulling things over and cogitating, listening

---

[5] cf George Lovell, *Consultancy* e.g. pp. 86–87, 91, and *Analysis and Design* e.g. Chapter 5.

to what they might say to us, pursuing thoughts that arise. *Prayer* is a listening to and a dialogue with God. *Meditation, reflection and prayer* are activities which allow the freewheeling association of mind and heart with all that is happening in the widest possible context.

*Formulating conclusions, drawing out implications and determining learning* requires a searching, active, mood. It involves standing back from things, looking for connections, surveying and scanning in order to discover anything that might emerge, and finding ways of expressing it accurately.

*Doing theology* is variously in the active and reflective moods and modes. *Applied or practical theology* is actively putting beliefs into practice. *Experiential theology* is reflecting on events. *Emergent theology* is about discovering God at work.

These different activities range from 'direct thinking' to what Koestler calls 'thinking aside'.[6] They draw and feed upon one another. Working at things systematically and praying about them in a context of pastoral care integrates them, creates a spirituality of its own, generates energy and enables preachers to be more effective. Sometimes the appropriate movement from one mood and mode of thinking to another occurs naturally. Otherwise, it is necessary to discern which approach to use: a structured analytical approach; a meditative reflective period to mull over what has emerged; a time of prayer, or, in St Ignatius of Loyola's expressive phrase, 'a colloquy with the Lord'.

*Reflecting*

Reflection is one of a cluster of words such as contemplation, meditation, rumination, and cogitation. Here we use it as an umbrella word to describe this sequence, and to indicate the use of any of the methods described above. Preachers who do this are 'reflective preachers' – to adapt Donald Schon's widely used concept of the 'reflective practitioner'.[7] Unreflecting preachers have little to contribute to the church and the world. Indeed it could be argued that the quality of preaching is directly related to that of the preacher's reflective praxis or, to put it another way, the capacity to preach effectively is closely related to the capacity for reflection. There are an infinite number of approaches to reflecting. Some of

---

[6] Arthur Koestler, *The Act of Creation* (London: Hutchinson, 1964) Chapter 7.

[7] See Donald A. Schon, *Educating the Reflective Practitioner: Towards a New Design for Teaching and Learning in the Professions* (San Francisco and Oxford: Jossey-Bass Publishers, 1990) cf. Lovell, *Consultancy* pp. 314–315, 330–331.

them are highly schematized; others are quite the opposite. Here we note some practical aids to reflecting.

- 'Wait on' the preaching issue or problem or situation or whatever you are trying to understand: 'attend' to it; let it speak to you; have a kind of conversation or dialogue with it by asking questions to or about it. As one person puts it, 'attend to talkback from the situation'. Or try to read the situation and ask questions of it.
- Address a problem reflectively and systematically rather than analytically by pondering questions such as those suggested in Chapter 10, p. 168.
- Explore the issue/situation in relation to scriptural passages that it evokes.
- Get the essentials of the issues down on paper through personal brainstorming. Just write without thinking. The main character in *Gilead*,[8] reflecting in his old age about a lifetime of preaching, says 'For me writing always felt like praying ...'. *Then* reflect on what you have written. *Then* reflect on your reflections. And so on ... These are rungs on what Schon calls the 'ladder of reflection'.
- 'Journalling' is a structured way of writing reflectively about aspects of life and experiences from different perspectives developed by Ira Progoff (See Chapter 9).
- Build up brain patterns[9] or mind maps by writing in the centre of a blank page in one or two words the preaching issues or problem or situation or whatever you are trying to understand, and noting the strands of your reflective thoughts on separate branch lines in different directions. The result is a picture of the pattern of your thought. An example is given in Display 4: 2.
- Consider the issue in relation to its effects on you, your vocation, relationships and overall context.
- Talk to God and/or another person about the issue, possibly using one or more of the approaches outlined above to structure the prayerful conversation.
- The above methods are about reflecting on *specifics* and drawing out *generalities*. An alternative is to reflect *generally* on various examples of an issue and draw out implications for *specifics*.
- Simply allow your mind to freewheel and receive what comes to mind!

[8] Marilynne Robinson, *Gilead* (London: Virago, 2004), p. 21.
[9] cf Tony Buzan, *Use Your Head* (London: BBC, 1974) cf pp. 186, 333, 336, 349. Tony Buzan, with Barry Buzan *The Mind Map Book* (London: BBC, 1993).

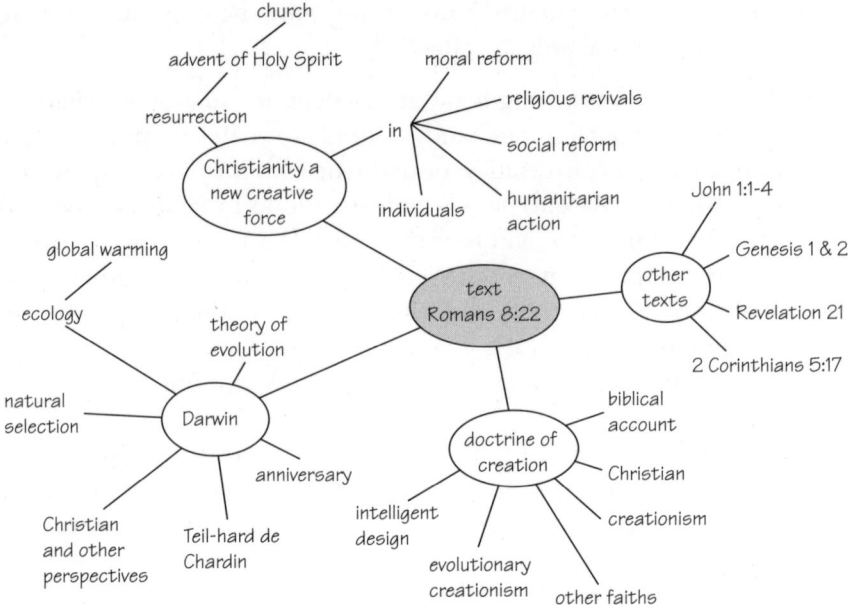

**Display 4:2** An Example of a Brain Pattern or a Mind Map

None of these ways of reflecting is necessarily better than others; they are all more or less appropriate to different preachers, their temperaments and moods at any given time, and the situation in which and the subject matter on which they have to reflect. Preachers need to discover and use reflective methods that work for them. But as David Smail says, 'our ability to reflect on our experience is only as good as the linguistic tools available to us to do so.'[10] Taking care, therefore, to find words and sentences which most accurately describe our thoughts and feelings pays high dividends whichever method of reflection is used. And that is something that preachers are normally good at.

Working through the preaching circle time after time is a potentially powerful formative process: it can build up the spirituality of preachers and develop the vocational and the professional nature and shape of their ministry. The value and impact of the outcome is profoundly affected by the depth of the preacher's spirituality and devotional life; the quality of their thinking and reflecting; and the discipline with which they approach their study and the rigours of the circle.

---

[10] David Smail, *Illusion and reality: The Meaning of Anxiety* (Guildford: Dent, 1984), p. 64. Cf Lovell, *Analysis* pp. 176–179.

## Chapter 5

# *PREACHERS AND THE NATURE OF CONGREGATIONS*

The purpose of this chapter is to help preachers to explore the nature and characteristics of congregations, both when their members are gathered in churches and when they are dispersed in the wider world. It concludes with an overview of the principal perspectives discussed in Part Two.

### I  Congregations, Churches and Services of Worship

Common speech blurs significant distinctions between congregations, churches and services of worship. For instance, people speak of going to church to indicate that they are going to a church building in order to join a congregation to share in an act of worship. What they mean is, of course, readily understood. But in order to think about the nature and function of congregations, it is necessary to distinguish between these three closely related but different entities.

*Local churches* are the sum total of many constituent parts: buildings, plant and capital assets; organized Christian societies; legal and ecclesiastical constitutions; meetings and councils; traditions and common practices; members, officers, clergy and lay workers; a range of activities including acts of worship; formal and informal power structures; and, of course, congregations. This is not to mention their denominational and ecumenical structures and social relationships. It is the responsibility of churches to organize and ensure the well-being of congregations. Whilst *congregations* are integral to churches, they are vital sociological and spiritual entities in their own right, with a life of their own. They are a public human face of a church and its predominant and most persistent activity, but they are not the church. Large or small *congregations* are open but structured groups, each with its own culture and ethos. It is *congregations, not churches*, through which preachers pursue their vocational preaching ministries, normally in the context of *services of worship*. Understanding them and how they work is essential to preachers: getting to know the congregations to which they preach is part of the preacher's craft (see, for instance, the section on 'congregational perspectives' in Chapter 11).

Congregations differ in all kinds of ways, for example in size and ethnicity, and less tangibly but just as importantly, in character and ethos. But they all have the potential to perform vital Christian functions and they have characteristics in common. Groups of these characteristics form the following four facets of a general model of congregations.

Facet 1: structural and constitutional characteristics of congregations
Facet 2: spiritual and pastoral services offered to members of congregations
Facet 3: missiological functions of both congregations and their members
Facet 4: formative processes in congregations

Awareness of these facets can help preachers to get a better grasp of the nature and dynamics of congregations in general. This helps them to explore these aspects of the congregations to which they preach and their interaction with them. It also helps preachers to profile congregations, to set realistic objectives for themselves and thus to relate more creatively to them.

FACET ONE: STRUCTURAL AND CONSTITUTIONAL CHARACTERISTICS OF CONGREGATIONS

As we have already noted, members of congregations vary enormously in character, ethnicity, size, theology, worldview, and in many other different ways. All of these have to be taken into account by preachers. But it is the following features, which combine to create the unique socio-spiritual structure and constitution of each congregation.

*Congregations are heterogeneous, ever-changing, free associations of people with open physical access and therefore unpredictable in size, composition and mood.*

They are normally made up of people who, in addition to the differences already mentioned, also differ in other ways: age, experience, intellect, emotional intelligence, faith development, knowledge of the Bible and understanding of Christianity, commitment to Christianity, the church and the congregation, and their social status and political outlook. (On this congregational diversity, see also Chapters 1 and 6.) In addition, they are presently experiencing radical change. (See Chapters 1 and 12.) Remarkable as it may seem, inspired preaching is able to communicate the Christian faith and spiritual insights to very different people in the same congregation when other methods fail. This is a treasured feature of preaching.

*Congregations are physically open, but access to the inner life and fellowship can be controlled, by design or default, by deacons, ministers, priests, core members and preachers.*

Congregations are variously hospitable or inhospitable, psychologically, socially, spiritually and theologically open and/or closed. For instance, secret inside knowledge, do's and don'ts known only to 'insiders', can operate powerfully in congregations to create and segregate some groups and cliques, and make other people outsiders and keep them so. Secret inside knowledge creates and maintains invisible impenetrable barriers. In sociological terms these barriers constitute 'symbolic boundaries.'[1] On the other hand, normally welcoming and friendly members of congregations can leave newcomers out of things unintentionally simply by concentrating on valued relationships with long standing friends.

---

[1] On how symbolic boundaries are created in society and their effects upon community life, see, for instance, books by Anthony P. Cohen, *Belonging: Identity, and Social Organisation in British Rural Cultures* (Manchester University Press, 1982), *Symbolising Boundaries: Identity and Diversity in British Cultures* (Manchester University Press, 1986) and *The Symbolic Construction of Community* (London: Routledge,1989). On symbolic boundaries in congregations, see Leonora Tubbs Tisdale, *Preaching as Local Theology and Folk Art* (Minneapolis: Fortress Press, 1997); see particularly Chapter 3.

*Congregations are human and divine meeting points and touching places, means of audiences with God and places to experience the real presence of Christ.*

They have been described as 'communities of commitment and conviction' where 'people express their deepest longings and understandings.'

*Congregations can be examples of the collective socio-spiritual nature of Christianity and thus antidotes to individualism.*

*Congregations are hubs of human networks and so have the potential for spreading the Christian faith whether or not they are representative of society and the communities of which they are a part.*

When dispersed, members of congregations are in association and contact with people in all kinds of Christian and secular groups who are not normally in the congregation. What can be described as secondary congregations are formed when they use what they have heard in services in their conversations and arguments with family members, friends, people in other church groups and organizations, workmates, colleagues and total strangers. So unknowingly, preachers can help and prepare members of congregations to be 'secondary preachers' and advocates and apologists of Christianity.

FACET TWO: SPIRITUAL AND PASTORAL SERVICES OFFERED TO MEMBERS OF CONGREGATIONS

Preachers and congregations together, through services of worship and sermons, offer and provide spiritual opportunities and pastoral services to members by assisting and enabling them to:

- worship and adore God
- seek forgiveness and renew their relationships with God and people
- be challenged and confronted
- be called and commissioned
- reposition themselves and take their bearings in the Kingdom, the Church and the world
- equip themselves for their Christian lives and vocations in the Church and in the world.

Preachers and members of congregations also offer pastoral care to each other when they meet for worship, through personal relationships, conversations in the informal mingling before and after services, and later through extended congregational networks, a precious feature of congregational life. All of these pastoral services and care are well known, but there is a subtle aspect of them that is not generally recognized. Robin Green, in a remarkable book, argues that *'Liturgy, which is the vehicle through which worship is expressed, creates an environment in which human beings confront those sides of themselves which under normal circumstances they dare not face.* ... Pastoral care and liturgy come remarkably close to fulfilling the same functions. Both offer ways of seeing God and ourselves'.[2] (Green's italics)

FACET THREE: MISSIOLOGICAL FUNCTIONS OF CONGREGATIONS AND THEIR MEMBERS

Congregations and congregational life are essential missiological structures of the Christian church as well as being instruments of worship. For instance, they:

- are means of evangelism and apologetic instruments
- witness to and proclaim the gospel publicly
- bring people to faith and nurture them in it
- inform and educate people in the church and in society
- enable congregations and their members to engage in Christian apologetics in relation to inter-faith dialogue, critical developments in society and contemporary events
- build up Christian relationships and resources through creating socio-spiritual communities and networks.

Congregations perform these missiological functions when they gather for worship through the liturgy, preaching, *koinonia* (fellowship) and the active presence of God and, as already noted, when they disperse, some members continue this missiological work beyond gathered congregational life by acting as evangelists and ambassadors of the Christian faith in family groups and in all kinds of community and secular settings. All this indicates that services of worship provide many opportunities for mission and that some of their members are missionaries. Congregations are anything but audiences for preachers.

---

[2] Robin Green, *Only Connect: worship and liturgy from the perspective of pastoral care* (London: Darton, Longman and Todd, 1987) pp. 8–9.

FACET FOUR: FORMATIVE PROCESSES IN CONGREGATIONS

It is beyond the scope of this section to trace out the complex ways in which congregations are formed. This can be explored in the burgeoning literature on congregations and their life cycles.[3] However, the following points are made with particular reference to our theme in this section of the book: working dynamics and relationships.

- Congregations are variously formed by divine and human action and interaction: over time they acquire their own culture, tradition and history.
- Life-cycles and vocations of members, their leaders, lay and ordained, and, of course, preachers pulse through congregations: sometimes creatively, at other times destructively. These have positive and negative effects on the life-cycles of congregations and upon their form, ethos and fitness for purpose.
- Congregations can generate individual and collective vocations.
- Successive sequences of services of worship make important contributions to the formation of the character and ethos of congregations when liturgies and preaching combine to be powerful existential events.
- Effective preaching depends upon several interpersonal and spiritual factors, such as the way in which preachers and congregations relate to each other during the preaching; the preacher's charisma, integrity, authority and ability to communicate; the relevance and power of the preaching; and the psycho-spiritual atmosphere, including the openness of preachers and members of congregations to the presence and activity of the Holy Spirit.
- Local churches maintain and develop congregations. Week by week a small army of people expend enormous amounts of

---

[3] See for instance: Edwin Friedman, *Generation to Generation – Family Process in Church and Synagogue* (The Guilford Press, 1985); J. Hopewell, Congregation: *Stories and Structures* (London: SCM, 1988); Barry Palmer, *Congregational Profiling: Developing the Concept, Research Report 2, November 1997/Cheshvan 5758* (Leo Baeck College, 1997); Tisdale, *Preaching*, Chapter 3, 'Exegeting the Congregation'; Malcolm Grundy, *Understanding Congregations: A New Shape for the Local Church* (Mowbray, 1998); Margaret Harris, *Organizing God's Work: Challenges for Churches and Synagogues* (Macmillan Press Ltd, 1998); Helen Cameron, Philip Richter, Douglas Davies, and Frances Ward, *Studying Local Churches: A Handbook* (London: SCM, 2005); Martin F. Saarinen, *The Life Cycle of a Congregation* (The Alban Institute, Special Papers and Research Reports, 1986). But even in this literature, frustratingly and confusingly, 'congregation' is sometimes used as a synonym for 'church'.

energy to facilitate and develop congregational life and worship. Preachers who hold official positions in the church or are pastors to the congregations influence congregational formation through these roles as well as through their preaching. However, problems can be encountered in doing this, and in some cases relationships between preachers and congregations can be adversely affected.

## II Some Contemporary Challenges to Congregations, Preachers and Churches

Parts One and Five of this book explore the contemporary opportunities and challenges to Christianity and therefore to preachers and congregations. Members of congregations face them too, as they try to live out their Christian faith in church and society. Challenges and opportunities present themselves, in one form or another, in their experiences at home, in their day jobs and in their social relationships. Some of these relate to the validity of Christianity and difficulties of living it out with faith and with integrity. Challenges come in various forms: from people who are dismissive of Christianity, from Christians and sceptics alike, disturbed by contemporary events, such as an earthquake, and from those who are reaching out for faith.

Another way in which they encounter opportunities and challenges is through decisions they have to make, and stands they have take in relation to difficult moral issues in the course of their working and personal lives. They know all about the tensions and problems of conflicting views and compromises to be made. And they have to do all this out of their own faith, together with all the doubts and unresolved questions that they may have. Unavoidably, they are engaged in situational ethics and apologetics and in doing theology in the messiness of the real world, not in abstraction. This is a very different context from that of formal church services dedicated to prayer and Christian preaching and worship. To complicate things further, they may feel that they do not have the biblical and theological knowledge or the intellectual ability to put the Christian case, or to work through some of the tricky moral issues. What are the implications for preachers? How can they help and support congregational members?

First and foremost, preachers can resource members of congregations by demonstrating in their preaching that they experience and grapple with these issues themselves. They can show that, while it is satisfying to have clear-cut answers, that is not always possible.

Of itself, this can be enormously important to members of congregations who identify with those who preach like this because they know that the preachers identify with them. This induces empathetic bonding between preachers and members of congregations, which, in turn, causes them to be attentive to what the preachers have to say, because they know that they have been there and know what it is like. Establishing this kind of bonding is vital to effective preaching. Experiencing bonding whilst preaching and afterwards in informal pastoral conversations are high moments in a preacher's life. Preachers are more likely to be able to bond with congregations if they are in touch with their own inner experiences, problems and doubts, and open about them. It also helps if they listen to and engage with the experience of others.

Another way in which preachers can help is by demonstrating how they actually work through these complex issues, how they do practical theology and how they apply it. That is, they demonstrate the inner processes and mechanisms by which they come to their own decisions and answers and live with their doubts. One such mechanism is the use of 'simplicities' (see Chapter 12 and Appendix I) to engage with moral and spiritual complexities. This is a very different approach from giving cut and dried answers, which are invariably simplistic; it is introducing congregations, through sermons which are models of worked examples, to ways in which *they* might be able to work at *their* opportunities and challenges. The emphasis here is upon learning from the preacher's way of thinking through the issues.

Through such sermons, almost incidentally, preachers make clear what everyone knows: thinking about and deciding what should be done is one thing, but doing it as another. Sermons that acknowledge this to be problematic and explore what is involved in making the transition from resolving to do something that is demanding to doing it can be affirmative and enormously helpful. They provide opportunities to indicate ways in which people of faith can be helped through prayer, interpersonal support, careful preparation, and the strengthening ever-present God. In short, this kind of preaching, what I call 'process preaching', expounds the *how* rather than the *what* of making the most of the opportunities of the Christian life and facing its challenges: or, more precisely, ways and means of arriving at a desirable outcome. Sermons of this kind indicate how people who differ significantly in belief and faith from the preacher can work constructively at their own beliefs and doubts. Transcending religious and spiritual differences in this way contributes to interfaith dialogue. (Appendix I is an example of this kind of preaching.)

This is not to say that there is not a place for preachers to address controversial issues directly from their own faith base. Similarly, there is a need to preach about the great doctrines of the Christian faith, which provide essential foundations for process preaching. Doctrinal, expository and process preaching complement each other and can be woven together in a sermon. Amongst other things, this kind of approach freely acknowledges that living the Christian life can be difficult, and involves struggling with complex issues to which there are often no easy answers and in which compromises have to be made: it is an antidote to any suggestion that living the Christian faith is without problems. It also indicates that we are always working with limited understanding, and with human phenomena that we cannot completely explain. So while we must use reason to work things out, much of what we do involves intuitive acts of faith, taking calculated risks and learning from what we do as we do it. Preaching true to the human situation makes it clear that we have to live within our limitations and accept the possibility of failure. And that leads to other sermons on how Christianity approaches failure and how it helps us to cope with it: they too can help congregations with *their* opportunities and challenges.

Not all the resources congregations need to live up to their calling in these circumstances can be provided through sermons and preaching. In addition to preaching of the kind sketched out here, they will need access to direct interpersonal help, fellowship groups and adult educational sessions. (See Chapters 2, 6 and 9). But this section indicates that there are very important contributions to be made through appropriate modes of preaching.

### III Pursuing the Implications

This overall profile of congregations might have implications for you and your preaching ministry or raise questions in your mind. Four ways in which you could possibly work at them are noted in this section.

**a.** *Reflect on the overall profile*

The following questions could help you to reflect on the overall profile of the characteristics of congregations.

What strikes you about the outline of the characteristics of congregations presented in this chapter?
Is there anything to which you feel you need to give further thought or on which you need to do more work?
What do you consider to be the most important challenges to preachers?
What is the most important challenge that you are facing, and what if anything do you intend to do about it?

**b.** *Do some further reading*

During the past fifty years there has been a growing interest in surveying local churches. In the 1960s, for instance, churches produced aids to help local people to carry out amateur sociological surveys of their churches, congregations and communities. More professional methods have evolved through drawing upon the growing literature on social and community studies and research. This chapter reflects this increasing interest in congregations as congregations.[3] Congregational profiling is now in vogue. Ways of describing and interpreting congregations have evolved, which draw upon semiology: the study of signs such as rituals, architecture etc. which indicate the character of congregations. (See the note in the next section on Leonara Tubbs Tisdale's work.) One of the projects in Chapter 11 describes how a group of preachers set out to discover what people were experiencing in congregations in twelve churches.

**c.** *Profiling congregations to which you minister*

Doing the following exercises could now be useful:

(1) Note the salient characteristics of the congregation(s) to which you minister.
(2) Describe the nature of your interaction with your congregation(s) and what would improve it.
(3) Describe the effect of your preaching that you most value and aim for.
(4) Note what would improve the impact of your preaching.
(5) Outline changes you wish to see in the congregation(s) to which you preach and what you could do towards bringing them about.

Should you wish to examine in more detail ways and means of surveying and profiling congregations, the books listed in reference 3 could be helpful. A chapter in the book by Leonara Tubbs Tisdale[4] is particularly useful for those wishing to use qualitative rather than quantitative methods to profile congregations. It is about preachers themselves observing and describing the telltale signs and symbols that indicate the character and culture of congregations; that is, she suggests, 'preachers ... become amateur ethnographers in their role as participant observers.'[5] The chapter has an intriguing title: 'Exegeting the Congregation'. Tisdale is rich in practical suggestions about how to profile congregations. For instance, she suggests noting and interpreting the significance of:

- the texts that have meaningful value to members of congregations
- the stories they tell
- events, activities and rituals that are important to them
- their humanitarian, relational and theological orientation
- their views of God (theology, Christology, pneumatology), of humanity (theological anthropology), of nature (theology of creation), of time (eschatology), of the church (ecclesiology), of Christian mission (evangelism, missiology, Christian ethics).[6]

The outcome can then be used as a basis for the imaginative task of conceptualizing the 'overarching "character" and "ethos" of a congregation.'[7]

**d.** *A review exercise*

A review of your preaching in relation to contemporary challenges to congregations could help you to earth aspects of this chapter in your own experience. First, note any points in Section II of this chapter and in Part One of this book which struck you as important Then think of a congregation, possibly one you have profiled, and bring to mind sermons you have preached recently, and any feedback you have received. Do you discern any evidence that what we described as 'process preaching' sermons could help members of the congregation to develop their ability to do theology on the issues they are facing?

---

[4] Tisdale, *Preaching*, Chapter 3.
[5] *Ibid.* p. 60.
[6] *Ibid.* pp. 80–84.
[7] *Ibid.* p. 86.

## IV. An Overview of the Principal Perspectives in Part Two

Part Two has presented four complementary perspectives of the working dynamics and relationships of the vocational life of a preacher. *Perspective one* gives an overall picture of the life cycle of a preacher and describes the principal phases. *Perspective two* depicts and examines the private and public domains of the preacher's working worlds. *Perspective three* delineates and explores the sequences in the preaching circle associated with preaching appointments. *Perspective four* outlines the characteristics of congregations, the living socio/spiritual entities with which preachers engage. These perspectives:

- show that the preacher's vocational life is holistic and that the various parts interrelate systemically
- indicate the respective contributions made by the parts
- help preachers to combine the art of preaching with the art of living the life of a Christian preacher
- demonstrate ways in which preachers can develop and improve their vocational lives in ways which also enhance rather than detract from family life and other relationships
- take seriously the inner and outer aspects of a preacher's life
- help preachers to understand, live with and manage the oscillation between the private and public domains and the personal, social and spiritual demands it makes upon them
- indicate the knowledge, insights and the wide range of personal and interpersonal skills and disciplines required of preachers (and congregations) to make preaching effective and to realize its potential
- help preachers to set their ministry in the context of the overall lay and ordained preaching ministry of the church.

The perspectives described here can be compared with the elevations of an architect's drawing of a building or an engineer's of a machine. Elevations, like perspectives, are verbal and diagrammatic flat plane pictures of multi-dimensional phenomena and processes, and as such can help preachers to conceptualize, examine and evaluate the dynamic model of their vocational life. Together, they produce an all-round picture of the life of the preacher, and at the same time make it easier for preachers to examine and evaluate their preaching.

## Part Three

---

# MAKING A SERMON

Introduction

Preaching is always preaching in context. The Christian faith and Gospel cannot be preached in an abstract or generalized way: a sermon is always for a particular congregation in a particular place at a particular time. Even though it may be re-addressed to another congregation, it will not be quite the same sermon as before. Preaching, we have argued, is an existential event – at its best, transforming lives. So sermons cannot be simply repeated as if nothing has changed.

Chapter 6 will therefore address the contemporary context: its pressures, challenges and opportunities, as well as the resources available to preachers. Then, since one of the preacher's vital resources is the Bible, Chapter 7 will explore the use of the Bible in preaching, looking at some of the interpretative issues, and offering some case studies. Chapter 8 will consider the next stages of making a sermon: the development of a theme, the sermon's structure and style, its introduction, illustrations and conclusion. Finally – a point all too frequently overlooked – we shall briefly consider the very practical matter of delivering the sermon.

**Chapter 6**

---

## *PRESSURES ON PREACHERS TODAY*

In Chapter 1 we surveyed the challenges of preaching in a fast-changing world, and Chapter 11 will look at the bigger picture under the themes of continuity and change. Here we are concerned with immediate practicalities: those pressures which impinge very directly on the preacher's task.

### I  A Busy Schedule:

*The Problem*

It is impossible to generalize about how busy preachers are. (The problem, however, was briefly noted in the introductory section of Chapter 1). Their situations vary enormously: some are ordained, some are lay; some live and work in urban environments, others in more rural contexts. Amongst those who are lay preachers, some are in full-time, some in part-time employment; others are retired. Patterns will vary from country to country, and the demands placed upon preachers by their church or churches will vary as well. But most are likely to be busy. This will be true of many lay people in full-time employment. Current economic and political pressures have ratcheted up targets, introduced more stringent levels of accountability, and scaled back workforces, adding pressure to those remaining in work. As for preachers who are ordained, they too often experience greater pressures, especially where a shortage of ministers or priests has resulted in heavier, more extended pastoral responsibilities. Additional administrative obligations, including more paperwork, add to the load. Even people who have retired from paid employment sometimes wonder how they used to find time to work.

There may be more specific pressures. In theory, the demise of the evening service in many churches in Britain and elsewhere should have eased the workload of preachers. But there have been other developments. The more widespread use of a lectionary has perhaps led many preachers to write new sermons more often. Church services vary more, with special Sundays, such as Racial Justice Sunday, superimposed on the liturgical Christian Year. On such Sundays preachers may want to add visual material to assist the spoken message; that can be valuable, but it requires more work.

Busy preachers with access to the internet will naturally be tempted to look there for their sermons. We do not underestimate the value of resources on the internet for preaching. But preaching someone else's sermon can never have the authenticity and authority of preaching one's own. The thought, toil and prayer – and often the pain – of preparing a sermon is an integral part of the cost of the preaching ministry (see Chapter 4). The particular needs of each congregation, together with the very specific context of each Sunday – the first Sunday after a devastating earthquake, for example – are less likely to be addressed by an off-the-peg sermon which the preacher has lightly adapted for his/her own use.

There are other pressures on preachers today, and we shall come to those later in this chapter. Our concern here is simply with the preacher's busy schedule, and we note that many lay preachers will have additional, often heavy responsibilities in their local church or churches. So what is to be done?

*The Discipline of the Preacher*

The greatest challenge lies in ensuring that the capacity of a preacher – whether ordained or lay – for reflection and prayer is not eroded by their busyness. What preachers are and do in the many hours when they are not occupying the pulpit will enrich or impoverish their preaching ministry. Everything in a person's life can contribute to or detract from it. In an earlier section on 'The life and prayers of the preacher' (Chapter 2 section iii), we drew attention to De Caussade's teaching on the sacrament of the present moment, and to Dietrich Bonhoeffer's reflections on Christian worldliness. So precious hours of study are not the only measure of a preacher's preparation. The spiritual challenge posed by a busy schedule is by far the most important. But there are others.

Forward planning and good organization are vital. Those who preach every week need to start work on their sermons at the beginning of the week, not at the end of it. Ideally, to begin to make notes two or even three weeks in advance is better still. (This preacher, however, must confess to only rarely attaining such awesome heights of forward planning!). But Sunday mornings, for ordained and lay preacher alike, are the climax of the week. There are very few tasks indeed which can be counted more important than preaching, and schedules, as far as possible, need to be built round the preparation, rather than *vice versa*. In this respect, the preacher, however busy, is no different from the person training for the London Marathon. It is a searching test, not just for preachers, but for all Christians, to ask themselves the question, 'What is it that we will make room for during the day, no matter how busy our schedule?'.[1]

Identifying spaces, even in a busy day, when the mind is not engaged in immediate tasks can be helpful, especially if preachers have already done some initial spadework on the Bible passages from which they will be preaching. Themes and ideas may have begun to form in the mind, and free spaces in the day, even if very short, are opportunities for mulling things over, and holding the congregation prayerfully in mind. Access to pen and paper during or soon after these free moments will be important, if new thoughts and ideas are not to be forgotten. But even if the free space seems entirely unproductive, a kindly Providence, we must trust, uses every heartfelt prayer, especially the 'arrow' prayer of a preacher getting increasingly desperate as Sunday draws near.

Apart from a life of prayer and reflection, what other practices belong to the discipline of the preacher? Studying the Bible is clearly a lifetime's work. There are two interrelated tasks here: that of studying the individual passages appointed or chosen for each preaching occasion, and that of broadening and deepening one's knowledge of Scripture as a whole. For example, the Gospel of Mark as a whole helps us to understand more fully the individual passages within it and, conversely, the more we find in each passage, the richer will be our knowledge of the whole Gospel.

Giving priority to a study group with fellow preachers is important. A weekly or fortnightly meeting may be impossible, and there may well be periods in the preacher's life when even a monthly meeting

---

[1] L. Johnson, *Sharing Possessions*, (London: SCM, 1981), p. 51. This question is one of a searching list of questions which, Johnson suggests, can help us to identify our personal centre, or, in his words, 'What is it, in my actual life, that functions as my god?' (p. 52).

is not achievable. But if that continues to be so year after year, preachers may need to ask themselves some searching questions about their overall schedule. Reading is another vital part of the preacher's armoury. Aims should be realistic, and books chosen with care, since time is limited, and there are so many books from which to choose. The Internet, as we noted earlier, has valuable resources, but there is no substitute for a book of real quality. Even a chapter or two per week is better than nothing. The test, after all, is not how much we read, but what we get out of it. The daily discipline of using some good Bible reading notes, based on the passage chosen for each day, will build up the preacher's stock of biblical knowledge.

Finally, under this heading, it must be said that the task of preachers does not get easier however many years they have been preaching. At least it should not. It is true that, as time goes by, they may have a growing stock of sermons which they honestly feel they could preach again with the same passion and conviction as they did the first time – with the proviso mentioned in the Introduction to Part Three above. They may also have a growing stock of illustrations and anecdotes to draw on. But an increasing confidence in one's own fluency and an ability to speak with less and less preparation is a great danger. That is not what preaching is about, and the toil and cost of this vocation remain the same until the last sermon has been preached.

*The Resources of the Preacher*

We have focused in this section on the pressures on preachers today. They are many and real. Yet every pressure is also an opportunity. That is not a cliché, but a Christian conviction. And preachers need to draw on the resources with which they can respond to the pressures. Those resources are easily neglected or overlooked. The great Albert Schweitzer, from his mission station in Africa, wrote that the busier he became, the more he prayed. For us lesser mortals, the opposite all too easily happens. The Bible, too, is an extraordinary resource, as we shall see in the next chapter.

Pressure can drive us into isolation: we haven't time to make that phone call, meet a fellow-preacher for Bible study and prayer, or engage in that little bit of reading which will make all the difference to whether our sermon is well-informed or not. But it may make us turn to the many resources available for tackling all kinds of difficult and controversial issues in preaching. (See section (iv) below). And above and beneath all the more tangible resources at our disposal, there is one supreme Resource. I end this section with verses from Ephesians which I have come to treasure:

> Now to him who by the power at work within us is able to accomplish abundantly more than all we can ask or imagine, to him be glory in the church and in Christ Jesus, to all generations for ever and ever. Amen
>
> (Eph. 3.20–1).

## II Conflicting Views of the Bible

### The Challenge

There is nothing new in conflicting views about the Bible. Ever since the Church's canon of Scripture was finalized – and, indeed, before – the interpretation of what came to be called the Old and New Testaments has continued to be the subject of lively debate. Are conflicts about the Bible sharper than they were? Only a person ignorant of Christian history could possibly say that. But we are where we are, and preachers today may be under pressure in two ways. They themselves may be confused by the conflicting views about the Bible swirling around them in and outside the Church; their confidence in interpreting may be undermined by an uneasy awareness that scholars are constantly coming up with new insights and ideas. As if that were not enough, there is an ever-increasing number of translations and paraphrases of Scripture available. So one of the preacher's pressing tasks is to begin to clarify their own working approach to the Bible, however open-ended and capable of continuing refinement it must be.

A second task consists in responding to the diverse views of the Bible held by members of their congregations. Preachers may not know the extent of that diversity, at least to begin with. They can assume, in many modern contexts, that many to whom they preach will have a very sketchy knowledge of the Bible, and probably more questions than convictions about it – apart from the conviction that the Bible is very difficult. Here is a worthwhile challenge for all preachers: will their sermons make members of the congregation *want* to read the Bible?

### Establishing a Foundation to Work From

The preacher clearly needs a working understanding of the Bible's authority. What does it mean? Its authority is experienced in its effects, and that is the best place to begin, rather than with a theory about the Bible's inspiration or inerrancy or some other concept. In this book we take the Bible's inspiration for granted, but believe that a theory of biblical inerrancy misunderstands or overlooks the nature of the Bible.[2] Instead, we ask: what is the Bible meant to do? The question is best answered by recalling the definition of authority offered in Chapter 1: an authority, ideally, is a source of life, truth and growth. So, Christianly expressed, the purpose of the Bible is to bring people to Christ, and to nurture them in the life of Christ. When that is happening, we may confidently feel the Bible is being used well, and is fulfilling its role in the life of the Church.

But what of the Bible's inherent qualities? We may be quietly confident about its inspiration; the more we study the Bible, and allow ourselves to be changed by it, the more we shall know at first-hand its mysterious depth and power. The biblical documents comprise a unique, indispensable witness to Christ, whom we should see as the supreme authority behind the Bible's authority – which brings us to the next stage of establishing a biblical foundation from which to work.

*A Canon Within the Canon*

In clarifying their own views about the Bible, preachers will do well to identify some fundamental perspectives from which to work. Every Christian with a growing knowledge of the Bible arrives, sooner or later, at their own 'canon' within the canon. By 'canon' here we mean a measure by which the reader evaluates or interprets the whole Bible. (The whole Bible, of course, is the Church's 'canon' – the measure by which the Church assesses its own life, doctrine, worship and teaching). The canon within the canon for Martin Luther was 'justification by faith', and so, not surprisingly, Luther regarded Paul's letter to the Romans as the most important book in the Bible, and somewhat harshly dismissed the letter of James as 'an epistle of straw'.[3]

Personal experience and preference, as well as our own personal reading of the Bible may all contribute to the canon we each arrive at. Members of church congregations may also have their own canon,

---

[2] For a good recent discussion of this, see K. Ward, *The Word of God. The Bible After Modern Scholarship*, (London: SPCK 2010).

[3] Luther objected to the Letter of James on the grounds – mistaken as most scholars now think – that James' insistence that faith without works is dead (Jas 2.26) contradicted the teaching of Paul that we are saved, not by the works of the law but through faith (e.g. Gal. 2.16).

even if they have not identified it as such. But whatever our own individual canon of Scripture may be, it must not be an eccentric one. We may love the Books of Ruth or Jonah, for example, but for all their undoubted worth they can hardly bear the task of being the measuring-rod by which we interpret the rest of the Bible. Two observations may be helpful at this point. First, choices have to be made, and, within the broad stream of Christian orthodoxy, there are many, though not unlimited, possibilities. For example, one Christian may place great weight on the Bible's dire warnings about eternal punishment, another on texts such as Rom. 11.32 and 1 Tim. 4.10 which appear to hold out the possibility that, in the end all will be saved.[4] But we need to be sufficiently self-aware to recognize how much we all bring to the Bible. For instance, 'the interpretation of biblical statements about God will largely depend on your view of what sort of being God is'.[5]

The most important canon within the canon, of course, is Christ. Many Christians around the world, implicitly or explicitly, recognize Jesus as God's incarnate Word, and the Bible as the written Word of God containing a unique range of testimonies to Jesus. (For this reason, many Christians prefer to say that the Bible *contains,* rather than *is* the Word of God). So, 'while Scripture is the book that shows us Christ, Christ is the person who must govern our interpretation of Scripture'.[6]

So a circular process is at work: we need the Bible if we are to learn about Christ, but He is the One in whose light we read the Bible, including those passages which, we cannot but conclude, do not express the mind or spirit of Jesus. With this crucial relationship between the Living and written Word in our minds, we must seek to let the Bible do its work.

*Authority and Revelation*

Building on this, preachers may find it helpful to think about another fundamental of their vocation: authority and the other fundamentals closely related to it, namely revelation, faith and freedom.[7] If Christ, the Living Word, rather than the Bible, is our supreme authority, preachers are more likely to have an understanding of authority

---

[4] Ward, *Word of God*, p. 138.
[5] *Idem*, p. 51.
[6] *Idem.*, p. 138.
[7] R. E. C. Browne, *The Ministry of the Word,* (London: SCM 1958, repr. 1976), p. 36.

and of revelation which is dynamic and life-giving, rather than static and authoritarian. The authority which comes from God is easier to recognize than to define. But always (Chapter 1, section (i)) it promotes life, truth and growth.

A properly Christian understanding of revelation is also mysteriously elusive, as a thoughtful reading of the gospels shows. Paul Ricoeur's phrase 'the non-violent appeal' of revelation implies much about the style (and perhaps decibel level) of preaching. But our working understanding of both authority and revelation will also 'largely depend on our view of what sort of being God is'. The New Testament, we suggest, leads us to conclude that authority and revelation, Christianly understood, are *transforming*: long and imperceptible though the process may often be, the outcome of that transformation is the likeness of Christ in those who experience the authority of revelation.

*Working With Diversity in the Congregation*

Having established an understanding of the Bible to work from, preachers turn to the bewildering range of views about the Bible which, they may readily guess, exist in the congregation before them. Christians can and do hold different views of the Bible. Some, in our view, may claim too much for the Bible and place on it more weight than it is meant to bear. Others have too low a view, emphasizing its all too human characteristics, but failing to do justice to its transforming power. This diversity, of course, is not the only diversity within congregations preachers will encounter. Differing views of the Bible usually give rise to differing views on political, moral and social issues as well, and so what is said here more specifically about the Bible may be applied to other kinds of diversity. How is the preacher to respond?

The task of preachers is not to correct from the pulpit what they consider to be defective views of the Bible, nor to challenge directly what they perceive to be prejudice, let us say, towards a marginalized minority in society. Such views, however inadequate or wrong, do not mean that the people who hold them are not Christians. A person's view of the Bible, for example, may be a serious obstacle to their Christian growth, but it may be counterproductive to challenge even that directly in a sermon. Attitudes and relationships are all-important here: it is vital that no individual should feel 'got at' from the pulpit. That is very different from being challenged by a word bearing the kind of authority to which we referred in Chapter 1 ('source of life, truth and growth').

Nor are preachers in the business of pushing their own views, whether of the Bible or a contemporary political issue. Their task is not to privilege one view over another – *unless it is clear that such a view is distorting, or even betraying, the gospel.* Such was the interpretation of Scripture, held by the Dutch Reformed Church of South Africa, during the years of apartheid. Instead, the preacher's responsibility is to enable the hearers, whatever their views, to hear the gospel, to encounter God, and to be enlightened and transformed by that encounter.

The way in which preachers use Scripture may be clear from the way they interpret the Bible readings. But the method is not the message. They do not want to lose anyone along the way if they can possibly help it. Such an approach does not mean a bland relativism which implies that any view or interpretation is just as good as any other. Rather, an approach which self-evidently reflects a sustained, respectful attention by the preacher, both to the text and to the diversity of views in the congregation, will lead both the preacher and the congregation in the right direction. The challenge of responding to congregations who hold widely differing views about not only the Bible but many other issues will be discussed further in the next section of this chapter.

In the light of the preceding discussion, it may be helpful for preachers to ask themselves what constitutes biblical preaching, and what are the hallmarks of a church which lives by the authority of the Bible. Whether preaching is biblical or not cannot be measured simply by whether the sermon has a text, or how many biblical quotations it contains. The measure is deeper and more pervasive. A sermon grows out of the biblical passage(s) in such a way that the biblical material 'leavens' the whole (Lk. 13.20–1). The question then becomes: how essential is the reading of those passages to the preaching and the understanding of the sermon? If you discover just before the service is due to begin – as I did once – that the reader is about to read the wrong passage, how much will it matter? That is a useful way of assessing how biblical the sermon is. It is a more delicate matter if the wrong passage is actually read. Then the preacher must find a way of inserting another reading at the beginning of the sermon in a way that avoids embarrassing the reader.

Another way of assessing whether a sermon is biblical is to ask whether it reflects 'how the Bible preaches'.[8] This may seem a strange idea, but it is an important one. The Bible 'preaches' in ways that teach us how to preach. Writers often draw on traditions they received, but rarely, if ever reproduce them *verbatim*. Luke and Matthew used Mark's Gospel, the Deuteronomist drew on traditions found in Exodus, and so on. They do so in a way which re-focuses the old material on new situations and new audiences. The style and language of the Bible are important too. The preacher's task is not to reproduce them; that would not be to preach as the Bible preaches since, as we have just observed, biblical writers do not simply reproduce what they had received. Rather, biblical writers deploy – with inspiration, devotion and conviction – all their resources of literary skill and imagination in the service of the message.

Much more could be said on how the Bible preaches. But it paves the way for a final point in this section. The task of preachers is that of all Christians: to love Scripture, warts and all, and to revel – if that is not too strong a word – in exploring its rich depths and extraordinary insights. The interpretative challenges and the difficulties are there, but, above all, the Bible is a wonderful resource.

## III A Diverse Church

'It takes all sorts to make a church'. C. S. Lewis' observation expresses a perennial truth about the Church. The prominence of Jew and Gentile in the Church almost from the beginning is testimony to that. So we cannot blithely assume that congregations today are more diverse than they were. It is possible, if not probable, that the Church has long been home to people with a bewildering variety of Christian convictions and opinions. But it may be that several influences today serve to increase that variety, and we need briefly to review these.

### *Information and Misinformation*

First, people are exposed to a greater variety of books, newspapers, TV and radio programmes which contain far more overtly or implicitly anti-Christian than Christian material. A few years ago, Dan Brown's *The Da Vinci Code* was read by millions. It was not always easy to sift fact from fiction. A craftily written introduction encouraged (wrongly)

---

[8] Fred B. Craddock, *Overhearing the Gospel*. (Calver, Sheffield: Cliff College Publishing 1995), p. 65.

the view that the book reflected more research and contained more facts than it did. A quotation from a non-canonical gospel was accurate, but it was a rare example of 'research'. But how was the average reader to know? (For example, a church member was heard wondering whether there was something in the allegation that Jesus and Mary Magdalene were married.)

*The Da Vinci Code* is only one example. Others can be readily recalled or imagined. A television programme about the origins of the universe may raise all kinds of questions about traditional Christian understandings about creation. New ethical issues raise awkward, unsettling questions for the Christian. Newspapers, with their beguiling concoctions of information, skewed information and misinformation, may exercise a greater influence on many church-goers than the Bible.

*Irregular Church Attendance*

A second factor at work in many countries – with countless local variations – are those social and economic forces which increasingly fragment a local congregation. Fewer people attend their local church every Sunday. Some who have retired from full-time employment may travel at weekends to visit either their children and grandchildren, or their own elderly parents. Those who can afford to do so take more holidays. Christians in paid employment may have to work on some Sundays; others, such as teachers, find themselves obliged to bring work home at weekends.

Preachers need to be deeply sympathetic to, and understanding of people who, for all kinds of reasons, do not get to church regularly. (Whether it is as often as they wish is not for anyone to judge.) At the same time, irregular attendance at church may have a subtly corrosive effect on their Christian faith. A historian has suggested that in Britain people did not stop coming to church because they stopped believing; rather, they stopped believing because they had stopped coming to church.[9] Even if that oversimplifies a very subtle, gradual process, the net result may be that many congregations today contain more half-believers and would-be believers, not to mention people distracted by pressures of work, than in previous generations.

---

[9] D. Hampton, *Methodism. Empire of the Spirit,* (New Haven and London: Yale 2005), p. 196.

### The Pace and Extent of Change

A third influence at work is the impact of a complex, fast-changing world on congregations today. That impact, because of the revolution in communications and the sheer volume and speed of contemporary change, is probably greater than in any earlier periods of the Church's history. We return to this subject in Chapter 12. Although we devote two separate sections in this chapter to the Church and 'the world', a diagrammatic representation of their relationship to each other would not be two adjacent circles, but two concentric or overlapping ones.

So the wider world in which the Church is set, and of which it is a part, impacts on Christians in many different ways. (Similar processes are at work in other world faiths). So an average congregation in many countries today is likely to include people some of whom have embraced and accepted many contemporary influences and changes, and others who haven't. An obvious example in ethics is the difference of views about same-sex relationships.

### A Missing Generation?

One worrying trend today – certainly in the North – is the decreasing number of people of working age in many congregations. There has long been a preponderance of older people in the churches, and that is perhaps not surprising. But that preponderance today seems greater. People in their middle years, struggling to bring up a family and to cope with the demanding pressures of their job, often find it hard to make time for church. What makes matters worse is the infrequency with which Christian preaching addresses the pressures and the ethical dilemmas of the world of work. As a result, busy working people who once in a while find time to attend church, may leave feeling that there was nothing in the sermon for them.

So powerful and pervasive forces are at work today, making for congregations whose diversity, even if only partially known, is a challenge to preachers. But it should stimulate and even excite them as well. The diversity raises interesting questions. How much diversity can a *Christian* congregation legitimately contain? How much of the diversity before them on Sunday should preachers acknowledge and endorse? And how can they possibly preach in a way which meets the needs of everyone? (See Chapter 11 on how a group of preachers in Leeds grappled with this challenge).

St Paul provides an interesting case-study. In his first letter to Corinth, he addressed a church sharply polarized by one particular ethical issue: should Christians eat meat which had been offered in pagan sacrifices, or should they not?[10] He presented himself as a role model, arguing that Christians should not 'do their own thing', regardless of the effects of their conduct on fellow-Christians, but act in the interests of others, as he sought to do in his apostolic ministry:

> For though I am free with respect to all, I have made myself a slave to all, so that I might win more of them. To the Jews I became as a Jew in order to win Jews. To those under the law I became as one under the law (though I myself am not under the law) so that I might win those under the law. To those outside the law I became as one outside the law (though I am not free from God's law but am under Christ's law) so that I might win those outside the law. To the weak I became weak, so that I might win the weak. I have become all things to all people, so that I might by any means save some. I do it all for the sake of the gospel that I might share in that gospel
>
> (1 Cor. 9.19–23)[11]

'All things to all men', as Paul's phrase in v. 22 has become in popular parlance, does not seem a promising slogan for Christian preaching of honesty and integrity. But in the original context in which Paul preached, it was a costly ministry expressing what one scholar has called 'the adaptability of love'. A minister or priest acting as a go-between unionist and republican communities in Northern Ireland at the height of the troubles in the late twentieth century offers a partial parallel to the costly, sacrificial nature of Paul's ministry. Other letters by the apostle hint at the misunderstandings he caused, e.g. Gal. 1.10 and Romans 3.8. It was a costly, boundary-crossing ministry, exposed to risk and misunderstanding on all sides.

Can preachers learn from this strategy of Paul's? I believe we can. In his book *Overhearing the Gospel* Fred Craddock argues that the teaching of Jesus (and of Socrates and Søren Kierkegaard), was 'servant-like' in that 'he gave his speaking to effect experiences within the listeners', adding 'I never cease being awed by anyone who can be so completely giving of self to listeners'.[11] Craddock is careful to argue that such communicators will also respect a certain distance between themselves and their listeners. He contrasts this with those over-enthusiastic preachers whose zealous sermons become counter-

---

[10] This passage is part of Paul's long discussion about meat offered to idols, (1 Cor. 8–10). On the background to this, see N. Richardson, *Paul For Today*, (London: Epworth 2009), pp. 44–8.

[11] The NRSV, but adapting its rendering of v. 23, which ends 'so that I might share in its blessings', a common mistranslation. (There is no reference in the Greek to 'blessings', only to 'sharing in it' – i.e. the gospel).

productive in their intrusiveness. Instead, communicators sacrifice themselves '*in the service of the listener*', (my italics).[12]

With the example of St Paul, and Craddock's advocacy of preaching in the service of the listener in mind, preachers can preach to people of different views, whether theological, ethical or political. Indeed, they must do so, simply because they are there in the congregation. They will pray that the sermon, and the worship of which it is a part, will refine and deepen the faith of everyone present. Attitudes and relationships matter even more than people's opinions and views. No-one should be made to feel that the preacher is having a go at them, singling out their views for criticism. Every word spoken has to be spoken in love – that is, in ministry to them.

How can this be done? Preachers will need to prepare and write their sermons from start to finish with all groups in their minds and in their prayers. To do so will inevitably affect their choice of language, illustrations – indeed, everything. Preachers will also keep in mind the aim and outcome of the sermon, (see section (v) below). The aim will not be so much to correct the views of some, and endorse those of others, but to bring everyone to a transforming encounter with God. And it may well be that as a result of that encounter, the political views (for example) of some people in the congregation will be changed.

This is not a policy of the lowest common denominator. Nor should it result in preaching which lacks integrity and transparency. The aim is preaching which seeks to offer the Bread of Life to all, irrespective of their views, and regardless of whether or not a person's views are similar to the preacher's. So while the diversity of many congregations today cannot but be a challenge for preachers, they should not despair, because it is a worthy challenge and a great opportunity. Let them love their people in all their rich diversity, keep that diversity in mind as they pray for them, and believe that a word of grace and power can be offered to all.

## IV A COMPLEX WORLD.

### *On Leaving the World Out*

The world often gets short shrift in Christian preaching and it deserves better. Some preachers can be dismissive of a world perceived as materialist, sinful, godless – a long list of words like these is

---

[12] Craddock, *Overhearing*, p. 128, 132.

not difficult to find. Such sweeping, negative generalizations are unhelpful. Perhaps they are heard from Christian pulpits less than they used to be. They certainly do nothing to advance the Gospel, nor, we suspect, to build up the Church.

There is another reason why the world at large sometimes receives little attention in Christian preaching. A pastor once observed that members of his congregation found it relatively easy to relate their faith to personal matters, and to personal relationships, but less easy to relate it to national and international issues. This is likely to be true of many Christians today. It is much harder to translate 'love your neighbour as yourself' into action in national and international politics than, say, in the village where I now live.

So the world at large can easily be left out of Christian preaching. It is easier, and more immediate, to concentrate on the Church and on people's individual faith and spirituality. So the Christian faith and the Bible are often spiritualized and privatized in a way that does scant justice to the central Christian conviction that this is God's world, and that God loves it, and seeks to redeem and heal it.

*Preaching on Controversial Issues*

There are some important 'do's' and 'don'ts' for the preacher in addressing complex political, social and ethical issues. First, preachers can't avoid them just because they are complex. At the same time, no preacher should ever feel they are thrown back on their own resources, including their study, however prayerful, of the relevant scriptural passages. A range of expertise will be available in local congregations, or amongst colleagues and fellow-preachers. A phone call to someone working in finance or business may save the preacher from crassly oversimplifying a complex issue, or from demonizing a particular group of workers, such as bankers. The Internet, or more directly a Church's own central offices, will supply the latest informed Christian judgement on, say, abortion.

In seeking to address a complex contemporary problem, there are a number of things a preacher has to avoid. The pulpit cannot be the place which is merely an extension of the contemporary press. While eminent Christians have advocated the image of a Christian with a Bible in one hand and a newspaper in the other, it is a misleading image if the Christian gives equal weight to them, or, more probably, is unwittingly influenced more by the newspaper than by the Bible. Some newspapers are far better than others, but even the best cannot be used uncritically.

Preachers are not in the pulpit to advocate personal points of view, however passionately they may feel about them. The more passionately we feel about an issue, the more self-critical we may need to be. In preaching to a diverse church, the preacher's aim cannot be to promote particular views, and that of course must include endorsing a political party, even if it seems to embrace policies which are more Christian than its rivals. Sometimes, however, it is the preacher's Christian duty to condemn a party – for example, an ultra-nationalist party – whose very philosophy is incompatible with Christian faith, and to articulate why this is so in a biblically and theologically informed way.

So what should the preacher aim to do? The preacher is 'seeking the mind of Christ through theologically well-informed reflection on well-researched issues' and to 'nurture discipleship'.[13] This does not mean settling for bland generalizations which are hardly worth turning up to church to hear. It does not meaning sitting on the fence either. Preachers who seek to practise what they preach and who passionately advocate Gospel basics such as love, justice and equality of regard, are not being neutral.

The preacher cannot, and should not, always avoid controversy. Even an angry response to a sermon may not be a sign of failure, as the New Testament shows. At the same time, preachers – not least through conferring with colleagues and other fellow-Christians – will seek to avoid alienating people by pushing their own views, or speaking in a simplistic, ill-informed or one-sided way about complex issues.

No preacher can hope to deal with every facet of a controversial issue, and should not even try. Preachers should not be beguiled into thinking that they have to have lots of answers to awkward questions. What people need is enough light and courage to live with the questions, even when they can't answer them. Faithful preachers, grappling honestly with complexities out of their own knowledge and experience, as well as the insights of Scripture and tradition, will do much to nurture the faith of their congregations.

---

[13] D. Deeks, 'Handling Hot Potatoes', *Ichthus*, Vol. 159, issue 3, pp. 18–19. The remainder of this section owes much to Deeks' article. (*Ichthus* is a magazine published quarterly for Methodist preachers and others.)

## V Aims and Outcomes

Preachers who expect little from their preaching deserve little. Their congregation is likely to sense that, too. As an earlier chapter noted, it is possible for both to become locked in a downward spiral of decreasing expectations, and absolutely vital to imagine, work and pray for the opposite. We suggested in Chapter 1 (section i) that the overall purpose of preaching is the communication of life and light. But we can also be more specific. Because the aims and outcomes of sermons can and should vary, it is important for preachers to clarify in their minds the aims and outcomes they hope for. A sermon with no particular aim is unlikely to have any noticeable effect. But what are appropriate aims in preaching? It will help to begin our answer to this question by identifying some inappropriate ones.

We have argued (sections iii and iv) that preachers should aim primarily to refine and deepen people's faith, not to change their views about a whole range of issues. To do so is likely to be counter-productive. Telling a congregation which way to vote in a forthcoming election is not a good idea. Of course, not to mention the election at all is implicitly to deny that Christian faith has to do with the whole of life. But however passionately preachers feel about politics, their business can never be to impose their own point of view.

Another inappropriate aim in preaching is what might be called general exhortations. Bishop Jeremy Taylor advised his clergy:

> Do not spend your sermons on general and indefinite things, as in exhortations to people to get Christ, to be united to Christ, and things of the like unlimited signification. ... Generals (i.e. general exhortations) not explicated do but fill people's heads with empty notions, and their mouths with perpetual unintelligible talk; but their hearts remain empty and themselves are not edified.[14]

There are many such exhortations heard from Christian pulpits, the most common of all being the exhortation to love. Why are they not appropriate? The short answer is that people know what they are supposed to do without hearing it yet again. What they lack is the grace and power to do it. What is needed is preaching which brings about, however gradually and imperceptibly, change far deeper than changing one's point of view about abortion, or which way to vote. The Greek word *metanoia*, 'repentance', points to a change of heart and mind, the outward proof of which is a transformed life.

---

[14] Quoted in R. E. C. Browne, *Ministry of the Word*, p. 97.

But it is far easier to exhort and cajole a congregation than to preach the gospel. There is a place for exhortation of a more specific kind, provided it is framed by the preaching of the gospel. One of the most frequent defects of sermons is that they lack good news. The good news of the gospel is the primary agent of change, whether that is increased weekly giving in the church collection, or a different way of perceiving and responding to the local gypsy encampment. (Jesus told a story about a racial group of his day which his contemporaries were inclined to ostracize – Lk. 10.25–37.) So preachers should ask – with every sermon – 'What is the *particular* good news I want the congregation to hear, and – with that good news – what *particular* challenge and encouragement?

The outcomes of preaching are not easily measured, and preachers simply have to live with that. (On this see the discussion in Chapter 4 on feedback). Sometimes the way in which a congregation sings a hymn after the sermon (always provided the tune is known!) is an indication that the sermon has revived drooping spirits and flagging faith. A remark from one or two people at the church door as they leave may testify that the sermon has been for them a transforming experience. More often the preacher must trust that the message will work unseen, like the leaven of Jesus' parable, increasing faith, renewing hope, and replenishing love.

So the effect of a good sermon will be to form, or re-form the Church. (See also Chapter 13 on the Church's essential vocation.) Here we note two vital outcomes of this process.[15] A proper confidence will be a mark of a church which has heard the gospel. Such a confidence will be a world away from a superficially grounded self-confidence whose chief hallmarks are likely to be intolerance and arrogance. Instead, it will be a quiet confidence in the God who embraces the whole world, and whose presence in the world they may trust absolutely. A second characteristic of a church which has heard the gospel is praise. Such praise is not measured by how many hymns or songs of praise the congregation sings. It is a praise which transforms – including the way in which Christians perceive life and the world. Such praise will be sure proof of that positive change misleadingly called 'repentance'.

---

[15] L. E. Keck, *The Church Confident*, (Nashville: Abingdon, 1993), especially Chapter 1.

## Conclusion

Preaching in a complex and fast-changing world can be a daunting, even intimidating task. But that would not be the appropriate note on which to end this chapter. So one sentence from our earlier discussion will, I think, be worth repeating: 'Every challenge is also an opportunity – and that is not a cliché, but a Christian conviction'.

## Chapter 7

# *USING THE BIBLE IN PREACHING*

This and the following chapter attempt two things: to provide an introduction to the essentials of sermon preparation and construction, and also to offer material for established preachers to review their working practices against the challenging background for preaching today, outlined in Chapters 1 and 6. We look first at fundamental questions to do with the use of the Bible in preaching, and second, at case-studies.

## I Fundamental Questions

### *The Authority of the Bible*

We take it for granted that a preacher will usually preach from the Bible. There may be exceptional occasions when, like Paul at Athens (Acts 17.22–31), the preacher addresses people with no knowledge of the Bible and no contact with the Church. (The sermon at Athens is different from almost all the other sermons in Acts in having no explicit references to the Old Testament.) In some countries today preachers have to take into account the fact that knowledge of the Bible is patchy, to say the least, and we shall need to return to this. Even so, if preaching is to realize its potential as a core activity of the Church, it will nearly always be, implicitly or explicitly, biblical.

The previous chapter (section II) defined biblical preaching in two ways: first, as preaching in which the biblical revelation, like leaven, pervades the whole, and, second, as preaching in the way that the Bible itself preaches. This does not necessarily mean that the sermon always begins with a text, even though that is a good discipline for the preacher, and may provide a memorable image for the congregation. Nor does Biblical preaching mean that the preacher always begins from the readings of the day. On Trinity Sunday the starting point may be the much misunderstood (and widely rejected) doctrine of the Trinity. But the revelation of God through Jesus, recorded in the Scriptures, remains the presupposition and the content, implicit or explicit, of preaching. With this foundation, we turn to practicalities.

*Which Translation?*

We need to take a moment in asking what a translation is. In old translations, such as the immensely influential English Authorized (King James') Version of 1610, the translators tended to adopt a word-for-word approach. More recent approaches have recognized that meaning is located as much, if not more, in whole phrases and sentences, rather than in individual words. So translators of more modern versions have adopted a theory of translation known as 'dynamic equivalence', asking, not just what each word means, but what the nearest equivalent can be to the phrase or sentence being translated. The Contemporary English Version (CEV) adopts this method, quoting Luther, 'Words must obey and follow the meaning, and not meaning the words'.[1] To give an admittedly extreme example, if we translated word-for-word what Jesus says to his mother in Jn 2.4, we should have to translate, 'What to me and to you, woman?' But translators recognize that behind the original Greek lies a Hebrew idiom reflecting a conflict of interest.[2] So harsh though it may sound, the translation of the Revised English Bible (REB), 'That is no concern of mine' is rather better than that of the New Revised Standard Version (NSRV), 'Woman, what concern is that to you and to me?' and certainly better than that of the Good News Bible (GNB), 'You must not tell me what to do'.

There is another point to make about translations. No translation can entirely avoid *interpreting at the same time*. Nevertheless, the translator of, let us say, Mark's gospel, should aim to be as self-effacing as possible. It is Mark's voice the reader needs to hear, not the translator's, even though Mark's voice is bound to be at one remove when the reader reads the gospel in a language other than Mark's original Greek.

So the preacher should not turn too quickly to modern paraphrases of the Bible. They have a role to play, certainly. But in paraphrases

---

[1] The introduction to the *Contemporary English Version*.

[2] The same Greek idiom is found on the lips of the demons addressing Jesus at Mark 1.24 and 5.7.

we are at two removes, not one, from the original. Not only is the paraphrase not in the original language; it is also the author's attempt, praiseworthy as it might be, to say what he/she thinks it means. That may sound very like the translation method of dynamic equivalence which we have just described, in which words follow the meaning. There is sometimes a fine line between such a translation and a paraphrase. But paraphrases are more – sometimes far more – an interpretation than a translation. In a paraphrase the emphasis tends to shift from what the text says to what the reader can or will comprehend. That at first sight makes the task of preachers easier, but they could pay a heavy price. The biblical writer's voice will inevitably be more distant, and possibly distorted or even drowned.

Few preachers will have had the opportunity or the time to learn the original biblical languages of Hebrew and Greek, and so their first resort should be a well-established translation; among the best English translations are the New Revised Standard Version, the Revised English Bible, the New International Version, and the New Jerusalem Bible. (The Contemporary English Version varies in quality: at its best it is refreshing, at worst, banal.) Paraphrases should at least be tested against a good translation if preachers wish to use them, whether in their own studies, or in a church service. What is read in church needs to be comprehensible, if at all possible. But accuracy is clearly important as well.

*Should the Preacher Follow a Lectionary?*

This has its pros and cons. In favour of a lectionary, we may say that it steers the preacher away from looking for a biblical passage which 'fits what I want to say'. A lectionary is also likely to direct preachers' attention to passages which they themselves might not have chosen, and so churches experience a wider range of the Bible than they might otherwise do, though of course that need not be so. A lectionary also facilitates biblical study with colleagues, for example, if my Anglican or Baptist colleague is going to preach from the same passage as me. Not least, following a lectionary makes it more likely that the preacher will observe the rhythms and festivals of the Christian Year.

But the arguments are not all one way. Preaching from the lectionary seems to rule out thematic preaching, or at least to make it more difficult. And most lectionaries are selective; at least one in widespread use today has omitted many problematical verses, when it may be valuable for preacher and congregation alike to read them, hear them, and think through the difficulties. So unwavering adherence to some lectionaries can mean that congregations are deprived of hearing parts of Scripture. It can also inhibit/deflect preachers from pursuing themes and issues which are concerning them. But, without dismissing these contrary arguments, we shall assume in the rest of this chapter that preaching from a lectionary which comprises Old Testament, Epistle and Gospel will be the norm for the great majority of preachers.

*Interpreting the Bible*

The message of the Bible can be heard and experienced in preaching only through the preacher's interpretation of it. Even if a sermon were a veritable tapestry of biblical quotations, (and that is anyway probably not the best use of the Bible), the preacher's choice and use of those quotations would still be an interpretation. Every preacher must have, or pray to have, the courage and confidence to interpret the Bible; it is their unavoidable responsibility.[3] In this task, the value of conferring with other preachers can hardly be overstated (Chapter 2, section II).

So what is involved in interpreting the Bible? First, a journey in self-knowledge. (On this subject, see also Chapter 8). Preachers need to ask themselves some searching questions: 'What kind of Christian am I? Am I a 'conservative' who tends to read Scripture through the lens of my own tradition and convictions? Or am I a 'liberal', keen to 'explain' the Bible, including its obscure, objectionable details, and to replace, if necessary, some traditional understandings with ones informed by modern scholarship?'

Neither of these approaches is entirely wrong; all of us read the Bible through the particular lens of our own Christian tradition or experience, and much of the Bible does need to be explained. A recent writer goes so far as to claim that anyone who ignores the work of biblical scholars, which has been going on now for at least three hundred years, 'cannot any longer be regarded as competent to interpret the Bible'.[4] So what is the way forward?

Preachers need to build on the approach advocated in the earlier chapter. When we work in isolation, never hearing that another equally committed Christian reads and interprets the same biblical

---

[3] W. Brueggemann, *Redescribing Reality. What We Do When We Read the Bible.* (London: SCM 2009), p. 14.

[4] K. Ward, *The Word of God. The Bible After Modern Scholarship* (London: SPCK 2010), p. 2.

passage differently from ourselves, we are less likely to grow. We may say: 'The reason I don't study the Bible with so-and-so is because they are wrong!'. But then we are closing ourselves to correction and growth. This is *not* to say that every interpretation is just as good as another. It is to say that we are members one of another, and where 'two or three' say their prayers and study Scripture together, the Spirit will bless their prayers and their sharing and lead them into truth they probably would not have seen on their own.

The goal of such growing self-knowledge in interpreters of the Bible can be simply stated: the deepening of their life in Christ. To express this more precisely, the interpreters are called to tread the way of the cross, 'emptying' themselves for the sake of those whom they seek to serve through their preaching, (Philippians 2.5–11). As always, we 'preach not ourselves', neither our views and opinions, nor our particular agendas, nor even our preferred interpretations. Instead, we choose, freely yet responsibly, that interpretation which seems to us the most faithful to the passage in question, and at the same time the most significant for the congregation. (From start to finish, the preacher, in preparing to preach, is studying *for the congregation*).

*Interpreting means listening*

What else is involved in the interpretation of the Bible? We seek to develop, as prayerfully and attentively as we can, the discipline of listening to the text. As we shall keep on suggesting, that can be especially helpful when we listen with others. But whether on our own or with others, this discipline has to be learned and cultivated. It is like listening to another person telling us their news or their problems. We are easily distracted, or we give them only half our attention, or we soon interrupt with our own concerns and views. Similarly, the interpreter of the Bible must *let the text have its say*. As this phrase implies, the interpreter is engaged in a conversation with the biblical passage she/he is studying. This conversation has been called the 'hermeneutical circle' or the 'hermeneutical spiral'. (The word 'hermeneutical' derives from the Greek word to interpret. On this see also Chapter 11). A conversation is a two-way process. We bring our questions, assumptions, even objections to the text. But if we listen well, we begin to hear what the text is saying. It may not be what we first thought. It may be something new that we have not heard before.

There is more to be said about this crucial process of interpretation. So far we have made some basic general points. We shall return to the process when we look at particular passages in section III. Before we do that, we urge the case for preachers giving the extraordinary breadth and diversity of the Bible its due place in their preaching.

## II PREACHING FROM THE OLD TESTAMENT, EPISTLE AND GOSPEL

For some readers this may be an unnecessary section. In some English-speaking contexts, however, there is a real danger of the Old Testament or the Epistle being marginalized in preaching; they are thought to be too difficult, their relevance is far from obvious, and time is at a premium: the preacher's in preparation, and the congregation's because the service is likely to be long anyway. (Here we voice a concern about time expressed in some parts of the world, but not in others!). But if we go on neglecting whole swathes of the Bible in this way, it will impoverish the Church, and perhaps distort our understanding of the faith as well. Not all Christians will need persuading of the importance of the Old Testament and Epistle in the Church's worship and preaching, but for those who are unpersuaded the following paragraphs are offered.

### *Why Preach from the Old Testament?*

The short answer is that they are part of the Christian Scriptures, and an essential, irreplaceable witness to Christ. As such, Old and New Testaments belong together. St Augustine's epigram expresses their unity well: 'the New Testament lies hidden in the Old, the Old is made plain in the New'. We might sometimes fail to see the New Testament in the Old, or the illumination of the Old in the New. But there is wisdom in considering that that failure may lie in ourselves, rather than in the texts.

But there is much more to be said about the need for preaching from the Old Testament. The New by no means renders it redundant. The creation narratives, the stories of the patriarchs, the Exodus, the long story of Israel through the years of the conquest of Canaan, the period of the judges, and the kings, with the accompanying witness of the prophets, constitute the interwoven stories of God and the human race. A three-year lectionary cannot possibly include all of this, but it is our story, and Christ is its fulfilment: the One in whom the stories of God and humankind meet.

There is still more to be said in favour of preaching from the Old Testament. Without it, there is a real danger of Christian faith becoming bland and domesticated. But Job and the Psalms of lament remind us that cross-examining God, protesting to God, and even doubting God's presence, come within life of faith, not outside it. The prophets will not let us forget the centrality of justice and the bias to the poor in the purposes of God. The books of Ruth and Jonah are wonderful testimonies to the God who crosses any and every boundary. The Wisdom literature, including Proverbs, Ecclesiastes and the Song of Songs, remind us that the whole of human life falls within the biblical horizons, and the whole of that life is the gift of God.

### The Old Testament as the Hebrew Scriptures

Christian preachers interpret the Old Testament as disciples of Christ; they can do no other. At the same time, we are sensitive that these writings are the Scriptures of another community of faith, the Jewish people. Jesus and his earliest followers, as devout Jews, heard and interpreted these Scriptures. All the texts had a pre-Christian context and meaning before the Church, perhaps following Jesus' own understanding, saw them as prefiguring or pointing to Christ. So it is a kind of theological shorthand to say that Isaiah prophesied the birth of Jesus in the famous text in Isaiah 7.14:

> Look, the young woman is with child, and shall bear a son, and shall name him Emmanuel.[5]

We have naturally followed the evangelist (Mt. 1.23) in this interpretation. But Isaiah had his eye on a more immediate crisis, so the likely original meaning of his prophecy cannot be regarded as messianic at all.[6] But a text's original meaning isn't the only one there can ever be. The Christian will interpret Isaiah's prophecies as a Christian, but still have an ear for earlier meanings. So in letting Old Testament texts have their say, we are sensitive to their pre-Christian history, allowing all of that to enrich our preaching wherever possible.

### The Old Testament in the New

Christians differ widely in their approaches to the Old Testament – yet another reason for studying the Bible together. But all can benefit from noting how New Testament writers used what we now call the

---

[5] The Hebrew, unlike the Greek of Isaiah 7.14, has 'young woman', not 'virgin'.

[6] Isaiah's prophecy was addressed, in the first place, to the crisis brought about in the reign of Ahaz in 733BC by the threatening alliance against Judah of Israel and Syria.

Old Testament. They were selective, privileging those texts which illuminated their understanding of Jesus: the Psalms, and the books of Genesis and Deuteronomy are quoted more than, for example, the books of Samuel, Kings and Chronicles. They also read these scriptures in the light of Jesus. So some texts are now seen in a new light, and, in accordance with contemporary Jewish practice, the New Testament writers often quote the texts with their own interpretation added. Matthew, for example, or someone before him, has added a negative '*not* the least' to Micah's reference to Bethlehem (Mt. 2.6, Mic. 5.2).

Before we leave the subject of the Old Testament in Christian preaching, we should note the practice of Jesus himself, as far as we can discern it. Jesus' own use of 'the Old Testament' (our term, not the New Testament's) has been described not only as authoritative (compare Mt. 7.29), but also creative and even subversive. His own practice, and his central place in the biblical story and revelation, underline a distinctive character of Christianity: it is a religion of a Person, rather than of a book, unique and precious though that book is. When preaching from the Old Testament, we still, however indirectly or implicitly, preach Christ.

*Preaching from the Epistles*

The epistles, too, have their own distinctive contribution to make to Christian preaching. Ignore the epistles, and you are more likely to concentrate on the life and teaching of Jesus, on Christianity as an inspiring ethical code with Jesus as your example. But Christian faith is far more even than this. The significance of the death and resurrection of Jesus are what we might call the epicentre of the Bible, and St Paul and the unknown writer of the Letter to the Hebrews are two of the greatest New Testament exponents of the meaning of the cross. Preachers cannot make them their central theme every Sunday, but they must do so more than once a year. In any case, that significance, together with the gift of the Spirit and the calling of the Church to be the Body of Christ in the world, must permeate most if not all our preaching, and for this the letters of St Paul will be our chief resource, not forgetting Acts, the other letters of the New Testament and the Book of Revelation.

*Preaching from the Gospels*

The case for preaching from the gospels hardly needs to be made. Yet even the gospels have many challenges for the interpreter, and a preacher may be tempted to sidestep difficult sayings of Jesus such as his declaration that it is impossible for rich people to enter the Kingdom of God (Mk. 10.25). Alternatively, a preacher may all too easily turn one of the parables into a little moralizing homily; for example, 'From little acorns oak trees grow' – so they do, but the parable of the mustard seed is first and foremost about the Kingdom of God (e.g. Mk. 4.30–32); the parable's Old Testament background, not to mention the context of Jesus' own ministry, provides a preacher with much material to work on.

*Let the Text Have Its Say*

Whether we preach primarily from the Old Testament, the Epistle or the Gospel, in our preparation we seek to listen: to let the text have its say, so that through persistent, prayerful attention we may hear God's word for our congregation. But now we must say a little more about what is involved in letting the text have its say.

Every text has a context – indeed, more than one. Older schools of thought emphasized a text's historical context: what events behind this text can shed light on its meaning? To give an obvious example, it helps to understand the Book of Revelation when we appreciate the vulnerable position of small Christian communities in the Roman Empire. Whether Revelation was written during or soon after the reign of Nero (AD 54–68), or during the reign of Domitian (AD 81–96), persecution can never have been far away. In the Old Testament, the message of the unknown prophet of the Exile (Isa. 40–55)[7] acquires much greater significance as we visualize the depressed, demoralized state of the Hebrew exiles in Babylon, far from home. (For their state of mind, see, for example, Ps .137).

Sometimes we can discover little or nothing about the historical background to a passage, or even a whole book. But every passage has a literary context, as well as a historical one. This is much more accessible. The literary context of a gospel story in Luke, for example, can be discovered simply by looking at what Luke had just written, and what he wrote next. After recording Jesus' saying that rich people cannot enter the Kingdom, though with God 'all things are possible' (Lk. 18.25, and 27), the evangelist narrates not only the healing and conversion of a poor man (Lk. 18.35–43), but also the conversion of a

---

[7] Most scholars recognize that most of the prophecies of Isa. 40–55 come from the period of exile in Babylon, and so must come from a prophet other than Isaiah himself, who lived a century and half before the exile.

rich man (Lk. 19.1–10)! After the earlier story about the rich man, we are entitled to wonder whether Luke wants us to see the conversion of the wealthy Zaccheus as Jesus' greatest miracle – even the climax of his entire ministry. (The very next verse – 19.11 – signals that Jesus' earthly ministry is drawing to a close.)

There is still more that preachers may do in their study of a biblical passage. Such study is like looking at a precious stone or a priceless painting from many different angles. Each angle helps you see something you had not noticed before. In this reflection, biblical writers tacitly encourage us to use our imagination. That is what they did, using words and images to the glory of God. The use of our imagination should be informed by a text's historical and literary context. Otherwise, imagination gives way to fantasy. But imagination has a vital part to play in preaching, and we shall return to this in the next chapter.

To explore the historical and literary contexts of biblical passages is to look behind and around them, respectively. But that is only the beginning. Preachers can hardly be said to be letting the text have its say unless they give it their most careful and prayerful attention. Some shrewd words of a friend of C. S. Lewis, the novelist and literary critic Charles Williams, are worth keeping in mind: 'Some people believe in the Bible, some people don't; either way, nobody notices what the words are.' (The author of this chapter had written a book on Luke-Acts before someone pointed out to him that Saul does not become Paul at the point of his conversion on the Damascus Road.) This sustained attention to the words is a kind of praying. It is, as I suggested earlier, a kind of conversation, in which we listen attentively to what the other is saying.

There is yet another angle we need to note. In addition to the historical and literary contexts of a passage, and its contents – what is behind, around and in it – we have to ask what is going on *in front of the text*. This is the stance of a relatively new approach to the Bible: reader-response criticism. This approach makes the valuable, realistic point that readers make their own contribution to the meaning of what they are reading, just as members of a congregation make their own contribution to the meaning of texts and sermons. So the English Puritan who remarked, 'Tell me what you see in your Bible, and I will tell you what kind of person you are' was not being cynical – just realistic and honest. That is not to say that what we contribute dilutes or compromises the 'pure' meaning of the passage (whatever that might be); rather, it is the interpreter's indispensable role.

## A Useful Rule of Thumb

In the light of the foregoing discussion, there is a useful test to keep in mind: *No interpretation can be wholly objective; no interpretation should be entirely subjective.* Complete objectivity is neither desirable nor possible, even in academic study of the Bible. But the parameters of the text and its contexts must be respected; the text says this, not that, and we can't make it mean just what we should like it to mean. So no interpretation should be so personal that a congregation can't discern its biblical roots. And at the end of the day, a crucial test of all our interpreting is whether people, through our imperfect efforts, are enabled to hear God's word, to come to Christ, and to grow in the life of Christ.

## On Not Being Overwhelmed

Preachers can easily feel, if not overwhelmed, disabled by an awareness of how much they don't know about the Bible, especially in the light of contemporary biblical scholarship. There are three resources to keep in mind, and each complements the other two:

1. 'Where two or three …': (Mt. 18.20): studying the Bible with others, with one of the group undertaking to research and prepare in order to resource the rest of the group, can be invaluable.
2. Not all commentaries will help preachers; some are written by scholars primarily for other scholars, while others are too simplistic. It is worth getting advice, and, where some books are not available, borrowing from those who have them. This would be an excellent implementation of the Acts 2 principle of 'having everything in common'.
3. As pointed out earlier, at the end of the day the preacher has to take responsibility for their interpretation. Prayerful study and reflection before, during and after drawing on the other resources outlined above will be important. What preachers must not do is to react with obscurantist bravado in the face of modern biblical scholarship. It's not an academic conspiracy, still less demonic, and it is not infallible either. But a good commentary can be, if not the preacher's best friend, at least one of them.

In the remainder of this chapter, we shall look at three passages from the Bible, and deploy at least some of the principles and methods just outlined.

## III Some Case-Studies

a. *Preaching from an Old Testament passage: Gen. 32.22–31, Wrestling Jacob.*
The literary context of this passage, the storyline of Genesis, is powerful and dramatic. This mysterious episode comes between two tense, emotional scenes: Jacob's elaborate, fearful preparations to meet and to appease Esau, the brother he had deceived and wronged so grievously (Gen. 27, especially vv. 41–5, and 32, vv. 3–21), and their actual meeting and reconciliation (Gen. 33.1–17). We might anticipate by saying that this will be Jacob's moment of truth; his past has finally caught up with him.

From the context we turn to the passage itself. It is a mysterious story, and the preacher should not attempt to dispel the mystery, or even, in a sense, the darkness: 'night' here is not just a chronological reference;[8] vv. 22–3 convey an atmosphere of crisis and desperation: Jacob dispatches his family across a stream at dead of night, and faces the darkness – his darkness? – alone. Except he is not entirely alone; he wrestles until daybreak with an unknown opponent (v. 24).

The preacher needs to recognize that this story, like many others in the Bible, is almost certainly multi-layered – the product of centuries of storytelling. Hosea 12.3–4 is a passage reflecting some knowledge of this tradition about Jacob. So the preacher's task is not to explain what happened, but rather, to help the congregation to appreciate the drama, the details and the mystery of a story laden with profound meaning.

How may preachers do that? They allow the text to have its say – in this case, listen to the narrator tell his story. To begin with, neither Jacob nor the reader knows what is going on. 'The darkness of the scene is matched by the opacity of the narrative. The reader is allowed to see no more than Jacob'.[9] Is Jacob's opponent Esau – or God? Whoever it is, Jacob seems to be winning. His opponent asks Jacob to let him go, as day is breaking (v. 26), though not before he has inflicted on Jacob a telling blow (v. 25). What follows next is the heart of the story. Jacob, as always with an eye to the main chance, refuses to let his opponent go 'unless you bless me' (v. 26).

> 'So he (sc. the unknown opponent) said to him, "What is your name?" And he said "Jacob". Then the man said "You shall no longer be called Jacob but Israel, for you have striven with God and with humans, and have prevailed' (vv. 27–8).

---

[8] C. Amos, *The Book of Genesis*, (London: Epworth 2004), p. 203.
[9] Gordon Wenham, *Genesis* 16–50 (Waco, Texas: Word, Incorporated,1994), p. 302.

This is indeed Jacob's moment of truth. 'Jacob' meant 'deceiver', and so to state his name was tantamount to a confession. This confession, however, is the prelude to a new name, which, as often in the Bible, meant a new beginning and even a new character. Even if some of the old Jacob remains, the sequel shows a new man: courage and humility replace fear and arrogance (33.3), and penitence replaces deceit (vv. 10–11).

This transforming encounter owes its power to the identity of Jacob's mysterious opponent; it is indeed God himself. Again, preachers must resist the temptation to explain; their task is not so much to explain as to help the congregation hear the story, sense its mysterious power, and to encounter – costly and demanding though the encounter always is – the God who helps us to face ourselves and to begin again.

One of the great religious poems in the English language is the hymn on this passage by Charles Wesley, 'Come, O Thou Traveller Unknown'. Any preacher tasked with preaching on wrestling Jacob would find Wesley's hymn an enormous inspiration.

Before we leave this Old Testament passage, it may be useful to underline one or two features of the method we have followed here. As so often in the Bible, the literary context is hugely significant. The preacher need not labour the point; a few crisp sentences will set the scene. But the details of the passage too, as well as its context, offer the preacher so much. The night-time crisis, the mysterious opponent, Jacob's injury, victory and 'confession' of his name are all important. So, too, is the opponent's withholding of his own name, whilst at the same time blessing Jacob (v. 30).

A third point needs emphasizing. As we have said, Biblical scholarship, usually in the form of commentaries, is an invaluable resource for the preacher. (The above summary drew on two excellent commentaries). Preachers should not consult them until they have thoroughly immersed themselves in the passage; they also need to be wary of getting so excited about all the fascinating details to be found in a good commentary that they overload their sermon.

b. *Preaching from the Epistle*[10]

The letter to the Hebrews presents a challenge to preacher and congregation alike. There is much to be said for a short series of sermons on

---

[10] This section is abstracted from an article by the author which first appeared in *Ichthus*, Vol. 159/3.

its central, closely-argued chapters. With that objective in mind, this section focuses on a key image in the epistle, that of the high priest, with a brief look at some of the passages where it occurs. Though the imagery and the arguments of this epistle will seem strange to most twenty-first century congregations, it is part of the Christian scriptures, with a profound potential for nourishing Christian faith and Christian imagination. Because the letter's argument is quite dense, preachers will find it helpful to immerse themselves in the letter's central section (4.14 to 10.18) as thoroughly as they can.

Two short passages (2.17–18 and 4.14–16) introduce the theme of Jesus:

> For we do not have a high priest who is unable to sympathize with our weaknesses, but we have one who in every respect has been tested as we are, yet without sin (4.15; compare 2.17–18).

There is an important contrast here with the Jewish high priest, who was required to keep himself apart from the people to avoid being contaminated, and therefore unfit to enter the holy of holies on the day of atonement; (Leviticus 16 and Ecclesiasticus 50.1–21 provide important details). Heb. 5.1–6 contrasts merely 'mortal' high priests (NRSV) with Jesus, whereas it is God who appointed Jesus (v. 5) for ever:

> 'You are a priest for ever, according to the order of Melchizedek', (v. 6, quoting Psalm 110.4).

In the Old Testament only this psalm and Gen. 14.18–20, where he is also described as a priest, mention Melchizedek. One of the Dead Sea Scrolls, however, speaks of a priest-king called Melchizedek who will be a future deliverer. (The name meant 'king of righteousness'.)

The preacher, of course, needs to avoid overloading people with details about Melchizedek. Approaches will vary according to the congregation. But everyone can grasp the fundamental ideas:

1. Jesus' High Priesthood begins and ends in heaven: God appointed him forever.
2. So this high priesthood must be superior to all others, including the Levitical priesthood. The writer works with a crucial distinction between the earthly, or the material, and the heavenly or spiritual. But Jesus as 'one of us' (e.g. 2.10–11), and as the eternal high priest, brings the earthly and the heavenly together: his 'blood' was real blood, but its significance was spiritual; his sacrifice was an historical event, but its efficacy is for ever.

3. This High Priest intercedes in heaven (7.25). This is another difficult image. Two things may help congregations to appreciate it more fully: first, the Greek word 'intercede' also means 'meet', and second, Jesus, according to Hebrews, is 'the exact imprint of God's very being' (1.3). So God goes out from himself, as it were, and returns to himself, having forged a way for us (10.20).

In preaching from Hebrews, it is vital that preachers look for contemporary points of connection. Behind the – to us – strange concepts of high priesthood and animal sacrifice lie human concerns which are enduring and universal. And behind the imagery is the writer's fundamental conviction: Jesus our 'great High Priest' is God with us and God for us .

c. *Preaching from the Gospels: The Transfiguration, Mt. 17.1–9.*
Modern scholarship has wonderfully illuminated the distinctive features of each gospel. Two of its findings especially stand out. First, each writer edited his gospel in his own way. (This is the approach of redaction-criticism.) Thus even the smallest difference between one evangelist and another may be significant. For example, unlike Matthew and Luke, Mark mentions Elijah before Moses (Mk. 9.4); the difference reflects the different emphasis placed by each evangelist on these two Old Testament figures. There are also details found in one version, but not in the other two: only Luke says Moses and Elijah were speaking of Jesus' 'departure'; the Greek word here is *exodos*, a word probably indicating part of the meaning of Jesus' death for Luke (Lk. 9.31), especially as he writes that Jesus was about to 'fulfil' this 'exodus'.

Another more recent development in biblical scholarship is called narrative-criticism. Derived from modern literary criticism, it focuses on narrative details such as the plot, and how it unfolds, on the characters and how the narrator has characterized them, and the many unobtrusive touches which guide the reader through the story. This may sometimes seem an approach more appropriate to fictional writing. But narrative-criticism builds on redaction-criticism's insight that each writer has composed his gospel in his own distinctive way. Most valuable for the preacher is the way in which narrative-criticism has illuminated the literary context of each passage; often, though not always, we can find special significance in why an evangelist has placed one story, or one unit of teaching, next to another. So here, the meaning of the Transfiguration derives, in part, from its position immediately after the first prediction of Jesus' passion and the call to disciples to take up their cross (e.g. Mt. 16.13–28).

So, as always, preachers reflect on the context of the passage they are about to study. Next, they begin to listen carefully to the text itself, noticing every word. Space here precludes a detailed study, but we note amongst other things the significance of mountains for Matthew: they are the place of revelation, including teaching (Mt. 5.1, 15.29–31, 28.16–20, as well as v. 1 here); the radiance of Jesus' face (v. 2), recalling the radiance of Moses' face (Exod. 34, 30); the inappropriate words of Peter (v. 4), putting Jesus on the same level as Moses and Elijah; and a cloud (v. 5) which, as usual in the Bible, symbolizes the presence of God.

But this story, like the story of wrestling Jacob, has a pivotal centre, and that, hardly surprisingly, is the proclamation of the divine voice:

> This is my Son, the Beloved; with him I am well pleased; listen to him! (v. 5b).

This centre is important – crucial to our full understanding of the passage. Yet preachers often settle for sermons on 'mountain-top experiences' when they preach on the Transfiguration. At first sight, that might appear to be what the passage is about. But this is hardly what most of us would call a mountain-top experience: there was no view, because a cloud came down, and the disciples were terrified (v. 6; see also Mark 9.6). So to be faithful to the gospel here – and on this central point there is no significant difference between the Synoptic evangelists – preachers need to give central place in their sermons to Jesus, as God's Son.

That needs much more thought, of course, if the sermon is to be more than a mere rehash of biblical language. Two lines of thought – and there are others – may help the preacher to take the next step. First, (and especially so, if this gospel passage is paired with 2 Cor. 3.7–18), the New Testament invites disciples to *share* the Transfiguration: to be 'changed from glory to glory'. Jesus does not keep his radiance to himself.

A second line of thought is suggested by where this story comes in all three gospels: it is the beginning of the way of the cross for both Jesus and his disciples. So the way of transfiguration is the way of the cross. But it is important to reverse the statement as well: the way of the cross is the way of transfiguration. Does this suggest a two-point sermon? Perhaps so. But that takes us to the next stages in the making of the sermon. (See Chapter 8).

## Conclusion

Although there is no hard-and-fast rule, faithful, patient reading of the Bible passages chosen or appointed for Sunday will be the most frequent way in which preachers begin to prepare their sermons. They need time for this. A cursory glance at the passage hardly does justice either to the importance of Scripture or to the solemn responsibility of preaching. Even if a passage bristles with difficulties and obscurities, or we feel that it is so familiar that there is nothing new to say, the preacher needs to trust that, sooner or later, a word will be given.

## Chapter 8

## *CONSTRUCTING A SERMON*

Why is preaching sometimes boring? There are many reasons. A preacher fails to engage in sufficient depth with Paul's letter to the Galatians, or gets too bogged down in background details; a sermon on loneliness offers mere platitudes and generalizations; the preacher talks over the heads of most of the congregation, or says so little that they feel they have heard it all before. There are many other reasons why listening to sermons can be tedious. But it need not and should not be. It is quite an achievement to make the proclamation of the Christian faith boring, but those of us who are preachers must admit to no little success in this. So we turn now to the challenge of constructing a sermon.

Chapters 6 and 7 argue that a sermon does not necessarily have its origin in Scripture, but assume that studying the Bible – by oneself and with others – is a normative and early stage in the preparation to preach. In this chapter we continue from where the previous one left off: the preacher has explored the biblical passage and its context, and begun to reflect on one or more of their central themes. We saw that a central theme of Gen. 32. 22–31 was Jacob's transforming encounter with God, and that, central to the Transfiguration story, at the beginning of the way of the cross, was God's affirmation of Jesus' identity as God's Son.

At this point, it is necessary to offer a warning. Having found a main theme, some preachers, at this still early stage, leave the biblical passage behind! They concentrate on 'their' theme, developing it in directions which may have no basis in the passage, and ignoring those details in the passage which would help them to develop the significance of the central theme. *The preacher must keep re-visiting the passage.* Alternatively, preachers may feel that they must always begin their sermon by 'explaining' the Bible passages. Sometimes that may be the way to begin: week after week, that will be tedious. In any case, a sermon can have many different forms; common to all of them is – or should be – the Word of Life.[1] With these caveats in mind, we now ask: what are the next stages in the process?

### I  Preaching for the Church; Keeping the Congregation in Mind

Unless preachers have an exceptional memory, they will have made some notes about the biblical passages to be read in church. They won't find a place in the sermon for all of them; that would lead to serious overload. But they have tried to express, in their own words, what they think the text is saying and doing. But now – although the congregation will have been in their thoughts and prayers from the outset – they face more squarely the fact that all they are thinking and writing is for them.

Preaching for the congregation does not mean saying nothing which will challenge or disturb people; it does not mean pleasing or entertaining them, even though parts of many a sermon may do both. But preachers are at their service (2 Cor. 4.5); Christ has called them to this service, and the Church has recognized that call. So their business is to awaken, re-awaken, or strengthen their faith. So whether preachers know the congregation well or not, they keep them in mind, and, of course, in their prayers.

There may be particular challenges here. Part Two of this book deals with the moods and cycles of the preaching ministry, including the possibility, if not likelihood, that the relationship of preachers with all members of their congregations is seldom plain sailing. Preachers need to face problems, and the feeling in themselves which those problems engender, because their relationship with the congregation is crucial. Whatever negative feelings they may have need to be dealt with – through reflection, conversation with a trusted friend, and prayer (on this, see especially Chapter 9) before stepping into the pulpit. What no-one should do is to preach *at* the congregation. That is an abuse of the pulpit – and usually counter-productive anyway.

If preachers have never preached to a particular congregation before, how can they help them to be trustingly open to their preaching? Preachers need to be wary of trying too hard. To establish

---

[1] Jonathan Hustler, *Making the Words Acceptable. The Shape of the Sermon in Christian History* (London: Epworth, 2009), p. 5.

some rapport with the congregation – whether through some brief personal remarks earlier in the service or just before the sermon – may be helpful. Much more important will be to enable them to recognize in the preacher a person of Christian integrity and commitment, a person of prayer who takes seriously the responsibility of leading worship and preaching for the congregation.

So at this stage the preacher is moving to and fro between what some have called two 'horizons'.[2] The biblical horizon we explored in the last chapter, and as we saw, preachers even at that early stage are aware of the congregation, and are studying the Bible *for them*, though careful always to let the text have its say. But now, as they reflect on what they believe the text is saying and doing, they place it alongside the 'horizon' of the congregation. Their 'horizon' is everything which goes to make up their life, both their life together as a church and their lives individually, at home, at work, at leisure and in the wider world. The preacher will reflect, too, on their known or imagined response to the biblical passages in question (Chapter 2).

Let us imagine a small, struggling congregation meeting for worship in a community which has neither many regular churchgoers nor – apart from them – another church. If there were another church, they might have given up their own isolated struggle and joined that one. But if they closed their doors, that community would not have a church at all. You are preparing to preach on the feeding of the five thousand (Mk 6.30–44). You begin to see how readily the congregation might identify with the disciples in the story: faced with an impossible command from Jesus ('You give them something to eat' v. 37), they protest ('Impossible!'); Jesus invites them to consider what food they have; it appears to be pathetically insufficient.

Already the preacher is beginning to see how the two 'horizons' – the Bible's and the congregation's – might meet. What of the passages we looked at in the previous chapter? So much depends on the identity of the congregation. But the Jacob story, with its central theme of a mysterious but transforming encounter with God, can be developed in a number of ways. Its setting was a personal crisis for Jacob; what inner resources did he have to meet that crisis? Through his 'wrestling match' with God, he came to the point of confession,

---

[2] Anthony C. Thistleton has done most in the English-speaking world to make more widely known the concept of the two 'horizons' derived from the German philosopher and literary critic Hans-Georg Gadamer. (On this, see also Chapter Twelve.)

and received a new name and a new character. An analogy with baptism comes to mind. There is much more. All of us, like Jacob, have a tendency to use God; what we most want from God is his blessing – preferably a blessing to our own specifications. What Jacob – and we – get from an encounter with God is both more than we bargained for, and far more than we could ever have hoped for. Even for a small, struggling congregation such as we have imagined, there is both a challenge and a promise here.

Before we look again at the story of the Transfiguration, it is worth observing how much easier it is to preach a moralizing sermon than a theological one. A moralizing sermon concentrates primarily on people: the world at large, or the congregation and the preacher, emphasizing what we 'ought' to be and to do. (It can be a useful exercise to go through a sermon checking how many times we use words like 'ought', 'must' and similar expressions.) By a theological sermon, I simply mean a sermon whose primary focus is God – and that, of course, includes all that Christian faith claims about what God has done in Christ, the work of the Spirit, and so on. Such a sermon is usually harder to preach, because it is much easier to talk about human beings, especially ourselves, than to talk about the transcendent Mystery we call God, about whom every word of ours is bound to be inadequate. But to be faithful to the Bible, we have to make the attempt. And if we preach 'as the Bible preaches', we are bound to show, implicitly or explicitly, that believing in God has moral implications. (The Bible makes that abundantly clear.)

So what does it mean to call Jesus 'God's Son', as the divine voice does in the Transfiguration story? No single definition suffices. But we can observe that 'son' in the Bible means likeness of character: like father, like son; it also denotes origin: Jesus' ultimate origin is God himself – as is his destiny. And all of this, so the context of this passage indicates (Mt. 16.24–5), is the promised inheritance of the disciples.

Preachers can also reflect on what the transfiguration *of life* might mean in practice for themselves and for their congregation. Not the removal of all difficulties and uncertainties, that's for sure. Nor a permanent glow in our Christian lives, though that gift does seem to be given to a few. This is where a reference to mountain-top experiences may be relevant – they are the exception, not the rule. But whether we call 'transfiguration' a foretaste of heaven, or the beginnings of our own transformation, ('changed from glory into glory'), *it is promised.*

Whatever the passage, as preachers continue to reflect along these lines, they make connections between Bible and congregation, conscious at the same time of the danger of what a New Testament scholar called 'forced relevance'. Eventually, they will be ready to move to the next stage.

## II Moving Towards a Summary, a Title and a Structure for the Sermon

One of the most common defects in a sermon is its lack of unity. There is much good material, but it does not have one memorable, single theme. We have been misled, perhaps, by the conviction that a sermon must have three points. Some preachers think they are more than halfway there if they have got what they call 'my three points'! But the bible passage may not lead naturally to a three-point sermon. A sermon on the Transfiguration, as we have seen, is likely to have one central point: the revelation of Jesus. It may have two or three subsidiary points around this one central point, but if instead we have one point on the disciples, one on Moses and Elijah, one on Jesus, we may be in danger of making a mistake similar to Peter on the Mount of Transfiguration (Mt. 17.4). It would be a travesty of the text to have three separate points, unless the three points derive from the centrality of Jesus.

Now is not the time to decide whether your sermon will have three points. First, let it have a relatively short but accurate summary. Can you express the heart of your sermon in one sentence? On the feeding of the five thousand, perhaps a sentence like this will summarize our reflections so far: 'God is always asking disciples to attempt the impossible; but God always provides resources for the task'. From the story of wrestling Jacob, we might arrive at a summary such as: 'An Encounter with God is always both a moment of truth and a transforming experience'. Or – on Matthew's story of the Transfiguration – 'The way of the cross is the way of transfiguration – and *vice versa*'.

Such a summary will need to be unpacked and developed. But this is an important step towards ensuring that your sermon will have the necessary unity, rather than being all over the place. A short but accurate title can also be very useful in keeping a preacher on track. The title needs to be thought of at this early stage, along with the summary. '*Mission Impossible, Resources Unlimited*' might serve as the title for the sermon we are planning on the feeding of the five thousand. But it must be an accurate title, as well as succinct.

There is another task required of the preacher at this stage: what form and structure will the sermon take? This is a question which is all too infrequently asked. Preachers get into a rut, the 'three-point' rut being the most common. But the Bible contains an extraordinary variety of literary forms and styles; so why should not Christian preaching have a variety of forms too, as long as it serves the Gospel? (Remember, preach as the Bible preaches.) In fact, the Bible reading, or readings, will often be a guide to our sermon's form and structure. 'Mission Impossible, Resources Unlimited' looks like a two-point sermon, although to do justice to the centrality of Jesus in the story, the preacher is likely to have a pivotal point between the impossibility of the mission (part one), and the unlimited resources (part two). So it may be a three-point sermon after all. But there is a vital difference: a pivotal point which focuses in the middle of the sermon on the figure of Jesus is not really the second point of three at all.

Structuring the sermon is worth taking trouble over. There are two particular dangers to avoid here: having no discernible structure at all, or – at the opposite extreme – setting out the whole structure at the start. A sermon must have a structure, and the congregation needs to have some idea of the direction in which the sermon is going. But – and this is where preaching can become dull – the preacher does not tell them everything at the outset. No novelist or dramatist would ever do that. Anticipation is an important factor in a sermon.[3] Predictable preaching is unlikely to be as effective as it might be. The Bible itself is full of surprises.

## III Taking Care With Words

> From circumlocutions and clichés
>
> Longwindedness and wooliness
>
> Padding and platitudes,
>
> Good Lord, deliver us.

Words matter, and the preacher should take trouble over them. To do so does not imply a lack of faith in the Spirit, nor should it cramp the preacher's style or spontaneity. Care over the words we use is one

---

[3] Fred D. Craddock, *Preaching*, (Nashville: Abingdon 1985), pp. 165–7.

thing; the style in which we write them another. The delivery of the sermon is different again, and we shall touch on that at the end of this chapter. We look first at the preacher's use of words.

Words are one of the Creator's most precious gifts to the human race. 'More varied ways of using words can enlarge the opportunities for all of us to hear the Word'.[4] Language as we know it is a uniquely human phenomenon. So, as with our stewardship of the planet, our ability to write and speak needs to be used responsibly and well. Words can be used to obfuscate and oppress, or to illuminate and to liberate. Words may be used manipulatively, deceptively and carelessly, or with integrity, transparency and care.

Paul's criticisms of the eloquence prevalent in the Corinth of his day (e.g. 1 Cor. 1.17) should not deflect us from taking care with words. Nor should Paul's strictures on 'human wisdom' (e.g. 1 Cor. 2.1–5), lead us to overlook the ways in which a sermon is a work of art. R. E. C. Browne, whose book *The Ministry of the Word* became something of a classic on preaching, suggests that preachers should take their cue from the way in which biblical writers used their imagination and their intelligence in the service of God: 'only thus may the preacher discover more clearly the nature of the creative effort he is to make in his own work with words'.[5] Even the construction of sentences and the shaping of paragraphs can be a 'spiritual exercise'.[6] This stage of making a sermon is obviously related to whether we write a sermon out in full or not – an important, but not straightforward issue, discussed later in this chapter. In whatever way we preach, we need to put whatever gifts we have with words at the service of God and of the congregation.

A sermon often lacks clarity because preachers have not fully thought through what they wish to say. The critic and poet, Matthew Arnold, wrote that the secret of style is having something to say, and saying it as clearly as you can. If we are still confused about what the parable of the talents (for example) is saying, we had better postpone the writing of our sermon. But there are other stylistic points to bear in mind.

Using the Bible well helps to save the preacher from two preaching diseases; a surfeit of generalizing and of moralizing. Both are very prevalent in Christian pulpits. We generalize when we use expressions

---

[4] D. Deeks in a pastoral letter to British Methodist ministers.
[5] Browne, *Ministry*, p. 16,
[6] *Idem*, p. 22.

like 'modern science', 'the materialism which is so widespread today', or 'family life today is under threat as never before'. Such sweeping generalizations are much loved by Christian preachers, but they contribute little either to the clarity or the effectiveness of a sermon.

The contents of the Bible provide an interesting contrast. We might say that 'Love your neighbour as yourself' (Lk. 10.27) and 'Love your enemies (Mt. 5.44) are generalizations; but the first is followed by a very specific, down-to-earth story of the Good Samaritan, and the second preceded by equally specific and down-to-earth pictures: for example, 'If anyone forces you to go one mile, go also the second mile ...' (Mt. 5.41). The letters of Paul provide a similar picture. On the issue of meat offered to idols, there is very specific teaching about where, what and with whom to eat (1 Cor. 8–10). As for family life, or more precisely the life of the extended household, Paul has more to say than simply 'Love one another'; he addresses specific groups in turn, very difficult though it sounds to us today: wives, husbands, parents, children, masters, slaves (Col. 3.18–4.1).

### IV On Introducing, Illustrating, and Concluding a Sermon

Why do so many preachers think that they must make a joke at the beginning of their sermon? Do they lack confidence in the compelling, attractive nature of their message? Do they think that humour is the best or the only way to get the congregation's attention? Of course, well-judged humour may get the sermon off to a good start. But in this matter, as in all others, the preacher must not become predictable.

Introductions to sermons should be short. If they are not, they have become more than an introduction. Introductions should simply introduce, and do no more than that. They serve as a signpost, indicating the direction, or main theme of the sermon. They must not serve up the entire menu; otherwise, the sermon loses its vital quality of anticipation. But the congregation's attention must be secured at the outset, and the introduction needs to be tailored to them. The introduction is what preachers are likely to think about after they have thought through and structured the rest of the sermon. But they will naturally write it before, not after the body of the sermon; if it is added on after the sermon has been written, it is less likely to fulfil its one necessary function: to introduce.

Bible readings lay one particular obligation on preachers in the introduction or near the beginning of their sermon. The preacher says, in effect, to the congregation, 'Look at the biblical passage this way, not that way'. For example,

> Some people think of the feeding of the five thousand as a nature miracle; some think it was a miracle of sharing. This morning I invite you to think of it as a *church miracle*. After all, this was a miracle story which the early Church seems to have treasured above all others. And you will have noticed what a prominent role the disciples play in the story ...

We turn to the task of illustrating the themes of the sermon. Just as introductions should introduce, so illustrations should illustrate. That needs saying, because great is the temptation to drag in, by hook or by crook, a compelling or humorous story which the preacher has just come across, and wants to share with the congregation. But there will be another occasion – and preachers should have a good notebook or filing system for material like this, with a good index, so that they can find it again when required.

One good illustration for every major point of the sermon is a good rule of thumb. A sermon without illustrations has been described as a house without windows: not enough light on the situation! But a sermon which was practically all illustrations – though what would they be illustrating? – would be, to pursue the analogy, a flimsy construction with no solid foundations.

'Mission impossible' is not a difficult theme to illustrate at all. There are plenty of examples in the Bible: Moses, Isaiah, Jeremiah, Ananias (in Acts 9) are only a few. But illustrations need to be contemporary as well, not forgetting earlier centuries of Christian history, and 'the communion of saints'. So if the preacher knows of a church or an individual Christian with an experience to illustrate both 'mission impossible' and 'resources unlimited', that would be ideal. It would be even more effective if he or she saved the second half of the illustration until the second half of the sermon on 'resources unlimited'.

What of personal illustrations? Preachers themselves will be an illustration: 'truth through personality' (Chapter 1, section II). More specifically, there are some important guidelines to bear in mind. Personal illustrations should be used sparingly, and not without some heart-searching: 'What are my motives in telling this story?' ('We preach not ourselves ...'). Anecdotes about the preacher's own Christian experience come very firmly into this category. This is especially so if that experience is a positive one – an answer to prayer, or an experience of healing, since the telling of the story may only serve to increase the despair of struggling members of the congregation, or their feeling that the preacher is on a quite different plane.

The congregation needs to be able to identify with the preacher's experience. St Paul's language in 2 Cor. 12 is noteworthy: when he refers to remarkable 'visions and revelations' which God gave him, he uses the third person, ('I know someone in Christ ...',v. 2); when he goes on to speak of the humiliation and frustrations of his 'thorn in the flesh' (vv. 7–10), he reverts to the first person, ('I was given ...', v. 7).

Finally, in this section, we turn to conclusions. Conclusions must conclude the sermon! Now is not the time to introduce new material, or to present the congregation with a new question or a new idea. But a conclusion should not be a prosaic summing-up either: 'our first point ... our second point ...' Instead, in the words of an American writer, the preacher should fix the *intention* of the sermon in the minds and hearts of the congregation – and quit! That has a bearing on the decibel level. The preacher should not seek to emulate the politician haranguing the party faithful and ending on a great crescendo. Quiet, even abrupt, endings are likely to be more effective.[7]

So far, the preacher may have been thinking out much of the sermon, including its introduction, illustrations, and conclusion, in his head, or with the help of jottings on a notepad. There remains one more question to consider before we turn to the preparation to deliver the sermon.

## V Do I Write My Sermons Out in Full?

As with other questions we have addressed in this book, such as the use of a lectionary in preaching, there are pros and cons. This is an important matter, and the arguments need to be thoroughly examined.

First, preachers must work out for themselves what is the best method not just for themselves, but also for their congregation(s). The issue is not what I, as the preacher, feel most comfortable with, but what approach will lead to the best sermon?

There is much to be said for writing a sermon in full, especially in the early years of preaching. That requires of preachers careful thought about what they will say about a difficult bible reading, or the way in which the New Testament calls us to make the cross of Christ our own, or the challenge of climate change. To write a sermon in

---

[7] J.S. Stewart, *Preaching*, (London: The English Universities Press Ltd., 1955), pp. 120–2.

full – to repeat a point made earlier in this chapter – does not reflect a lack of trust in the Holy Spirit. When Jesus told his disciples not to worry beforehand about what they should say (Mk 13.11), he was referring to a situation of persecution, not the regular ministry of preaching. Nor does writing a sermon out in full commit you to taking the full manuscript into the pulpit. (We shall come to that shortly.) But it does ensure a more exact and precise use of words.

There is a real danger for the preacher here, particularly ordained ministers who preach regularly. The more public speaking we engage in, the more fluent we become. But that doesn't necessarily mean we shall use words effectively or well. A politician once lamented to a friend how difficult he found the task of composing speeches. 'You need not be disturbed as long as you feel like that', his friend replied. 'The time to become alarmed is when you find that you can speak quite easily without having anything to say'.[8] Indeed, many preachers will have noticed that the fewer notes they have the longer they are likely to preach. That is not good news. So we urge the discipline of writing the sermon in full: unless you are quite sure that your preaching and your ministry will suffer if you do. As always, honesty with ourselves is crucial.

If you write out the sermon in full, imagine speaking it as you write. Theological students who have not preached before beginning their theological training may write their first sermons in the way they might write an essay. But the styles are quite different. A sermon is more conversational in tone, without being chatty, trite or bland. Sentences will be shorter; there will be direct speech, and the occasional rhetorical question, as long as it is appropriate. (A Scottish preacher unwisely asked, towards the end of a long sermon, 'What more shall I say?', and received the retort, 'Sit doon, man, and shut up!')

It will be important to leave time to revise the sermon. If that sounds laborious, well, it may be. But if you are fired up by the message you are planning to preach, and looking forward to Sunday, then hopefully every extra effort will be a labour of love. (And if you are not enthusiastic about your sermon, should you really be inflicting it on others?)

Reading through the sermon gives you the chance to identify and simplify the sentence which is too long. If people were reading your sermon, its length might not matter. But they will be listening to

---

[8] *Idem*, p. 98.

it, and they won't cope with a sentence which is so long that by its conclusion they have forgotten how it started. Reading through the sermon also provides an opportunity to check whether your trend of thought will be as obvious to your congregation as it is to you. This is one reason why last-minute sermons are best avoided if possible; often such defects only come to light when you read the sermon a day or two after you have written it.

Having written and read through your sermon, you are now in a position to decide how much of it, in written form, you will take with you into the pulpit. Again, there are pros and cons, and the preacher must decide what is his or her best course. If you have a full manuscript, it will be important not be too tied to it: have you read it through – speaking it mentally or out loud as you read – enough times to be able to look at the congregation without either losing your place or forgetting what comes next? Some preachers virtually commit their full manuscript to memory, taking into the pulpit just a series of headings. That may be a better course, provided the spadework of writing and oral reading has been done beforehand, and provided too that a memorized sermon does not become a recital.

A few preachers may preach effectively with few or no notes. That may be the right way for them. But it will still be important to work just as hard at the style and language to be deployed. A demanding subject, or a not-so-clear biblical passage require hard work from all preachers, whether they write their sermons out in full or not. Without that thorough preparation, a sermon on a complex subject is likely to be full of airy generalizations and vacuous platitudes.

In this matter no one should be beguiled by their own or other people's admiration for preachers who preach without notes into managing without notes themselves, as if it were a kind of test in preaching virility. Being fluent and articulate is by no means the only or the most important factor here. This is where St Paul's reservations about contemporary eloquence have some relevance. The fundamental test is simply this: whichever methods and ways of preparing I adopt, what will best serve the Kingdom of God?

## VI Delivering the Sermon

Although the title of this chapter is 'Making a Sermon', it is important to give due attention to the preaching of it. That, after all, is the object of the whole exercise. But here, it must be said, preachers are often negligent. We finish writing our sermon, put down our pen or switch off our computer, and think our work is done. But writing the sermon is not an end in itself. It has been written in order to be preached. The preacher's sermon really 'only comes into existence as he preaches it'.[9]

In the previous section we recommended reading the sermon through, imagining speaking it as it is read. But there is more to this important task. Imagining speaking it also involves holding the congregation in mind, with pastoral sensitivity and prayer. How will Mr A, who struggles to believe, receive this paragraph of my sermon? How will Mrs D, with her strongly held views about biblical authority, respond to my comments about the passage? Of course, these questions will have kept recurring in the preacher's mind in studying the Bible passages, and in the writing of the sermon. But now, as he imagines speaking the sermon, he thinks of the congregation again, so that each sentence can be delivered to maximum effect.

Preachers need to know if their delivery detracted from the effectiveness of what should have been a powerful sermon. Some basic guidelines may be helpful here. 'Be yourself' and 'Forget yourself' are fundamental maxims. Preachers who are natural in the pulpit are more likely to use their voices naturally. Preachers who forget themselves, because they are entirely caught up by what they have to say – though all for the benefit of their congregation – are also likely to use their voices well.

The feedback process, discussed in Chapter 4, will be valuable. In particular, the preacher needs honest comments on three things: pitch, pace and pause. Was there enough variation in the pitch of the voice, so that the sermon was not delivered in a dull monotone which belied the quality of the words? At the same time, were the quieter sections not so quiet as to be inaudible, nor the louder ones so loud as to be contrived and alienating? Was the pace of the sermon about right, neither too fast nor too slow, and again, with some variation? Did the preacher pause effectively in the right places, but not so long as to make the sermon harder, not easier to listen to?[10]

There is a further practical point, not to be taken for granted: 'Look after your feet and your hands will look after themselves'. In other words, stand firmly and comfortably, and then other body

---

[9] Simon Tugwell, O.P. *The Way of the Preacher*, (London: DLT, 1979), p. 77.

[10] The emphasis on 'pitch, pace and pause' in public speaking I owe to my late mother-in-law, Gwyneth Bradshaw, a professional speech therapist.

language is likely to be more relaxed and natural. (I write this paragraph with feeling, since there was a time when I had to write 'Don't wobble!' at the top of my sermon notes, after a gentle word from my then wife-to-be.)

But it is difficult to overemphasize the importance of being natural, and using your voice naturally. Self-conscious preaching is a contradiction in terms, and contrived preaching is not much better. Speaking simply and naturally – and attractively – is vital. Preparing ourselves – with all the heart-searching and prayer which that involves – and loving and praying for the congregation will contribute enormously to the effective delivery of the sermon.

The detailed practicalities of the church building, and its equipment or lack of it, need to be thought about too. Is there an amplification system? If so, do I need to try it out before the service? Are there particular features of the church which will affect how I deliver the sermon? Should the age range of the congregation affect how I adapt my manuscript or notes, or the speed at which I deliver the sermon?

Finally, every sermon is likely to have a liturgical context. Should the nature of the hymn sung immediately before the sermon affect how I begin my sermon? If, of course, the preacher is responsible for the whole service, the question will need to be a different one: which hymn will be a good prelude to the sermon? So, for example, if the congregation has just sung a prayerful hymn such as 'Out of the depths I call to Thee', a joke immediately after it may involve too sudden a change of mood. Preachers, from their knowledge of both the sermon they have prepared and of the congregation, must decide what is appropriate. Similarly, the preacher, as far as possible, needs to enable the congregation to respond to the sermon, whether through the hymn they sing immediately after it, or through the prayers led by the preacher, or by someone else.

CONCLUSION

This chapter has attempted to offer some guidelines in constructing a sermon. It is important for preachers to keep their methods and practices under review. This is why this and the preceding chapter, 'The Use of the Bible in Preaching' are set firmly in this book between sections on 'Working Dynamics and Relationships' and 'Sustaining Developmental Support: Cultures, Services and Networks'. This new setting, we believe, can raise the sights of preachers and congregations alike. It is a programme for sustaining preachers and preaching in a fast-changing, demanding world. With such resources and support, (and, in the light of Chapter 5 on congregations, resources here very definitely include the Bible), preachers may begin to believe that their preaching will make a difference, and congregations start to expect it to make a difference.

**Part Four**

# SUSTAINING DEVELOPMENTAL SUPPORTIVE CULTURES, SERVICES AND NETWORKS

INTRODUCTION

Experience shows that preachers need support of many kinds – intellectual, moral, spiritual and theological – to engage with the practical and theoretical problems which may occur at any stage of their vocational life cycle. Apposite support is developmental: it helps preachers, as they study, prepare, preach and reflect. But it is also palliative: it comforts and supports them when they are in pain; it accompanies them as they recuperate from the stresses and strains of preaching. Furthermore, it helps them to live out their retirement.

No amount of ability, knowledge or initial training obviates the need for support, although these and other things will affect the nature of the help required. Conversely, support should not be seen as a substitute for instruction or study or formal training even though it may result in profound learning experiences. In fact, it may reveal the need for further study and then help preachers to pursue it and make good use of what they learn. Increasingly, new ways of providing preachers with the support they need are available. Effective in-service support is vitally important to the development of preachers and their preaching in the present challenging context. The intention of Part Four is to make these means of support and ways of acquiring them better understood and more accessible.

A wide range of professional support services, such as mentoring and consultancy, is provided for those who work with people in health, social care, business and industrial organizations. The theory and practice of the methods used have been well researched and described by behavioural and social scientists and practitioners.

Agencies provide them for individuals and groups. Lay and ordained people in churches looking for professional supportive help have quite naturally been attracted to what is so effective in the secular world, especially if they have had good experiences of these services outside church life. Sometimes this works very well. Unfortunately, but not surprisingly, the simplistic transfer of these services from secular to religious settings has not worked and brought them into disrepute in some quarters of the Christian community. Gradually, however, the negative effects of these bad experiences are being overcome. Extensive ecumenical application, theological reflection and action research have demonstrated that forms of support developed in the secular world can be adapted for effective use in churches, integrated into their culture and become a valuable part of the resources of practical pastoral theology. As a result, they are being used to good effect by increasing numbers of lay and ordained church and community workers of all denominations.

Drawing upon this experience of their successful application to general church and community work, these forms of support have been used to equip preachers to support themselves more adequately and to provide interpersonal support to individuals and groups. Chapters 9 and 10 describe these forms of support and the qualities required of those being supported and those providing and facilitating it. Chapter 11 describes how a group of lay and ordained preachers used and thoroughly tested out several of these support services in Leeds over a period of ten years and continue to use them. As they engaged together in this programme, lay and ordained preachers gained much from each other through sharing their knowledge, their experiences of preaching and their vocational lives in the church and the wider world.

The distinguishing feature of all of these interpersonal developmental support arrangements is that they engage directly and exclusively with preachers, individually and in groups, on the day-to-day issues of *their* ministry as they arise in relation to *their* needs, concerns, circumstances and uniqueness. So they are a means of fine-tuning each preacher's development and professional skills. In fact, they support preachers as they journey from general initial education and training through the long succession of specific applications of their vocational craft and into their retirement.

## Chapter 9

## *SUSTAINING PERSONAL AND INTERPERSONAL SUPPORT*

Human support and mutual help networks and systems are integral to all forms of secular and religious community life. Continuously or intermittently, individuals and groups reinforce each other physically, psychologically and spiritually. Interpersonal support civilizes and harmonizes life at all levels and helps people to realize their potential.[1] It is invaluable at times of crisis. Without this support human societies simply cannot function adequately.

Much mutual support emerges naturally and spontaneously. Preachers benefit from it enormously. Some forms of support, however, have to be created or strengthened or specially adapted in order to meet the requirements of preachers. Against such a background, this chapter examines what is involved in the provision of both self-support and interpersonal support. These two kinds of support interact with each other, providing, at their best, a strong core of human and spiritual reinforcement. The emphasis here is on developmental support for able and normally self-sufficient preachers, who on a short or long term basis:

- need help to tackle challenging preaching opportunities or tricky issues
- need palliative support
- are in crisis.

---

[1] A classical text that illustrates this is Gerald and Killilea Caplan (eds) *Support Systems and Mutual Help: Multidisciplinary Explorations* (New York: Grune and Stratton, 1976). They explore and illustrate interpersonal relationships in families, mutual help organizations, self-help treatment, single parents, mental health, transition, widows, caregiving and peer consultation among clergy.

The aims throughout are not simply to prop up and underpin, but to help preachers to develop themselves and their ministry, and to be self-dependent reflective practitioners. Pursuing these aims builds up healthy independence and interdependence and when facilitators and supporters engage with preachers non-directively, avoids unhealthy dependence.

## I  The Approach to Support

Obtaining wholesome support is not always easy. Many factors influence its quality, including the manner in which it is offered and received, the psychological and spiritual disposition of those seeking and offering it, and their hidden and overt objectives. When everything goes right, the support received is invaluable; when it goes wrong, the outcome can be injurious.

Self-support is the only means of support permanently and directly accessible to a preacher, apart, that is, from the ever-present help of God. Reliable means of self-support enhances a preacher's self-esteem and autonomy, and contributes to his/her development. It is the first level of substantive support. Crucial to self-support is the ability of preachers to think for themselves, especially about those things about which they feel deeply. Without the use of this competency, no matter how much they may believe what they say, their preaching does not emerge out of the crucible of their own intellectual and spiritual efforts.

Interpersonal and group support can enhance the ability of preachers to do their own thinking. However, there is always the danger that preachers become unhealthily dependent upon their supporters and their support. Generally this happens by default, but sometimes preachers and their supporters desire it, consciously or unconsciously. This danger is minimized if preachers are reflective, 'inner-directed'[2] practitioners and also if facilitators and supporters are committed to helping preachers to be more proficient and confident in supporting themselves. The interpersonal support arrangements described in this chapter are intended to do that, and to minimize the danger of supporters trespassing upon those things that preachers simply must do for themselves, albeit with help when

---

[2] The term is borrowed from David Riesman, *The Lonely Crowd With An Essay 'Ten Years On'* (Forge Village, Massachusetts: Yale University Press, 1967) He identified three main cultural types: inner-directed; tradition-directed; other- or outer-directed.

necessary. Effective support systems do not usurp independence nor do they drift into a counselling mode. Preachers need to ensure that they enter into relationships with supporters committed to these kinds of approaches. When they do, support systems can:

- enhance the preacher's critical self-awareness, creativity and ability to collaborate
- help preachers to build up patterns of integrated thought when working with complex intellectual and emotional material
- help preachers to be open to the Holy Spirit's leading
- earth preaching contextually in the realities of their own experience and beliefs.

## II THE RIGOUR OF DEVELOPMENTAL SUPPORT

Achieving these aims involves commitment to the discipline of developmental support both in preparing for preaching and also in the evaluation of it. Intensive interior activity is a crucial aspect of these phases, and, of course, it occurs in a different way during preaching itself. Engaging in this activity can be variously inspiring, taxing, and depressing. It involves preachers working prayerfully and meditatively on insights, challenging ideas, difficult problems, spiritual insights, thoughts and doubts. Doing this is not simply an exercise in reasoning or logic; it makes demands upon the preacher's confidence, their intellectual abilities and on their emotional and spiritual awareness and intelligence.

Preachers develop their own ways of engaging with these interior activities. Providing support to preachers in relation to these personal processes is unavoidably invasive. Great sensitivity and skill are required of supporters. Preachers have to go deep into themselves to allow supporters to accompany them. This involves preachers engaging with their subjectivity, exploring their own needs, and using their own learning methods and styles.

### Engaging with subjectivity

Some denigrate 'subjectivity' and extol 'objectivity' and *vice versa*. Both are important to preachers. Healthy subjectivity, but not morbid introspection and preoccupation with self, helps preachers to be inwardly and outwardly creative; objectivity enables them to set their subjectivity in context with that of others and the world generally. Preachers need to know their own subjective world and to be able to explore its realities, not least because it is one of the places in which they find God active through the Holy Spirit. In short, knowing and being on good spiritual terms with their subjectivity helps preachers to:

- build an inner base for outgoing action
- get purposeful purchase on things within and beyond themselves
- lay inner foundations which will sustain all other forms of support.

Professor David Smail[3] comments that *intuitive sensitivity* is the faculty that gives access to our 'intricate and finely balanced worlds'.[4] An illustration of what this can mean in practice was given in an earlier section on the preparation sequence of the preaching circle in Chapter 4. It demonstrated the vital importance of preachers recognizing and trusting the ways in which their subjective creative systems operate and how God works through them.

Some people are helped in understanding themselves and their subjectivity/objectivity through using the Myers Briggs Type Indicator or an enneagram to obtain a profile of their personality. An enneagram is a nine point psycho-spiritual model of personality types derived from an ancient Sufi tradition. Some clergy and laity find the Myers Briggs Type Indicator helps them to do their work more effectively by gaining confidence and insights into human behaviour. On the other hand, it has been misused to pigeonhole people and to interpret human behaviour in ways that are unreliable and disrespectful.

My own experience of the Myers Briggs Type Indicator revealed aspects of what I already knew of myself, but aspects of the analysis were unconvincing. I have residual doubts about its scientific veracity and real concerns about its potential for misuse. But it has its uses as a catalyst for discussion of human personality. Leslie Francis concludes that Christians who take the Indicator's psychological and theological challenges (and I would add spiritual ones) seriously are enriched, while those who accept it uncritically are as impoverished as those who reject it out of hand.[5]

---

[3] David Smail, *Illusion and Reality: The Meaning of Anxiety* (Guildford: Dent, 1984).

[4] Smail, *Illusion*, p. 88. There is a brief discussion of his ideas in George Lovell, *Analysis and Design: A handbook for practitioners and consultants in church and community work* (Tunbridge Wells: Burns and Oates, 1994) pp. 263–265; cf. pp. 50 and 176.

[5] *Movement*, Autumn 1996, p. 6. Leslie Francis published a book about the application of the Myers Briggs to preaching, *Personality Type and Scripture: Exploring Mark's Gospel* (London: Mowbray 1997). It is a useful introduction to Myers Briggs typology

## Sustaining Personal and Interpersonal Support 141

*Exploring needs*

Preachers who know their development needs are most likely to identify and find appropriate means of support and further training. Conversely, support and training can help them to see their needs. So they should define their needs themselves or get help to do so, before deciding about means of support. Display 9:1 is designed to help preachers to do so. Starting at the top with the 'felt need to be a more effective preacher', it guides and prompts preachers to articulate basic aspects of that need. It distinguishes developmental needs related to ability, faith and spiritual growth, knowledge and technical skills and suggests appropriate ways of meeting them. Working through this exercise can reveal what preachers know and do not know about their developmental needs and how they can be met. As the results are rooted in the realities of the preacher's situation, they provide a basis for further clarification of his/her needs and ways of meeting them. Would-be supporters and trainers can be asked whether what they can offer is likely to meet those specific needs.

Such a process is much more likely to be successful than second-guessing the value of various means of personal and interpersonal support and training that might be on offer. It provides information about the conditions to be met for effective supportive learning. It enables preachers to make better-informed assessments of whether or not what is on offer will help them. So the resulting statement of need becomes a support or training agenda. This is a very different approach from simply looking around for something that might help. Preachers who adopt this kind of structured approach take responsibility for their own support and development programmes. It is the antithesis of preachers being told what they need, but it provides for the input and critical consideration of what others perceive to be a preacher's needs. Knowing yourself as a preacher in these and other ways bolsters self-confidence, engenders independence and the ability to collaborate.

*Using learning methods and styles*

Preachers will have some idea of the various ways in which they learn through courses, experience, private study, reading and reflection, as

but the internet on Myers Briggs is possibly more accessible! Francis's book gives alternative sermon outlines on the same texts for each of the four basic Myers Briggs Types, i.e. it illustrates preaching in and through one Myers Briggs type to many types at the same time.

**Starting with your felt need to be a more effective preacher:**
1. Reflect on your calling to preach.
2. Articulate what you believe about preaching and leading worship and your purposes and assumptions.
3. Note what is prodding and motivating you to do things better: problems? frustrations? ambitions? hopes?
4. Write down what you want to be able to do better, to know, to understand.
5. Pool, edit, prune and decide what is key in relation to purpose and situation.
6. Note anything to be avoided in making arrangements for training programme groups or for interpersonal support.

**This could lead to several training, study, research, personal development needs:**

| *The need to develop your ability:* | *The need for enhanced personal faith and spiritual development* | *The need for more knowledge and understanding of:* | *The need for technical skills related to the use of equipment.* |
|---|---|---|---|
| • to preach;<br>• to lead worship;<br>• to address young people and children.<br><br>The need for human and spiritual relational skills in formal and informal groups. | | • The Bible.<br>• Christianity and its history.<br>• Theology.<br>• Other faiths.<br>• Contemporary world and philosophy.<br>• Current affairs.<br>• Etc. | *The need for information.* |

**Appropriate ways and means of meeting these needs:**

| Instruction, study, discussion, reflective practice, guidance.<br><br>Interpersonal developmental support. | Study, spiritual direction, counselling.<br><br>Interpersonal developmental support. | Instruction, study, discussion, essay writing, research, courses.<br><br>Interpersonal developmental support. | Instruction and practice.<br><br>Coaching<br><br>Interpersonal developmental support. |
|---|---|---|---|

**Display 9:1** A Guide to Thinking About Preachers' Developmental Needs[6]

well as through other people and role models. Some learn most from their failures, others from their successes. People who know how they learn are best able to improve the ways in which they do so by developing their strengths and attending to their weaknesses. Should you wish to refine your understanding of your learning styles, much has been written on the subject, and various aids are available which help people to explore how they learn best. For instance, there is a mass

---

[6] This is an adaptation of a chart originally designed by T. R. and M. Batten, and published in *The Non-Directive Approach in Group and Community Work* (Oxford: University Press, 1967) p. 93

of material on the Internet under 'Learning Styles'. Peter Honey and Alan Mumford have a helpful learning style questionnaire with notes on learning preferences of 'activists', 'reflectors', 'theorists' and 'pragmatists', the 'learning cycle' and 'learning as a continuous process'.[7] (See also Chapter 12.)

### III SELF-SUPPORT

In the first section we established the importance of self-support and in Chapter 4 we discussed how preachers can be self-supporting reflective practitioners through, for instance, processing feedback creatively. Here we turn to three methods, all of which can help preachers themselves to think things through constructively. They are: facilitating structures; reflective writing; and depicting.[8] The combined use of these multipurpose tools enables preachers to maximise their thinking range and power by helping them to draw upon their left brain which is linguistic and logical and that of their right brain which is holistic and intuitive.[9] The ability to use these methods is a key to all forms of self-support.

### a. *Facilitating Structures*

A facilitating structure is a series of questions or tasks which help people to think through things more thoroughly and systematically, such as a sequence for tackling problems.[10] Examples are Display 9:1 and the problem-solving sequence described in the next chapter. They enhance the functioning of the left hemisphere of the brain, which 'excels at the kind of one-step-at-a-time and logical sequences that are the basis of language.'[11] Standardized facilitating structures

---

[7] The Peter Honey and Alan Mumford 'Learning Style Questionnaire' can be downloaded online.

[8] I have written about the interrelated uses of these in relation to working with people in church and community in *Analysis and Design* pp. 175–188.

[9] See for instance Thomas R. Blakeslee, *The Right Brain: A new understanding of the unconscious mind and its creative powers* (London and Basingstoke: The Macmillan Press Ltd, 1980). There is a related useful book on creativity and writing confidence by Gabriele Lusser Rico, *Writing the Natural Way: Using Right-Brain Techniques to Release Your Expressive Powers* (Los Angeles: J. P. Archer Inc, 1983)

[10] See *Analysis and Design* for a discussion of different kinds of questions and the ways in which they can be used to form facilitating structures, pp. 184–188. It also describes facilitating structures for studying 'cases', that is, a sequence of events in which people experience interpersonal difficulties, pp. 29–48.

[11] Blakeslee, *The Right Brain*, p. 9.

are to be found in many forms. Once their value is realized, formulating them is not too difficult. It is of course important that preachers choose those structures that fit them, their mood and circumstances. Working through them slavishly is to be avoided; over-structuring as well as under-structuring can inhibit thought;[12] creative thought may require abandoning structures, and brainstorming ideas instead in the way described in Chapter 4.

b. *Reflective Writing*

Reflective writing has many uses. It can help preachers to think through sermon ideas, process feedback and tackle issues and problems as they arise by formulating them on paper or on the computer. Sometimes this process flows smoothly, at other times haltingly as ideas are refined. The purpose can be to communicate to others or to create a personal working document. Writing can also be used to transfer muddled and inconclusive thinking from the mind to paper, 'to get it down', as a colleague of mine says, 'without reference to merit.' This is a similar process in prose to what brainstorming is in forming patterns of thought. Transferring thought to paper in this way reflects what is going on in the mind, objectifies it in the text and enables preachers to gain a much more objective purchase on it; it helps them to think more creatively about it and to edit it until it represents them as accurately as possible.[13] This can be described as 'thinking writing' i.e. writing which makes you think, and thinking which enables you to write. Such reflective writing enables preachers to re-examine and reassess their ideas and to capture them on paper. This can be both exhilarating and painful as new insights emerge, attitudes and perceptions are corrected and revised patterns of thought evolve. It is writing that shapes our thinking and thinking

[12] See notes on this in *Analysis and Design*, pp. 143–146.

[13] This method has been used effectively to get people to dictate or write their 'life histories' which have then been researched by anthropologists, sociologists and educationalists and by people engaged in community studies. Information on the internet can be accessed through Google, 'life history research methods'. Two of the texts I have drawn upon are: John Dollard, 'The Life History in Community Studies' (*American Sociological Review* Vol. 3 No. 5, 1938) pp. 724–737; Ken Plummer, *Documents of Life: An Introduction to Problems and Methods of a Humanistic Method* (London: Unwin Hyman, 1983 revised 1990). Sister Margaret O'Connor and Father Richard McKay used this method to research their religious and priestly vocations in the Roman Catholic Church. Their dissertations are in the Avec Archives in section [72] in the Wesley Studies Centre, Westminster Institute of Education, Harcourt Hill, Oxford OX29AT.

that shapes our writing. Given the importance of words to preachers, the application of reflective writing to the preparation of sermons and thus to preaching is obvious. Both writing and preaching are forms of 'talking work'[14] in contradistinction to craft or manual work.

A few preachers can compose sermons in their heads and do not commit them to paper until they have preached them. Most sermons, however, are preached from notes or manuscripts. However this might be, it is the act of preaching that transforms them into sermons: sermon manuscripts are not themselves sermons. No matter how closely preachers stick to their text, sermons have to be preached from the heart as well as the mind, not simply read from manuscripts, if they are to come to life. (cf Chapter 8, Section VI)

Facilitating structures described in the previous section can be used to stimulate reflective writing about unresolved complex and emotionally-charged issues. Frequently, for instance, when I am absolutely stuck in the preparation of a sermon that will simply not take shape, I turn aside and attempt to answer questions such as: Why am I stuck? How did I become stuck? How do I explain to myself what is happening and the stultifying effects it is having upon me? What are my options? What am I going to do, when and how? What am I learning? Generally, tackling questions such as these helps me to tease my way forward and contributes to the sermon! In addition to these do-it-yourself-facilitating structures two other methods warrant mention.

*Journalling* is a structured way of writing about life experiences devised by Dr Ira Progoff.[15] It is an 'integrated system of journal writing exercises', used in privacy or quiet, which enables people to deepen their awareness of diverse aspects of their lives. Many people find it helps them to develop more meaningful lives through considering and writing about themselves and their experiences from different perspectives.

The second way is *recording*,[16] which was developed in the first instance as a creative way of making carefully structured records

---

[14] I owe the phrase 'talking work' to Michael Argyle, *The Social Psychology of Work* (Harmondsworth: Penguin, 1972) pp. 129 ff. See also *Analysis and Design* p. 176.

[15] Ira Progoff, *The Practice of Process Meditation: The Intensive Journal Way to Spiritual Experience* (Dialogue House Library, 1980). There is also material on the internet about Progoff and journalling.

[16] See *Analysis and Design* pp. 178–9 for notes on records and recording. See also George Lovell, *Consultancy Ministry and Mission: A Handbook for practitioners and work consultants in Christian organizations* (Tunbridge Wells: Burns and Oates, 2000) p. 98 for their application to consultancy.

of meetings, encounters and incidents in church and community development work. Records describe purposes, content, interactive effective processes, decisions and implications of an event or meeting. Clearly, they differ from minutes. I have used this method extensively with great profit in relation to all aspects of my personal and working life, including those related to my preaching ministry, and especially to sermons and to incidents before and after preaching events that went wrong.

c. *Depicting*

With the advent of PowerPoint presentations, visual aids are increasingly used in worship and preaching. Here we focus on depicting thoughts and concepts in diagrams and models as aids to thinking, talking, writing and preaching about things difficult to describe in words alone. Ian Ramsey said that theological models 'enable us to make sense of discourse whose logical structure is so perplexing as to inhibit literacy' and 'to talk of what eludes us.'[17]

Some models are what Ramsey calls scale models: a drawing of a building indicating how it is used, or a map of an area showing where organizations and churches are located, are examples of this kind. Others he calls 'disclosure' models. They reveal something of the inner structure and essential shape of things; they disclose how things fit together and interact. Both kinds are useful but it is the latter that are the creative tools for preachers. (Flowcharts are also useful but their function is to plot 'critical paths' of events and tasks.) Diagrams of models are invaluable aids to thought and discussion: they stimulate and facilitate creative thinking with the use of few words; points can be made simply, directly and vividly; they objectify things and are memorable; they stimulate thinking processes and discussions. There are illustrations of their use in Chapters 3 and 4. However, while diagrams are useful in highlighting key characteristics about complexly related entities, they can mask the need for accurate verbal descriptions of nuances that they do not convey. Some diagrams communicate widely; others do so only when people see them built up. The effectiveness of others is restricted to those involved in their construction – they simply do not travel! Most

---

[17] Ian Ramsay, *Models and Mystery:* The Whidden Lecture of 1963 (Oxford University Press, 1964) pp. 14, 15; cf pp. 5, 13, 48, 53.

people are not as adept at producing disclosure diagrams as they are at producing the other forms.[18]

Diagrams can also be useful in preaching. They can be projected on to a screen or drawn on a flip chart. Alternatively, they can be described. For instance an imaginary diagram can be signed in the air as the preacher says, 'these three things form a triangle'. Though invisible, the diagram remains available on the screen of the collective memory of the congregation to be used to indicate where points being made are located.

Some people find they are most creative when they work at things through these three complementary activities of talking, writing, and depicting. This is not surprising, because when used together, they draw upon the resources of the left and right hemispheres of our brains.

IV INTERPERSONAL SUPPORT

Preachers are supported in all kinds of ways naturally and freely. This section examines ways in which preachers can supplement this rich informal source with formal interpersonal support based on proven codes of good practice. It describes nine forms of vocational (not psychotherapeutic) support and indicates how they operate and the learning that can occur and points to some further reading and professional services. Chapter 10 discusses what is involved in using and providing these services. The aim is to provide basic information about forms of interpersonal support, which helps preachers to review them in relation to their needs.

Many different forms of interpersonal support are on offer under a range of titles. A brief overview may help at this point. Broadly speaking peers and support groups help each other through critical support; consultants help preachers to work at the substance of their concerns; facilitators help preachers to think and act constructively; coaches help preachers to develop confidence and skills; mentors enable preachers to draw upon the mentor's experience; supervisors, accompanists and appraisers help preachers to be more effective

---

[18] Diagramming and modelling are central to my praxis in church and community development work and consultancy. See: George Lovell *Diagrammatic Modelling: An aid to Theological Reflection in Church and Community Development Work* (William Temple Foundation, 1980; An Avec Publication, 1991); *Analysis and Design* pp. 175–184 et al; *Consultancy, Ministry and Mission* pp. 88–91 et al.

reflective practitioners; spiritual directors help preachers in their soul-searching. They draw upon a common pool of concepts, insights and methods that they use in various ways. Nine forms are described using the titles chosen by those who practise them and focus on the methods they emphasize.

*Form 1 Peer Support: critical and soul friends*

Peers can provide invaluable personal and inter-professional support especially when they are critical friends or soul friends. They can affirm, rebuke, challenge and, if they are perceptive, help each other to see things differently. As these involve relational transactions, their quality depends upon their mutual respect, the strength of the bonds between them and the value they place upon each other's wisdom. Soul friends are very special sources of support. They can perform the function that critical friends do, but in addition they are more likely to minister and bring blessings to the preacher's spiritual life: they are 'soul-making' as well as aids to practice. 'True soul friends', says Edward Sellner, 'do not depend on each other alone, but root their relationship in God'. He says that in the early Celtic Church a person who listened to you, guided and loved you was referred to by the Gaelic term, *anamchara*, 'a friend of the soul' or a 'soul friend'. The word came to be used to describe a person who acted as a teacher, confessor or spiritual guide.[19] Soul friends do not need to be preachers or even Christians; they can vary in age and experience and transcend gender differences.

*Form 2 Consultancy and co-consultancy support*

Consultancy is an established and growing discipline in various professions as well as in the church. Other professionals use aspects of consultancy as an allied discipline to help colleagues, staff and students. Identifying and securing appropriate consultancy help can be difficult: ending up in unhelpful and even damaging consultancy relationships is all too easy.

Professional approaches to consultancy range from 'systems thinking' through 'organizational management' to 'complexity and chaos theory'.[20] The one I have found most appropriate to providing consultancy help to preachers emerges from non-directive group and

---

[19] The quotations in this section are from an essay by Professor Edward Sellner, 'Early Celtic Social Friendship'. It is on the internet under Edward Sellner.

[20] Six different modes of consultancy and twelve associated models are described in

community development work in churches.[21] Broadly speaking, this mode of consultancy is to reflective preachers and their preaching ministry what counselling is to people and their lives. In this form of consultancy, preachers remain responsible for their ministry, while consultants have primary but not exclusive responsibility for the effectiveness of the consultancy services they offer. It works through an alliance of minds between consultors and consultants. Consultants need not be preachers themselves, but they need to be knowledgeable about preaching. Consultors decide what they wish to consult about. It could be one of many things: a preaching problem, congregational relationships that have gone wrong, recurring difficulties with preparation, coping with feedback, aspects of their preaching ministry, vocational doubts or unease about their ministry as a whole.

Consultancy can be offered in various ways. A professional or ascribed consultant normally works with a consultor on their concerns in formal confidential sessions whenever the consultor feels the need. There are many variations to this basic arrangement; for instance, one or more consultants may work with two or three consultors. In another arrangement two or more people who have basic consultancy skills offer each other consultancy help in small 'co-consultancy groups' of two to six people.[22] This reciprocal consultancy has proved to be extraordinarily effective for ministers and lay workers.

The members of a co-consultancy group operate by focusing directly and exclusively first on one consultor's situation and concerns and then on another. They work at that situation specifically, scrupulously avoiding comparing them with others. Various experiences may well prompt them to ask unloaded questions of, or test out suggestions with, the consultors while avoiding anecdotes. Other members act as consultants and note-takers. Roles are exchanged, as different members become consultors during a session or in a succession of sessions. This leads to egalitarian consultancy relation-

Lovell, *Consultancy*. For information about consultancy courses and services see: www.theologyinthecommunity.org.uk and www.sysleadconsult.com.

[21] This approach is described in detail in *Consultancy* and summarized in *Consultancy Modes and Models*, pp. 143–163.

[22] Co-consultancy and stages of a continuing group, originally of three and now of four which started in 1997 is described in *Consultancy, Ministry and Mission*, p. 356; *Consultancy Modes and Models*, (Cliff College Publishing, 2005), pp. 164–167: and in an article by David Copley, George Lovell and Charles New in the *Epworth Review*, Vol. 27, No. 3, July 2000, 'Take Three Presbyters ... The Role of Co-Consultancy', pp. 6–9. Groups have been operating effectively in London for several years.

ships and avoids the ever-present potential of patronage, intrinsic in one person invariably helping another without receiving help in return. Great care is taken to respect the autonomy of consultors; the process is aimed at getting consultors reflecting and thinking creatively; it is essentially non-directive. Of course, within this basic framework members will develop their own ways of relating and organizing themselves and develop their own co-consultancy ethos. People acquire consultancy skills quite quickly by participating in co-consultancy groups and, as a consequence, build up their ability to act in a consultancy capacity to others.

*Form 3  Support through facilitation*

Support is available to preachers through facilitators (sometimes referred to as 'catalysts' or 'enablers') who specialize in *how* to help individuals and, more generally, groups to work with people, to think through complicated practical, theoretical and spiritual issues. (A particularly interesting use of these processes is the facilitation of pastoral and spiritual exercises with individuals and groups.[23]) Doing this involves facilitators taking into serious account interpersonal behaviour and feelings without focusing upon them exclusively. Their expertise lies in processes, structures and working relationships: they may or may not have specialist knowledge of the subject matter under discussion, which consultants would normally have in addition to the ability to facilitate. An example may clarify the distinction. I acted as a facilitator when I helped a group of Benedictines to examine their monastic life and the theology on which it was based. My expertise was in the process, not in the subject matter. I would have acted as a consultant if I had helped the same group to design a church and community development project, because that is a field in which I have some experience.[24]

*Form 4  Coaching support*

Coaching is a pragmatic approach to helping people manage their acquisition or improvement of skills.[25] It focuses on how to do

---

[23] See Lovell, *Consultancy* on 'facilitating spiritual exercises', pp. 368–370.

[24] Lovell, *Consultancy*, p. 366.

[25] For this definition see: D. Clutterbuck, *Learning Alliances: tapping into talent* (London Institute of Personnel and Development, 1998). I owe this reference to Peter Jackson, 'How do we describe coaching?' An exploratory development of a typology of coaching based on the accounts of UK-based practitioners. (*International Journal of Evidence Based Coaching and Mentoring*, Vol. 3, No. 2, Autumn 2005.) Diane

things in the same way as coaching does in the world of sport. So, for instance, coaching for preachers concentrates on: their pulpit behaviour and preaching skills; the way they use their voices and hands and make eye contact; their non-verbal communications; their use of preaching notes. Coaching helps preachers to be creatively self-aware of themselves in action without being disturbingly self-conscious. It builds up self-confidence and tempers over-confidence. Coaches need not be preachers. Coaching can be a one-to-one activity or one or two coaches to a group of preachers. Like consultancy, coaching lends itself to mutual coaching partnerships.

*Form 5 Support through mentoring*

According to one tradition, the practice of mentoring derives from the Greek myth in which Odysseus entrusts the education of his son to his friend Mentor. Mentoring is widely understood as a way in which experienced practitioners support, guide and advise those less experienced. Mentoring relationships are not normally supervisory. They facilitate access to the experience and wisdom of mentors, which can be helpful and reassuring during periods of induction and difficulty. Generally speaking, mentors do not supervise; 'mentees' are not their apprentices. This, however, is only one of the understandings of the nature of mentoring and the diverse ways in which it is practised.

*Form 6 Support through formal work reviews*

Work reviews can provide support to preachers and help them to be reflective practitioners. They take many different forms and are often described as 'appraisal' and 'assessment' and sometimes as 'audit', and 'evaluation'. Unfortunately, as Michael Jacobs shows, the terminology is not used in a consistent way.[26] Depending on the skills of those facilitating review procedures, they can proceed to provide consultancy services. More generally, however, they restrict themselves to reviewing, evaluating and setting objectives.

---

Clutterbuck is a founder director of '3D Coaching', an agency, which provides 'organizational and career development through top quality coaching, training and group facilitation.' See http://www.3dcoaching.com

[26] Michael Jacobs, *Holding in Trust: The Appraisal of Ministry* (London: SPCK, 1989), pp. 19 and 21 give an analytical overview of the subject.

### Form 7  Supportive supervision

'Support' and 'supervision' seem to jar when they appear together: support suggests underpinning from below or buttressing alongside; supervision suggests imposed surveillance and control from above and carries with it suggestions of 'line management' and being kept in order by superiors. Administrative, educational, supportive and non-managerial professional supervision[27] do not fit these stereotypes. These forms of supervision can help preachers to deploy themselves in the best possible way, to work within their resources and not to overstretch themselves, thus enhancing their well-being and reducing the dangers of burnout. Supervision of this kind is most likely to serve the reciprocal interests of preachers, congregations and churches when it is voluntary, non-executive and rigorous.

### Form 8  Support groups

Clergy and lay church leaders of all denominations are increasingly making use of support groups. These groups, normally formed by clergy and leaders themselves to fit their needs, enable them to get help through exploring their concerns in the security of confidentiality. Groups can be orientated to general or pastoral or professional support.

### Form 9  Spiritual support and direction

Spiritual support can come through any of the forms of interpersonal help and relationships already described. Equally, it can come through biblical and theological underpinning discussed in Part Three; the 'means of grace' (private devotional practices and communal acts of worship); fellowship or *koinonia*;[28] and pastoral care and support.[29] Another form of spiritual support is spiritual direction. Kenneth Leech defines it in this way:

---

[27] To pursue this approach further see: M. K. Smith, 'The Functioning of Supervision' The Encyclopaedia of Informal Education, update September 03, 2009 on the internet.

[28] *Koinonia*, a New Testament word (e.g. 1 Cor. 1:9; 2 Cor. 13:14), commonly understood as 'fellowship' but has a wide range of meanings including: community, communion, sharing possessions, partnership, solidarity and spiritual relationships which are profound means of grace.

[29] Alastair V. Campbell, (ed.) *A Dictionary of Pastoral Care* (London: SPCK, 1987) writes, 'Pastoral care is to be distinguished from pastoral counselling ... although it may include it, and from pastoral theology ... or practical theology, which are its theoretical counterparts.' It has 'four main pastoral functions – *healing, guiding,*

> Max Thurian's definition is a useful starting point. 'Spiritual direction, or the cure of souls, is seeking after the leading of the Holy Spirit in a given psychological and spiritual situation'. Here the stress is on *seeking* and the seeking is mutual. The director, and he (*sic*) who is being directed, are both seekers; they are both parts of a spiritual relationship. 'Spirituality' and 'spiritual life' are not religious departments, walled-off areas of life. Rather, the spiritual life is the life of the whole person directed towards God.[30]

The stress on *seeking* resonates positively with the other approaches to support described above. Understood in this way, spiritual direction can be an invaluable non-authoritarian form of help to preachers with the spiritual aspects of their lives and ministry, especially when they are experiencing faith and vocational crises. Spiritual directors, according to Leech, help people to direct or redirect their whole being towards God. Focusing on the preacher's personal and vocational relationship with God introduces other vital dimensions and perspectives into the pattern of support arrangements. A central feature, for instance, of the Ignatian method of spiritual direction is that it aims to facilitate colloquies with the Lord, which properly complement dialogues between preachers, consultors, coaches, mentors etc., and their own inner dialogues.[31] This indicates that, whilst there are similarities between spiritual direction and pastoral counselling, there are real differences which must not be blurred.

Undoubtedly, God is actively involved in these various forms of support: in many different ways they can be God's agents of ministry. Interpersonal support systems have their counterparts in the spiritual support preachers receive directly through their personal relationships with Jesus Christ and their experiences of the Holy Spirit. At best, these human and spiritual forms of support fuse and complement each other.

---

*sustaining* and *reconciling*' and deals with problems and issues 'within the context of ultimate meanings and concerns.' p. 188. It is also to be distinguished from spiritual direction, although it may include elements of that. Pastoral care can be palliative *and* developmental *and* salvific.

[30] Kenneth Leech, *Soul Friend: A Study of Spirituality* (London: Sheldon Press, 1977, seventh impression 1985) p. 34. This is a penetrating study of schools of spiritual direction in the Christian tradition and the relationships between spiritual direction, counselling and therapy.

[31] See Lovell, *Consultancy*, p. 128 and G. Lovell, 'An Experience of the Ignatian Exercises' (*Epworth Review* Vol. 21:3, September 1994).

## V Support Systems: Uses and Learning

This section reflects on the needs that can be met by interpersonal support, the uses that preachers might make of various forms of support and the experiential learning that can occur.

### a Needs Met

Support arrangements and aids operate through helping preachers to engage more creatively with anything to do with their preaching ministry that requires attention. For instance, they may help preachers to sort out their wants from their needs and to tackle dissatisfactions they may have about their preaching. Support arrangements do not provide instruction in technical skills nor courses of study, but they can help preachers decide on and secure appropriate courses and instruction, and support them as they pursue them. This assistance helps preachers to take responsibility for their further training and it reduces the chances of them attending inappropriate courses with all the difficulties this can cause.

### b Experiential Learning

There are times when preachers may be intimidated and stressed and all they need is empathetic loving support. On countless occasions I have found this kind of support of inestimable value. Providentially, many people provide it. But it is equally important that complementary forms of support are made available to help preachers to develop their preaching and themselves, seize opportunities, cope with stress and work through problems and setbacks.

Doing this through the kinds of support discussed in this chapter promotes learning through the careful examination of actual experiences. There can be three kinds of experiential learning. The first involves preachers adjusting the way in which they pursue their preaching ministry to conform to accepted ways of doing things. This has been described as 'adaptive learning'. A second form involves them in discerning and learning new ways of doing things: 'thinking outside the box', originally and creatively. This kind of learning is about opening up closed circuit thinking and breaking out of 'groupthink'.[32] Feedback, for instance, which challenges

---

[32] Groupthink is a term used to describe a form of bad decision making in groups based on group conformity thinking and uncritical misplaced loyalty to highly directive and manipulative leaders. It engenders defensive avoidance, illusions of invulnerability, and collective rationalization. It operates in many ways including

basic assumptions and accepted procedures, can induce this kind of learning. Some commentators claim that it is critical to success during times of rapid change. A third form involves preachers developing creative processes for revising codes of good practice. Supporters need to be able to identify and facilitate these different kinds of experiential learning and to get preachers to engage in them appropriately.[33] These approaches to learning throw light upon preaching, and particularly upon the way in which preachers and members of congregations approach contentious, moral and doctrinal subject matter. Some preachers, for instance, aim to adjust human behaviour to long established norms; others aim to change the norms. The current debates about homosexuality and the consecration of women as bishops illustrate these different approaches.

Preachers will vary considerably in their commitment to and their ability to negotiate these three approaches to learning and change. Naturally they will be inclined to operate within their comfort zones and be stressed when they are prised out of them. When that happens, they need support, as indeed they do when they are trapped in an approach which is becoming untenable. This brief incursion into these three learning zones shows the potential scope for support services if they are to operate effectively across this broad experiential learning front during periods of change.

### c  Uses

Self-support is a must. Different forms of interpersonal support are not mutually exclusive. Some of them can be used on a regular basis, others occasionally as required. Preachers can form their own support portfolio. Support overload, however, is to be avoided, not least because it can induce unhealthy dependence and generate unhelpful dissonance between the different sources of support. In securing effective forms of support much depends upon finding able

---

self-censorship and through self-appointed mind guards. In its chronic form it is extremely dangerous. For a critical analysis of it see Irving L. Janis and Leon Mann, *Decision Making: A Psychological Analysis of Conflict, Choice and Commitment* (New York: Free Press, Collier Macmillan, 1977) pp. 129–133 et al. There is a note of its features in Lovell, *Consultancy*, pp. 322–324.

[33] These forms are described as single, double, and triple-loop learning. See: Robin Snell, and Man-Kuen Chak, 'The Learning Organization: Learning and Empowerment for Whom?', *Management Learning*, Vol. 29(3), 1998; Gareth Morgan, *Images of Organization* (Beverley Hills, California: Sage Publications, 1986) pp. 87–95; 957–958.

and compatible support partners and/or supporters, and that in turn depends upon them being available. A first step is to determine the kind of support that you need. As said earlier, the facilitating structure in Display 9:1 can help you to do this. The next step is to think about the characteristics of congenial partners or supporters who can help you to meet these needs. Sections of Chapter 10 will help you to do this. Working out the criteria for a support group, for instance, can help you to form a group that is most likely to meet your needs. This preparatory thinking clarifies what you are looking for and provides a basis for discussing and contracting with potential partners and supporters, and developing together the necessary skills to support each other or to develop self-support systems. Trying out support relationships before formalizing them is advisable. Some denominations have lists of enablers, and some agencies that provide consultancy, coaching and mentoring help have been noted.

## Conclusion

Personal and interpersonal support can help preachers to pursue their vocation stage by stage thoughtfully and prayerfully. It leads to improved performances, deepening and increasing vocational satisfaction. It enables preachers to work through difficult periods and to keep their feet on the ground when plaudits are showered on them. It helps preachers to work within their strength and competence and to maintain professional boundaries, preventing dysfunctional isolation. It helps preachers to develop professionally and spiritually. Preachers whose own needs are met are best able to support family and friends most affected by the ups and downs of their ministry, as well as members of congregations and other preachers.

## Chapter 10

# *FACILITATING LOCAL DEVELOPMENTAL PROGRAMMES AND INTERPERSONAL SUPPORT*

This chapter provides practical help to anyone interested in facilitating in-service training and support arrangements. Equally, it is useful to preachers using or intending to use these services: it will, for instance, help them to choose suitable facilitators and supporters. The chapter has five main sections. The first describes the nature of the in-service training advocated; the second is concerned with helping preachers to think through their needs for training and interpersonal support; the third and fourth sections explore the abilities required of trainers and of preachers and supporters engaged in interpersonal support; and the fifth indicates ways of equipping yourself as a facilitator and/or a supporter.

### I IN-SERVICE TRAINING

Programmes and interpersonal support arrangements may be for individual preachers or for denominational or ecumenical groups of preachers, both lay and ordained. Experience has shown that there are advantages when groups of preachers engage in in-service training together. Sharing their experiences of preaching and their vocations in the Church and in the world can be enriching. So, again, the term 'preachers' will be used inclusively.

The facilitative approach advocated here is a 'bottom-up' one, with the emphasis on tailor-made rather than ready-made training and support programmes. It aims to get preachers actively involved in the development of their preaching and of themselves as preachers by helping them to determine their training needs and explore practical ways of satisfying them. In this approach preachers themselves assess the strengths and weaknesses of their abilities and performances and consider seriously but critically what others say about them and their training needs. Programmes emerging from these processes could of course include or even consist of ready-made modules or sessions designed and conducted by others which the preachers themselves decide are a good fit with their purposes, temperament and situation. Facilitators, enablers or trainers who are preachers themselves have certain advantages in promoting these programmes. However, those who are not preachers but are acceptable to the preachers concerned can be equally effective, provided they are sympathetic to the preaching ministry, and equipped with sufficient understanding of the art of preaching and of relevant biblical and theological issues. An example of this kind of approach to preacher development in action is described in the next chapter, 'An Ongoing Ten-year Local Programme.'

## II GETTING AT APPROPRIATE AND VIABLE TRAINING AND SUPPORT PROGRAMMES

In order to determine appropriate forms of in-service training and support for preachers, it is first necessary to obtain reliable information about their training needs. To determine viable forms of training, it is then necessary to obtain reliable information about the time and energy that they are able and willing to give to it. These obvious conditions need to be stated because, in my experience, they are not normally given the attention they deserve. It is common practice for trainers to assume and second-guess training needs, organize a course and then try to persuade preachers to get involved in it. As preachers themselves are the only reliable source of some of the information required for the responsible planning of training and development programmes, it is necessary to listen to them and to think through their needs with them until a realistic assessment of their needs is established. Establishing preachers' needs is a part of their in-service training, not a prelude to it as some might think.

A facilitating structure for getting at a reliable understanding of training needs is presented in Display 9:1, which we will refer to as the Chart. Facilitators and preachers themselves can use this tool to review their own needs, or it can be used by the participants in any of the interpersonal support arrangements described in Chapter 9. This section describes how facilitators can use it to review their own needs

*Facilitating Local Developmental Programmes and Interpersonal Support* 159

and to help preachers, individuals and groups, to work through it to determine their training needs and how to meet them.

The structure consists of a sequence of tasks that starts at the top of the chart with six reflective exercises and concludes at the bottom with ways of meeting needs that have emerged. This section describes the action required of facilitators at various stages in the process. The personal pronoun 'you' is used to preface what facilitators should and should not do in order to help them to read these things off directly. This makes the text as easily accessible as possible, without reducing it to a list of rubrics or instructions.

**a** *Start Where You Are*

If you are a preacher yourself it will be important to establish what your own training needs are, before you take up the role of facilitator to a particular group of preachers. Knowing where you are reduces the danger of you being, consciously or unconsciously, unhelpfully preoccupied with your own needs, and it makes it easier for you to share them without imposing them. Consequently you are better able to give yourself to the demanding tasks of clarifying with the preachers *their* position and of connecting constructively with *their* needs. This avoids dysfunctional gaps between meeting their needs and yours. Having done this, you might go on to establish what are your purposes as a facilitator in general and in the particular work you are about to do. (It can also be helpful to articulate what you wish to avoid.) Establishing these reference points puts you in a strong position to offer constructive facilitative help.

**b** *Start Where the Preachers Are*

At all costs avoid the all too prevalent practice of starting where you, the facilitator, consider the preachers are or should be. Orientate yourself to start where the preachers actually are, not with assumptions of training needs and prescribed programmes, no matter how attractive they may seem. You could do so by getting the preachers to articulate their felt needs by working at tasks 1 to 4 on the Chart. They could work through them privately, for instance, to prepare for a group discussion in which you help them to share and examine their thoughts in relation to each of the four tasks. Share needs that you identify for critical consideration along with those identified by others. Getting at real needs, and therefore at appropriate programmes, involves scanning *all* ideas and felt needs, expressing

### c  Establishing the Preachers' Training and Support Needs

Now we move to exercise 5 on the Chart, 'pool, edit, prune and decide what is key'. Rigorous thought at this stage will pay dividends. Compare and contrast each and all the needs expressed in relation to purpose, interests and situation. To avoid being myopically introspective and the danger of arriving at a distorted programme, consider whether the preachers and you are missing anything out. What, for instance, do members of their congregations say about preaching and preachers in general and their strengths and weaknesses in particular? Is there anything they need to take into account? Again, is there anything in standard training programmes about preachers' needs that is relevant? (After the preachers had articulated their felt needs at the beginning of the project described in Chapter 11, the facilitators suggested that a prior requirement was a shared understanding of some fundamentals about preaching. The preachers had not mentioned that suggestion but they readily accepted it. Considering some fundamentals took a year but gave a firm basis for tackling what the preachers felt they needed.) Reflect on all that emerges on your own and with the group of preachers. Share your thinking. Look at one need in relation to another. Test them out. Do they point to deeper underlying needs or significant common denominators? Can they be grouped or classified? Take time and care over this seminal phase of the exploration.

When this kind of rumination has run its course, you and the preachers are in a position to decide what is key in relation to *their* purposes and situation. Alongside what you want to achieve it is helpful to note what you want to avoid, *noxiants* as they might be called: we steer well by plotting paths which move towards *purposes* and away from *noxiants*.[1] What needs to be tackled first? What requires long-term attention?

What is becoming clear is that as a facilitator you have two main tasks: to help the preachers to do these things as thoroughly as they can, and to feed into the processes for critical appraisal any ideas or relevant information you may have which are otherwise unavailable to the preachers.

---

[1] See Lovell, *Analysis*, pp. 122–123.

*Facilitating Local Developmental Programmes and Interpersonal Support* 161

d *Establishing Needs to be Met and Viable Training Programmes*

Using what has emerged from the previous exercise, get the preachers to draw up what can be called a 'development agenda'[2] This involves determining just what the preachers themselves need to do to pursue the implications of their examination of their developmental needs. This is a brooding mood stage, a standing back before going forward. The objective is to find a manageable in-service training agenda which will meet the identified needs. Get the preachers to mull over the list of needs that have been established, to mark those which are substantive, to look for links between them, and then to group them. One way of doing this is outlined in the lower half of the Chart, which correlates needs with appropriate ways of meeting them:

- instruction, study, discussion, reflective practice, guidance and/or
- study, spiritual direction, counselling and/or
- instruction, study, discussion, essay writing, research, courses and/or
- instruction and practice and/or
- interpersonal developmental support.

Facilitator and preachers could try to fit them into such a framework and read off the implications. Encourage the preachers to stay with these processes until they have put their needs into an order and shape that makes you and them feel that together you can and want to work at them. The following questions could help you, the facilitator, and the preachers to turn the classified needs into a training programme.

*Which needs if any are we, preachers and facilitators, going to tackle?*

All the members of the group could decide to work on some things, for instance, while sub-groups worked on others and shared their findings.

*Is there a natural order in which we should approach these needs and if so what is it?*

It may be best to tackle some needs in sequence and others in parallel and cross-reference them.

---

[2] Lovell, *Analysis*, pp. 81, 83 and 119.

***What kinds of in-service training and/or interpersonal support are appropriate to each of these needs?***

See the 'appropriate ways and means of meeting these needs' at the bottom of the Chart. Some needs could be met, for instance, by self-programming groups of preachers facilitated in the ways suggested in this chapter, but in some cases it may be necessary for groups to recruit the services of people with specialist skills or knowledge. Other needs might best be met through 'preaching projects', i.e. reflective preaching exercises. Examples are given in Chapter 11. Yet other needs might best be met by one or more of the forms of interpersonal developmental support described in Chapter 9.

***Can we do it ourselves? Have we the necessary resources? If so, in what ways? If not, what specific additional help or helpers do we need?***

The group may decide to get others to facilitate some sessions or to give talks or lectures or to instruct them. The work done on the needs of preachers can be variously used: to check out whether people you approach can be of help, to discover whether they see 'needs within the needs', and/or to give precise briefings to anyone invited to help. Doing these things can save everyone's time and minimize the risk of frustration and disappointment.

***How much time are we able and willing to give to this training and support programme?***

Clarify with the preachers the training programme and support that is emerging and test it out for viability and acceptability by asking questions such as:

> What do you think and feel about this proposed programme?
> Is it a programme that we, preachers and facilitators, are able to make time for?
> Is it acceptable to you/us? Is it manageable?
> Do we commit ourselves to it?

Hopefully the outcome will be a viable development training and support programme, which the preachers and the facilitators own as theirs and are able, committed and eager to get on with!

III REQUIREMENTS OF TRAINING PROGRAMME LEADERS

Now we turn from processes and procedures to the attributes required of would be facilitators.

## a Disposition and Approach

Chapter 9 and the previous section are about facilitators and supporters helping groups of preachers with their needs in various ways. A particular kind of disposition and cluster of skills are needed to help preachers examine critically and reflectively their vocations, issues they are confronting, disaffections they are experiencing, problems they are facing, needs they might have and contemporary socio-religious and contemporary theological issues that challenge them. What is known as a *non-directive disposition and stance* is crucial. But such a disposition clearly must include a belief in preaching, an empathy with preachers and a conviction about the need for in-service training and interpersonal support and enthusiasm for self-help programmes. Accompanying these characteristics must be a deep desire and real commitment to get preachers, individually and collectively, to think rigorously and actively engage in promoting their own development as preachers. Such attitudes are central to working *with* preachers in contrast to working *for* them. These are features of the non-directive concept and its approach to promoting holistic human and spiritual development.

## b The non-directive concept and approach

Being non-directive is the antithesis of being directive, authoritarian and didactic. But it is not to be confused with being laissez-faire or permissive, which by definition involves avoiding and withdrawing from people and situations, rather than approaching them forthrightly as occurs in both the directive and non-directive *approaches*. Adopting a non-directive approach involves robust, energetic leadership directed towards stimulating and enabling preachers to engage in thoughtful action through which they are primary instruments of their own development and that of each other. It can involve facilitators making strong interventions and original presentations and, paradoxically, at times taking firm directive action. The description of the project in Chapter 11 shows what it can be like in operation.

Those committed to a directive approach decide what they consider people need, ought to do, or ought to value, and then plan, organize, and administer to influence people to follow the pre-determined pattern of behaviour and thought (this can be described as the *for* approach). In the permissive approach people are allowed to do and to be just what they wish to do and to be. In the first approach the worker assumes an authoritarian role, in the second a passive, if not indifferent, role.

The non-directive approach (or the *with* approach) should not be thought of as on a sliding scale between permissive and directive. It is a quite separate type of approach. Facilitators are concerned not with the introduction of pre-determined content into the discussion but with structuring and deepening the discussion. They help by supporting, stimulating, clarifying, summarizing where necessary, and avoiding taking sides; they put their verbal skills at the service of others. Where necessary they provide information and suggest sources of help and support. They assist people to see the balance of advantages and disadvantages of their plans and its implications, and to make decisions on the basis of a proper evaluation of the consequences of any proposed action. By these means, in the words of the original proponents of this approach, T. R. and M. Batten:

> Non-directive workers try to get people to decide for themselves what their needs are; what, if anything, they are willing to do to meet them; and how they can best organize, plan and act to carry their project through. Thus they aim at stimulating a process of self-determination and self-help, and they value it for all the potential learning experiences which participation in this process provides. They aim to encourage people to develop themselves, and it is by thinking and acting for themselves, they believe, that they are most likely to do so.[3]

Briefly stated, facilitators:

- try to strengthen preachers' incentives to act by stimulating them to discuss their needs in the hope that they will come to see them as specific wants
- provide information where necessary on, for example, what similar groups have done
- help preachers systematically to think through and analyze the nature and causes of any problem they encounter
- suggest sources from which the preachers may be able to obtain personal or material assistance or technical advice.

Commitment to the non-directive approach does not mean that in certain situations and at certain times directive or permissive approaches may not be used. The most appropriate and efficient approach and method must be selected in relation to purpose, situation, context and resources.

---

[3] T. R. and M. Batten, *The Non-Directive Approach* (London: an Avec Publication, 1989) Inclusive language version.

## c. Key Abilities Required of Facilitators

This section highlights abilities and skills that equip people to be non-directive facilitators to preachers. Four key aspects are described which form a closely interrelated cluster variously integrated in good praxis.

### *Key aspect one: the ability to engage in non-directive 'talking work'*

A particular form of 'talking work' is a core activity in preacher development in-service training, which differs significantly from that of preaching and lecturing but is complementary to them. It involves preachers in unrehearsed conversations and discussions in small or large groups that promote creative dialogue between and within the participants. Achieving this involves putting language to work for human and spiritual development openly and freely while being focused, disciplined, courteous, structured and purposeful. It aims to give a voice and say to all participants and to take all contributions seriously. Doing that involves using language carefully, as indicated in the following translation of Eph. 4:29: 'Do not use harmful words in talking. Use only helpful words, the kind that build up and provide what is needed, so that what you say will do good to those who hear you'[4] To promote this kind of interaction facilitators have to:

- work diligently with the words of others as well as with their own
- help people to find words to express themselves adequately
- help people to move from arguing, debating and using rhetoric to win points to thinking things through together using all their resources, insights and verbal abilities collaboratively
- help people, when words are being used hurtfully in anger, to change their ways of speaking to each other so that they begin to confront the issues constructively and to care for each other
- act as translators and find words to cross chasms of misunderstanding and disagreement as they help preachers in groups to find a *lingua franca*. (A large ecumenical team of well-educated professional people to whom I acted as consultant eventually came to the conclusion that to overcome the acute difficulties they were facing they needed a 'more adequate, mutually acceptable working vocabulary'.)

---

[4] As translated in *The Divine Office: The Liturgy of the Hours According to the Roman Rite III*, (Glasgow: Collins, Dwyer and Talbot, 1974) p. 114.

Used in this way – words, the tools of thought and communication – are the instruments of reflective discourse of the kind described above. 'Our ability to reflect on our experience', says David Smail, 'is only as good as the linguistic tools available to us to do so'.[5]

For me, a preacher by vocation, to become involved in this kind of talking work involved a conversion as shaking, painful and liberating as any I have experienced. It was from habitually using what verbal facilities I had for my own purposes (and often, to my shame, unfairly against others) to a commitment to use them for others, in other words, to put them, such as they were, at the service of others and their well-being and development. This meant, for instance, making sure that all contributions, whatever I might think of them, are equally well articulated so that the quality of the description is not misrepresented by or confused with the quality of the idea. When this is done, people are more likely to select ideas on their merits; the better idea is not lost to another simply because it is badly phrased or expressed. However, there are of course occasions when it is right to use verbal abilities against others. This conversion took place in me in the late 1960s and I have been working out its implications ever since!

Set pieces or questions, introducing unrehearsed free discussion, are extremely important in this kind of talking work. They must represent the essence, tone and feel of this approach – as must the responses to participants' contributions, especially the initial ones. In fact, *the quality and effectiveness of preacher development training are directly related to the quality of the verbal exchanges that suffuse it.*

There are many difficulties of promoting this kind of talking work and adopting a non-directive approach. It goes against so much of the common grain of verbal intercourse in general, and the way in which preachers are inclined to use words in particular. In all walks of life, words and talking are used in all kinds of ways: for example, to sell, persuade, cajole, manipulate, threaten or impress. Then again, those with the greatest facility with words in positions of authority may not have the deepest insights or the best ideas, but they often have the will and the power to dominate and quash others. Consequently more perceptive, less articulate people can be marginalized by less perceptive, more articulate and powerful ones. What follows explains further ways of engaging in this talking work.

---

[5] Smail, *Illusion and Reality*, p. 647; cf. Lovell, *Analysis*, pp. 51–69.

*Key aspect two: the ability to identify and use facilitative questions*

Unloaded questions (e.g. 'What do you aim to achieve through this preacher development programme?') are more likely to promote direct, open, honest exchanges than leading or loaded questions (e.g. 'Do you agree/I am sure you will agree that the aim is to …?'). Unloaded questions require, stimulate and enable people to think personally and collectively. Leading questions are manipulative devices, which can induce unreliable, superficial responses and relationships. Formulating effective questions can be difficult but it pays dividends when you get the right ones. Other kinds of questions to be avoided are those that are trick, multiple, marathon, ambiguous, rhetorical and discriminatory. The following further distinctions between different kinds of questions can be helpful.

- factual or closed questions
  - e.g. 'How long have you been a preacher?'
- investigative questions
  - e.g. 'Who did what ?', "Where?', 'When?', 'How?', 'Why?'.
- questions about patterns of relationships and interaction between people, their actions and events
  - e.g. 'How does your spouse respond when you are over-anxious about a preaching appointment?' 'What effect does that have upon you/ your spouse/children?' (Some call this circular questioning, possibly because it is aimed to see a pattern of interactions in the round.)
- reflexive or probe questions
  - e.g. 'What do you feel about that?' 'What do you mean?' 'What would you do if …?' 'What do you think you could do better?' 'How would/ do you explain that to yourself?' 'Why is it, do you think, that people respond positively to your preaching?'
- link questions.
  - e.g. 'How do you connect this with that?' 'What is the relationship between this and that?'

*Key aspect three: the ability to identify, design and use facilitating structures*

As already noted, when questions (or tasks) are ordered so that one question (or task) follows another constructively, they form a facilitating structure. They enable us to break down the analysis of a problem or the examination of a topic into interlinked, but discrete and manageable parts. This helps individuals and groups to tackle a topic systematically and holistically, stage by stage. A seven basic question approach to examining problems is a good example of a facilitating structure.

1. What is the problem?
2. What has been tried so far?
3. What specific changes are required and why?
4. What are the causes and sources of the problem that we need to examine?
5. What is sustaining the problem?
6. What are we/am I going to do about it?
7. What are we learning from our study of this problem?

These questions relate to five activities: definition; diagnosis; decision making; action; and reflection. Questions 1 to 3 help to define but they also help to diagnose a problem; questions 4 and 5 help to diagnose it further; questions 2 and 6 are action questions about what will and what will not work. The order is not invariable: 2 and 3 for instance, are readily interchangeable. Answers to question 4 to 7 may well lead to a redefinition of the problem; 1 to new insights into what has been tried previously; 2 and 7 to new learning; 5 and 7 may lead to going through the sequence again![6]

### Key aspect four: the ability to draw diagrams and to use diagrammatic models and flow charts

Diagrams, models and flow charts appear in the text of this book and their use was discussed in Chapter 9. The ability to draw diagrams and to construct and/or use diagrammatic models and flow charts is generally an asset but not an essential requirement. They are generally found to be useful but not universally so. They help people to talk about things that are difficult to describe. They can help people to make points with verbal economy. They bring into play in our praxis the non-verbal side of our brains.

## IV ABILITIES REQUIRED OF PREACHERS AND SUPPORTERS

The effectiveness of these support systems depends on each and all of the participants making the contributions required of them. This elementary and obvious condition of engagement needs to be made to counteract the undue emphasis generally placed upon the abilities and skills required of developmental supporters and the neglect of

---

[6] The point is made in relation to consultants and consultancy in Lovell, *Consultancy*, pp. 25–27.

those required of the people they support. For support to be viable and to build up the participants, matching skills are required of supporters and preachers that enable them to collaborate in egalitarian and respectful relationships.[7]

*Preachers and support systems*

Preachers will get most out of support arrangements of any kind, and avoid some of the pitfalls and downsides of using them, if they aspire to know and accept themselves and keep in touch with their feelings. And if, with due humility, they:

- keep in mind that they are the expert on themselves and their circumstances and context
- take themselves seriously
- know when to, and when not to, trust their own judgements and challenges to them
- are committed to do their own thinking
- guard against being unduly influenced by others
- avoid unhealthy dependence and anything else that compromises their autonomy
- are able to discern what support they need and want
- seek interpersonal support when they cannot support themselves adequately without undue strain.

These abilities and commitments provide a good foundation for supportive arrangements. They help preachers themselves to assess whether what is on offer is likely to be of help to them, to be their own 'analytical instruments'[8], and to be equipped to explore, negotiate and contract with supporters. Preachers who adopt this kind of approach are well-placed and orientated during support sessions to test the veracity of anything supporters say about them and their situation, and the viability of any suggestions made. They are able to guard against the erosion of their autonomy and the creeping tide of dependency. Above all they are in touch with and able to articulate essentials of themselves as preachers, and the realities of their context and needs, and to correct any distortions by supporters when they misunderstand or misrepresent them. The ability to do these things depends on several other things: preachers knowing themselves and

---

[7] Cf. Lovell, *Analysis*, pp. 136–137.

[8] I have developed this principle in relation to consultants focusing on consultors' work views and the interaction between the work views of consultants and consultors: see Lovell, *Consultancy*, pp. 51–71.

being able to discern those elements that must be in the discussion frame; communicating them clearly and economically; and ensuring that they are properly understood, respected and taken into account.

Closely related to these key abilities is the capacity to be attentive to what supporters say and to explore it respectfully but critically, even if initially it seems inappropriate. Alongside this, they need to have the confidence to question and challenge things with which they are not comfortable, especially when they feel they are being pressurised to accept them. So they need analytical skills and the ability to use them confidently on their inner and outer realities, in other words, they need to be able to operate subjectively and objectively. Developing the aids to self-support described in Chapter 9 Section III will help them to do this. All in all, preachers have to provide the vital subject matter for support sessions and to be active partners in working at anything supporters introduce.

*Developmental supporters*

As we have seen, those who provide the various means of support described above have their own terminology to describe what their system aims to achieve and the way in which it works. It is not possible here to describe these, but some general commonalities in their approach and methodologies can be indicated. By and large they would want those preachers they support to participate in the ways described above, and would encourage and help them to do so by:

- adopting a facilitative disposition and stance
- establishing effective working relationships
- getting an accurate and deep understanding of how preachers see and feel about themselves and their context (Among other things, this involves listening, reading body language, questioning, reflecting back and checking out what is emerging.)
- helping preachers to express and look at their feelings as well as their thoughts
- working to the preacher's view of their ministry and situation
- getting alongside preachers while maintaining the objectivity required to remain independent and reflective and to provide reliable feedback
- using their own perspectives on the preacher's situation constructively during their exchanges
- respecting and enhancing the preacher's autonomy
- evoking and facilitating creative and challenging thought
- working with the preachers through an alliance of minds and souls

*Facilitating Local Developmental Programmes and Interpersonal Support* 171

- checking out thoroughly with preachers whether any ideas that emerge are ones which *they* feel they can pursue and are what *they* want to and intend to do.

Supporters put different emphases upon approaches and methods, and cluster and order them into coherent codes of good practice to form their particular support system. What they do not do, however, is to tell preachers what they should do, take control, or do anything for them that they can and need to do for themselves. Ways of doing some of these things are discussed in more detail in Chapter 9. Soul friends, consultants, coaches, mentors and others can use this methodology and its associated attitudes and approaches in various ways. But, however used, it derives from the non-directive concept and is consistent with it, even if those using it do not describe themselves as non-directive supporters. Many people do some of these things quite naturally; others acquire them through reading about them, trying them out or attending training sessions and courses.

## V Towards Equipping Yourself

If you want to adopt the approaches described in this chapter or better equip yourself to be a group facilitator or an interpersonal supporter, you could do so in ways described below.

*Describe the attributes you require*

In the light of what has been said in this chapter, make a note of what you consider to be the essential attributes required of facilitators and supporters. Then note which of the attributes you have and those that you will need to develop or acquire. Now consider which if any of the following possibilities will help you to become better equipped to be either a facilitator or a supporter.

*Study appropriate approaches and methods and how to use them*

There are several ways in which you might do with this:

- reflect on the ways in which groups were facilitated in chapter Eleven;
- study the approaches described in this chapter, and particularly the non-directive approach, which is basic to the approaches advocated in this book[9]

---

[9] See reference 3 and visit www.avecresources.org

- follow up the brief descriptions of the forms of interpersonal support in which you're interested, and examine the methods and codes of good practice associated with them.

*Attend training courses*

Explore the possibilities of acquiring the skills that you have decided you need through a training course organized or recommended by your denomination or a local college.[10]

*Have a go!*

You do not necessarily have to jump in at the deep end, although sometimes it is an effective beginning. You can gradually work at acquiring new skills in many different informal ways without being designated as a facilitator or a supporter. For instance, you can practise using unloaded questions and making objective summaries of issues emerging in discussion groups, committee meetings and private conversations. (A minister took up this suggestion. Quite quickly members of committees that he chaired were asking why their meetings had improved so much recently!) Or again, quite informally, you can use what you are learning about being a supporter when people turn to you for help without being thought of as a professional supporter. Many things can develop from small beginnings. You can be a first-rate supporter to good effect.[11] Or you could look for opportunities to act as a facilitator to a group. If you are doing it for the first time, you might level with the group, tell them what you would like to try to do, ask for their permission and cooperation and, if they agree, get them to help you to learn how to do it. Another way is to find someone who is also prepared to have a go with you at being a facilitator. To have a co-facilitator is enormously helpful. It is an arrangement I adopt whenever possible. It enables you, for instance, to mull over the approach together; plan how you are going to use it; share facilitative leadership; act as observers and note takers to each other in turn; and reflect together on your performances.

---

[10] All denominations have extensive in-service training programmes. One college has a course in consultancy ministry and mission: see www.theologyinthecommunity.org.uk

[11] One of my earlier booklets was about this kind of informal use of the non-directive approach in youth clubs. It had a somewhat grandiose title: 'The youth worker as a first-aid counsellor in impromptu situations'!

## Chapter 11

# *AN ONGOING LOCAL DEVELOPMENT PROGRAMME*

A group of Methodist lay and ordained preachers in Leeds have been using some of the interpersonal group work methods and support services described in Chapters 9 and 10 in an ongoing programme that started in 2000. This project, in which both authors were involved, led to the writing of this book. It is a local 'bottom-up' development programme organized and controlled by the preachers themselves and has enjoyed some ecumenical participation. It demonstrates how preachers can engage in in-service training in their very busy lives; it also reveals their interests and concerns. This programme is presented in this chapter as a case study to illustrate the use of methods already described and to demonstrate their relevance to the support of preachers of any denomination.[1] This chapter describes the programme, key features of the work done, the facilitation of the programme and indicates the general relevance and application of the approach and methods in other contexts, settings and denominations.

### I Preachers, Context and Facilitators

#### a *Preachers*

The preachers involved in this programme preach in local churches comprising, in Methodist terminology, a 'circuit'. At any one time there are about thirty lay and ordained preachers available to preach in these churches. Naturally the membership and numbers fluctuate. In total, over the past ten years, almost sixty preachers have been

---

[1] Information about this programme is on a website, which is regularly updated, http://www.preacherdevelopment.uk7.net/, referred to in the text as the website.

active in the Circuit. Most of the members of this heterogeneous group of lay and ordained preachers, men and women in equal numbers, have participated in various aspects of the programme. Eighteen were ministers including four probationer and two retired ministers. Some forty were local preachers (lay persons accredited by the Methodist Church to lead worship and preach on a regular basis) or preachers in training. Together they composed a strong preaching force. The majority willingly took on the training programme and brought to it considerable Methodist, ecumenical and professional experience. Some had been preaching for forty years. They came from a wide range of occupational and professional backgrounds. They varied greatly in their academic ability and education and in their biblical and theological training and scholarship. A few were wary of intellectuals and intellectualism. Some of those involved in the training programme preached in other churches in Leeds and a few preached nationwide. They met quarterly in the preachers' meeting, which is responsible for them and their preaching work in the local churches.

*b  Churches and their Settings*

The twelve churches in which all the participants preach regularly are situated in a geographical wedge-shaped area of Leeds stretching from the city centre to the outer suburbs and beyond. All have lively ecumenical connections. One of the churches is a small inner city church, three are village churches, one is on a large housing estate, and four are strong suburban churches. Four of them have sizeable congregations. One is a united Methodist/URC church, another houses Methodist and Anglican congregations with some shared services. There are two churches with black majority congregations and the small inner city church hosts active foreign national congregations.[2]

*c  Facilitators*

The programme operated under the aegis of the preachers' meeting. This gave it official authority, maximized its learning potential and prevented the programme becoming the pursuit of an enthusiastic elite. During the first four phases, three of us, two local preachers and myself, formed a facilitating team. We worked closely with successive

---

[2] For further information see website www.leedsnemethodist.org.uk and particularly Circuit newsletter on change, December.

Superintendents of the Circuit. Several other preachers became actively involved in organizing and leading self-programming groups and projects as the programme evolved. So, in essence, it was a self-development programme for lay and ordained preachers, planned and resourced locally by preachers and ministers able to draw upon several disciplines. Visiting lecturers have helped with some, but not all, the day conferences. The preachers' meeting and its officers are now directly responsible for the management of the programme.

## II Programme Overview: 2000–2010

It is not necessary to give a detailed account of the extensive programme from 2000 to 2010, which is still evolving; an overall annotated picture will serve our purposes. It will indicate the evolutionary nature of the programme, trace out the principal stages of its development and note the subject matter covered.

After what is best described as spontaneous beginnings, six distinctive phases have emerged so far. All phases were inaugurated and given their initial shape by thoroughgoing discussions about their content and form. They were rounded off by equally thoroughgoing discussions about the work that had been done, its implications, possible future agenda items and suggestions about ways of tackling them. These discussions were informed and stimulated by position papers prepared by the facilitating team. Decisions were made about programme development by the preachers and the facilitating team only when they had had several weeks to mull things over. Each phase had its own timetable, determined by the preachers and the work they decided to do; they varied in length from one to almost three years. Importantly, they represented the learning cycles and rhythms conducive to the particular group of busy preachers and facilitators.

A study day was an integral part of Phase One. This inaugurated a series of independent annual study days organized by the preachers' meeting which made important contributions to the in-service provision. Biblical scholars staffed the first six, and preachers who are medical practitioners the seventh. It is only necessary here to note the subjects. The Gospel of St Matthew (in phase 2); the Gospel of St Luke (in phase 3); the Gospel of St Mark (in phase 4); the Writings of St Paul (in phase 4); the Book of Psalms (in phase 5); Feminine perspectives (in phase 5); and Medical ethics (in phase 5). Information about some of them is on the website. An overview of the programme and study days is presented in Display 11.1.

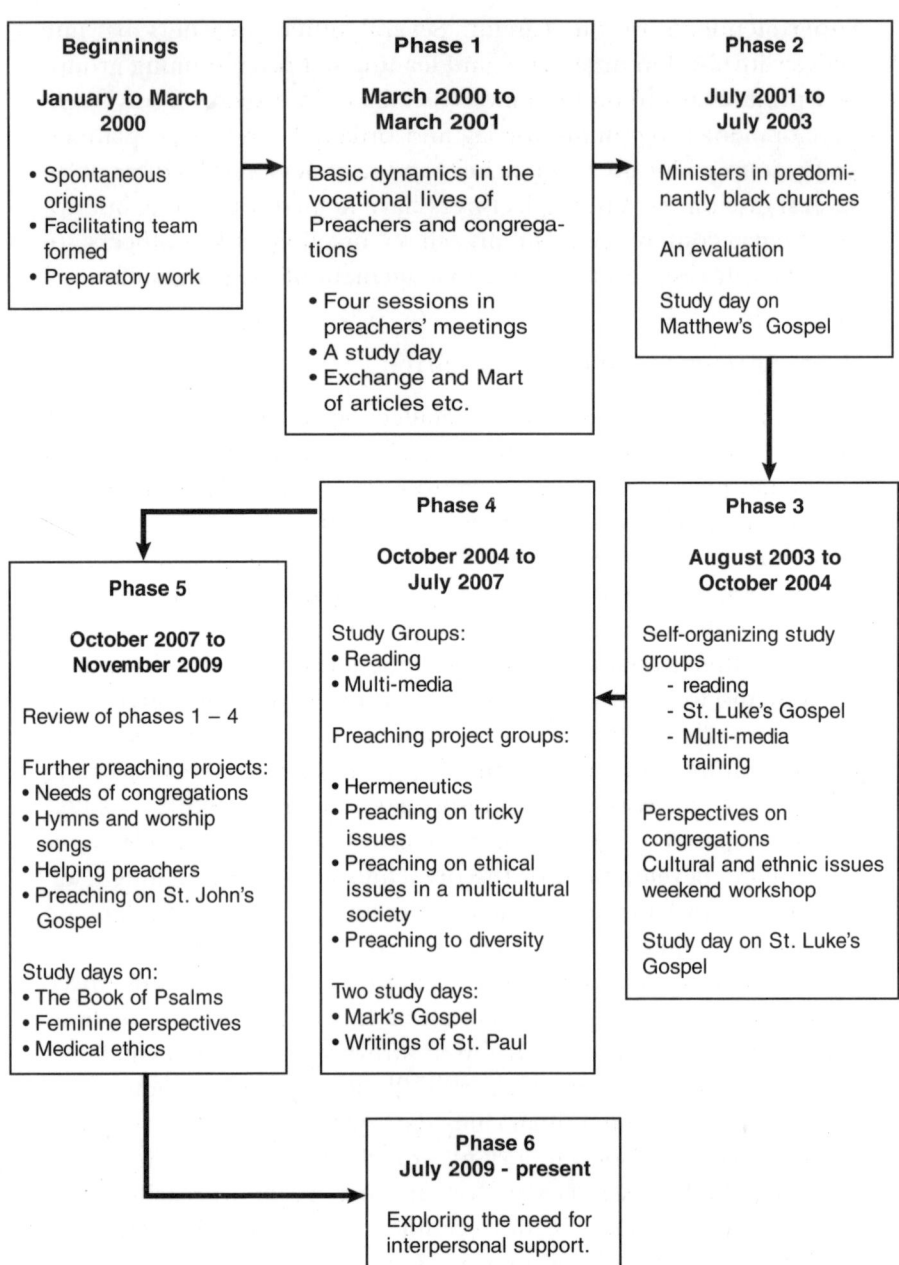

**Display 11:1** Overview Of The Programme and Study Days, 2000–2010

## a  Beginnings

The beginnings of the programme emerged spontaneously at a preachers' meeting in January 2000. Some of the preachers had been following a Methodist in-service training project known as the Continuing Local Preachers' Development Programme (CLDP). Attendances had been disappointing and the sessions uninspiring. There was a half-hearted conversation about revamping the programme. I found myself classifying the points emerging on my agenda sheet, my normal practice. I shared my summary of the topics: communication; sermon content and construction; all-age worship; promoting congregational participation; using visual aids; leading prayer; self-reflection. They were taken aback as they realised the importance of their discussion. A moment of silence was followed by animated exchanges during which they asked me to help them to devise a new programme. In accepting, I said that I would prefer to do this in partnership with local preachers. Without hesitation two preachers volunteered, Catherine Frieze and Anne Vautrey. We became the facilitating team for seven years, adopting the approach described in the previous chapter.

The team's first task was to decide how best to get the programme off to a good start. An obvious way of proceeding would have been to arrange seven sessions covering the nominated topics. However, as six of the topics were about preaching methods, this would have meant tackling practical concerns and attempting to promote self-reflection (the seventh topic) without a shared understanding of some basics about the ministry of preaching. Convinced that this could adversely affect the programme, they felt that sessions on the following aspects of the preaching ministry would provide a foundation for tackling practical, theoretical and theological issues:

- The 'preaching circle' (preparation, public performance and management of post-preaching experiences)
- The nature, attributes and functions of congregations and ministering to and through them
- Personal and collective vocations of preachers and presbyters.

This meant that, while they took seriously the felt needs of the preachers, the team had a responsibility to introduce possibilities not so far mentioned by the preachers for their consideration. This interactive process continued throughout the programme. It distinguished the programme from those based exclusively on either a personal assessment of needs by preachers themselves or on independent ideas or assumptions by others about what preachers need.[3] However, the final say and ultimate responsibility for *their* in-service training was with the preachers. So the programme was non-directive; it was not 'top-down' and directive even when there was input from 'above'.

### b  Outline of the First Six Phases: 2000 to 2010

Outlines of the six phases give an overall picture of the programme to date.

### Phase One: Basic Dynamics in the Vocational Lives of Preachers and Congregations, March 2000 to March 2001

The preachers willingly adopted the team's suggestions and put the original agenda into abeyance. Sessions were held during their meetings about the private and public lives of preachers (described in Chapter 3); aspects of the preaching circle (described in Chapter 4); leading collective acts of prayer resulting from the silent and spoken prayers of both people and preachers; and, lastly, the attributes and functions of congregations and ministry to them (described in Chapter 5). The preachers saw that the study of congregations as congregations is of fundamental importance to the ministry and mission of the church and some were enthusiastic about the possibility of congregational members being advocates and apologists of Christianity in secondary congregations. (See Chapter 5.) Sharing their personal reflections on their vocation to preach led to rich exchanges and generated a deep sense of togetherness. Exploring their collective vocation as a group of preachers and ways of pursuing it broke new ground for them. They were engrossed as they considered the concept in relation to the contemporary challenge to preaching, current emphases upon collaboration and their interest in teamwork. Ideas for the next phase proliferated. Considering these along with the initial cluster of felt needs led to the following proposals for phase two: sessions on Methodism and a study day on Matthew's Gospel; getting a better understanding of the churches in which they preach and of their ministers; and evaluation

---

[3] Felt needs, i.e. those of which people are conscious, are not infallible guides to those things that promote holistic development. Exclusive attention to them can bring satisfaction and at times be developmental. Getting people to consider and act upon them, and human and spiritual needs of which they are not aware is fundamental to any education or development programme. It differentiates them from programmes of self-help.

of the programme. Various preachers undertook to organize the first two of these items and the facilitating team was asked to organize an evaluation, which at their request would conclude their present overall responsibilities. The preachers agreed that an effective developmental programme should provide safe places in which they could:

- learn from experts
- develop themselves
- engage in substantive biblical and theological study
- explore the praxis of leading worship, preaching and pastoral ministry through study, experiential learning and reflective collaborative practice
- develop understanding of and relationships with local churches and congregations
- promote evangelism and mission through, for example, planting new congregations
- develop new forms of worship and congregational participation, and preaching the gospel beyond existing congregations
- deepen and extend socialization and fellowship between preachers.

Progress was made during this phase in relation to the initial requests for help with 'self-reflection which enables us to grow' through the way in which the sessions were conducted rather than by attempting to teach reflective practice. Increasingly preachers listened to each other and helped each other express and work at the points they were trying to make rather than arguing their case. A useful 'exchange and mart' of papers, articles and books was organized, but interest was short-lived. (Quite independently around the beginnings of this programme one of the preachers, John Summerwill, organized an extensive preachers' library.[4])

During this phase an explosion of thinking set preaching in its systemic context and in the collective vocation of a local group of preachers. Locating sessions within the three-monthly preachers' meetings proved to have two problems: shortage of time and continuity.

### Phase Two: Ministers in Predominantly Black Churches and an Evaluation, July 2001 to July 2003

Three of the four events planned for this phase were carried through. At a useful session on *Understanding churches and their ministers*, two

---

[4] Classified indexes of this library are on http://www.preacherdevelopment.uk7.net/

ministers of the two well-attended black majority churches shared and discussed with the preachers what they were trying to achieve, critical aspects of the church situations, and hopes and plans for the future.

For various reasons the evaluation did not take place until July 2003, a year later than planned. By this stage, the programme had lost its original momentum. Concerned about the situation and how to go about the task, the team realized that there were no agreed statements of purpose and criteria for effective programmes against which to evaluate phase one and design future work[5], so they made explicit the purposes implicit in previous discussions. These were to enable preachers, lay and ordained, individually and collectively:

- to continue their development through all the stages of their ministry
- to minister more effectively to the given needs and wants of local churches
- to address more effectively, in the light of the Christian gospel, complex socio-religious-political issues.

Reviewing past experience indicated that criteria for effective programmes were:

- agendas must be seen by the participants to be appropriate and workable
- effective use of apposite approaches to in-service training education
- quality time to pursue the agenda profitably
- effective overall leadership and facilitation
- all-round commitment to the programme, preparation, collaborative learning and participation
- suitable premises and facilities.

The team prepared a position paper, summarizing the work done so far and presenting these statements of purpose and criteria. Worksheets were sent out to the preachers to help them prepare for the discussions at the evaluation meeting by reflecting on the content of the programme, methods of study, the time they would be willing to give to the programme, and the above criteria for an effective programme. At a lively meeting, the preachers said they wanted the

---

[5] Assessing change in relation to purpose is a form of directional analysis. See Lovell, *Analysis* pp. 132 and 155.

programme to continue, expressed their commitment to it, and decided that the next phase should include the following items:

1. Building up pictures of local churches and their contexts.
2. A study-day on cultural and ethnic issues.
3. Sessions on Luke's Gospel, apologetics and Methodism.
4. Multi-media training.
5. A reading group.

Naturally, the facilitating team was delighted by the outcome of the evaluation and offered to facilitate the next phase, an offer that was accepted.

### Phase Three: Self-Organizing Study Groups and Perspectives on Congregations, August 2003 to October 2004

The team made suggestions about the implementation of the ideas for this phase. First, they outlined a way of building up pictures of local churches (item 1). Second, they suggested ways of overcoming the problems of holding sessions in preachers' meetings, where time was limited to one and a half hours and vulnerable to pressure of other business. This suggestion retained the involvement of all preachers and ensured that the programme remained under the authority of the preachers' meeting. They suggested the formation of self-organizing and programming groups that shared their progress and findings in the sessions allocated to the programme at the three-monthly preachers' meetings.[6] Preachers with an interest in a particular subject would form a group, agree among themselves on the subject matter to be considered, decide how the group was to be facilitated, determine the amount of time that they felt able to allocate to it and wind it up when they felt the group had run its course. In short, they were autonomous task-oriented groups.

The preachers enthusiastically adopted the programme and the suggestions made by the team. They asked the team to design the local churches project, which they committed themselves to staffing. Preachers offered to organize groups on the other topics with the help of the team. Adopting this ambitious programme, however,

---

[6] This is an application of a helpful approach to using the learning of one group to stimulate another round of interactive learning in another group, and repeating the process in a succession of groups of increasing size. An exposition of this is given by William W. an Loureide J. Biddle, *The Community Development Process: the rediscovery of local initiutive* (New York: Holt, Rinehart and Winston, inc, 1965) pp. 88–126).

meant the following subjects were once more reluctantly put in abeyance: praxis of leading worship and preaching; evangelism and mission; and preaching and pastoral ministry.

*Self-Organizing and Programming Groups*

In the event, three self-organizing and programming groups functioned well.

*The Reading Group* ran for two years. Six or seven preachers met monthly for two hours at the home of one of its members. The books studied ranged from Monica Ali's *Brick Lane* and Philip Pullman's *Northern Lights* to *Barchester Towers* by Trollope to non-fiction works, including Vanstone's *The Stature of Waiting* and Brian Wren's, *What Language Shall I Borrow? – God-Talk in Worship: A Male Response to Feminist Theology* and Clive Marsh's *Christianity in a Post-Atheist Age*; The author of this last book joined the group for that particular discussion. The conversations informed and challenged the members. In an unforced way the reading and discussion linked to their preaching ministry. For instance, *Brick Lane* led to considering multiculturalism in Britain with particular reference to the challenge of evangelism and inter-faith relationships.

*The Multi-Media Training Group* organized a useful Saturday morning session attended by twelve preachers led by a local minister. He demonstrated how to use PowerPoint and other software programmes in worship.

The group on *St Luke's Gospel* organized a study day led by the Rev Dr Peter Doble, a New Testament scholar. The thirty people who attended were asked to prepare by reading through Luke and Acts in one sitting! An overall introduction to Luke-Acts was followed by workshops on the Emmaus narrative and using parables; a Eucharist concluded the day.

The *Study-day on Cultural and Ethnic Issues* became a weekend workshop on contemporary cultural and ethnic issues entitled, 'Strangers No More'. It was based at a predominantly black church in which the preachers regularly took services and was led by the Racial Justice Secretary for the British Methodist Church. Black and white church members and preachers participated in the Saturday workshops. Throughout, the interest was intense and the interactive sessions boisterous, exuberant, spirited and at times a little unruly. The conference was a frank outpouring of the experiences of black people in church and society. The mood and content were salutary and moving and some of the disclosures painful. On the Sunday the findings and reflections of the workshops, challenging to preachers and people alike, were presented to the church during a service of worship.

*Perspectives on Local Congregations, July 2003 – October 2004*

Two years after the initial sessions on congregations the preachers decided to explore what people were actually experiencing in congregations in each of the twelve churches. The purpose was to understand and serve churches and congregations better and to build up collaborative working relationships with them. Deciding against a questionnaire survey of congregational members, they adopted a twofold approach: structured conversations with small congregational groups, followed by preachers reflecting together on what emerged in relation to how they themselves saw things. This is known as a 'qualitative approach'.

Six different pairs of preachers had conversations with groups formed by each of the congregations for the purpose; one preacher led the conversation while the other observed and took notes. Visitors, as they were called, were prepared for these conversations by the team through a briefing paper and an orientation session. Emphasis was placed on the use of open rather than loaded questions, and on listening rather than putting words into people's mouths or arguing with them. This was a demanding and fascinating reversal of roles for preachers, who normally talk while members of congregations listen; not surprisingly they became known as talk-back sessions. Visitors were encouraged to use what has been described as 'circular questioning'[7] which encouraged people to explore their own experience in relation to that of others and how they interacted with them as they agreed or disagreed about things.

The visitors went for depth through open conversations structured around a sequence of topics: congregational life; people's feelings and attitudes to various forms of worship; congregational energy levels, moods and ethos; world- and church-views of members and their effects on congregational life; their congregation's approach to mission; and relationships with other congregations. They drafted reports of the conversation with each church group on one or two sides of A4, checked them out with the group, invited comments from the church and discussed them in preachers' meetings. Subsequently, they shared the outcome of the preachers' discussion with the group

---

[7] On circular questioning, see p. 167 and Lovell, *Consultancy*, pp. 65–66, 333.

and, with their permission, with church authorities. This ambitious programme took some eighteen months to complete.

Valuable conversations took place between preachers and congregations. The impact was positive and extensive. New perspectives on preaching and worship were generated which helped local church leaders, preachers, ministers and councils to think more comprehensively about congregational life and worship in the churches. Empathic bondings were deepened. Discussions of the reports in the preachers' meetings were impressive and memorable experiences that deepened the members' preaching and pastoral relationships with congregations. As they grappled with the issues raised, they spoke about the congregations with deep concern and affection. New information, insights and understandings emerged. Preachers who had ministered to congregations for many years said, 'I never knew that. Goodness! That explains so many things'. An abiding memory of the discussions is of preachers sitting forward in their seats totally engrossed in the whole experience as sessions went well over the allotted time. The project revitalized the training programme by generating a new wave of energy.

This brief and orderly presentation could leave the impression that everything went smoothly. By and large it did, but not without hesitations, hitches and some anxiety. Initially some preachers saw the exercise to be an unprofessional attempt to survey and profile congregations and foresaw the danger of obtaining distorted information of little value and at great cost. Gradually, their concerns were allayed by clarifying that the exercise was a limited one about perspectives on congregations, informed by the contemporary emphasis on the importance of conversations in organizational development.[8] Others were concerned about the danger of intimidating people by taking lids off cans of worms, or of arousing unrealistic expectations by inviting members of congregations to have their say. This they feared might make demands upon them, which they could not or did not want to meet. Through careful consideration of these inherent risks, the preachers saw that they could reduce them by explaining the nature of the exercise to participants, discussing with

---

[8] On the importance of conversations in secular and religious organizations, see for example Patricia Shaw, *Changing Conversations in Organizations Approach: A Complexity Approach to Change* (London: Routledge, 2002); George Lovell, *Consultancy Modes and Models* (Calver, Sheffield: Cliff College Academic Series, Cliff College Publishing, 2005) pp. 214–228.

them how to cope with possible dangers and how they would use the information and decide what action they could and would take, and by keeping open the possibility of further dialogue. Finally the preachers and facilitators saw going ahead as an act of faith in each other, the potential of the project, and belief in the integrity of what was being attempted.

## Phase Four: Self-Organizing Study Groups and Preaching Projects, October 2004 to July 2007

Four years had elapsed since the preachers' last reviewed the programme and significant developments had occurred. So the team prepare a comprehensive position paper and organized previous reports into a sequence of background notes. This massive undertaking enabled the preachers to get a grasp on the overall situation and, greatly encouraged by what had been achieved, make plans for this phase using the criteria for effective programmes established earlier. Developments are outlined below.

### Study and Training Groups

Two self-organizing and programming groups were operative in this phase, the Reading Group and the IT Group, both of which were described earlier.

### Developmental Preaching Projects

The preachers opted to tackle a large number of interrelated agenda topics. Tackling them serially in self-programming groups might well have taken years and could have been tedious and drained the lifeblood from the programme. On the other hand, prioritizing by selecting a few topics could sever important links between the subjects. Eventually the team came up with the idea of 'developmental preaching projects'. Each project would tackle holistically a cluster of subjects related to identified needs. Doing this could, for instance, involve a self-programming group working on team preaching, evangelism and lectionary readings. Similar kinds of projects could be designed around other clusters. This idea was enthusiastically accepted. Small groups accepted responsibility for eight projects. In the event only four got under way but they did much good work.

### Project 1: Hermeneutics: Interpreting and Teaching the Faith for Today

Six people tackled this theme during five evening sessions spread over a period of several months. Hermeneutics, they said, 'is about how we read the Bible: how we interpret it, find meaning within it which is true both to the text and to the way in which it has been heard in the past, but which also carries meaning within our own context and experience and that of our hearers. That is, a sort of conversation with the text, the hermeneutical circle or spiral.

They discussed this in relation to various theological themes and ways of studying biblical texts and found themselves coming back to the word 'conversation' and their understanding of hermeneutics as a form of prayer-like listening to God, tuning in to conversations others have had with the text over the centuries, and listening to the needs and thoughts of those to whom we preach and of the world in which we live.

*Project 2: Preaching on Topics Related to Church and Society which Raise Tricky issues*

A group of four people pursued this subject in four one-and-a-half hour sessions over a period of six months. They wanted to be more adequately equipped to tackle tricky socio-religious issues in their preaching in order to help members of congregations to think more profoundly about such topics and to have better conversations about them with secondary congregations (family members, friends, colleagues etc). They distinguished three modes of responding to them:

- *reactive preaching* forced on us by events such as the Boxing Day Tsunami, 9/11and the London Bombings
- *proactive preaching* which reflects on socio-religious concerns related to issues such as sexual orientation, asylum seekers, multiculturalism
- *educative and preparative preaching* on Christian apologetics and ways of dealing with challenges to faith.

They explored the practice of these three modes of preaching by discussing notes of sermons each of them had preached. (See Appendix I.) Drawing on this, they listed characteristics of services and sermons which would help people to think for themselves about tricky issues, and produced a two-page review of the work they had done, which they discussed at a preachers' meeting.

An important need was identified which the group could not pursue because two of them were about to leave the area. It was the need for a group dedicated to helping preachers with their preaching through mutual support, appraisal and exploration by variously attending to different aspects and phases of preaching.

*Project 3: Ethnic Issues: Worship and Preaching in a Multi-Cultural Society*

A preacher and a minister, both white, signed up for this project. They were convinced that they and the preachers generally needed to hear authentic ethnic voices on congregational life in the mainly black churches in a predominantly white circuit. Two ways forward were considered: to study reports and read books like *Brick Lane* and to converse with black members of congregations. They opted for the latter and arranged a meeting in a private house for church members and preachers. Nine people responded to the invitation: five black (Afro-Caribbean and West African) congregational members including two preachers, and four white congregational members including two preachers. Black members shared in a moving way just how it had been for them when they first came to this country and how it was now. Working together at the key issues that emerged led to a rich discussion on cultural identity and worship. In relation to ethnic issues, the black people said they valued worship and preaching that enhanced their cultural identity through music and dancing and celebrating Emancipation Day and other 'black' events which induced creative cultural, racial and spiritual interaction between black and white people and preachers in a religious setting.

A four-page report of this moving and informative evening disturbed a preachers' meeting and promoted rich discussion. Speaking for many in the meeting, the leader said, 'This breaks new ground'. Subsequently four people met to consider the report in more detail. One was in the last year of a distinguished thirteen-year ministry to a strong black local congregation. Quite spontaneously he reflected on his ministry in an impressive and deeply moving way. Other members felt that he should do this at a preachers' meeting, which he did. On that occasion, he shared openly his experiences, his vicarious pain over the suffering of his members and what he had learnt from and through them. The effect was an electrifying experience; preachers expressed admiration for the black people and their 'white guilt' feelings. Fittingly, it rounded off much discussion about ethnic issues over the years and opened up a challenging agenda yet to be taken up.

*Project 4. Preaching to Diversity*

Preachers became increasingly aware that there was a wide range of orthodox, agnostic and – surprisingly – atheistic beliefs amongst members of congregations. Some church members who were sympathetic to the radical restatements of Christian faith as represented by The Progressive Christian Network movement and the writings of Bishop John Spong represented an example of the diversity. Inspired to consider the implications for preachers, they set out to explore what was involved in preaching to diversity.

In the first phase, four local preachers and three ministers spent five sessions over a period of nine months identifying key issues for further work. The first three sessions were lively discussions about Paul's preaching at Athens (Acts 17) and his claim to be 'all things to all men' (I Corinthians 9: 19–23). These discussions, however, left the group bemused. Insightful papers were written and discussed on theism and atheism. These sessions were enlightening, but did not bring the help required, nor did an exchange of reflective notes. At the request of the group, I produced a paper outlining the history and content of the project, summarizing and indicating a structured way of approaching the issues. This led to a series of open seminars on key issues on which there is diversity of views among preachers and within congregations.

After these initial explorations, a summary of the paper and an outline of the programme were presented to the preachers' meeting. Enthusiastically, they encouraged the group to go ahead with bi-monthly sessions under the general title 'Preaching to Diversity: Critical Topics for Preachers'. The topics focused on were: experiencing the presence of God in worship; the authority of scripture; concepts of God; prayer and the concept of an interventionist God; Christ's divinity and humanity; sin and salvation; styles of spirituality; and sermons and PowerPoint presentations. (Unfortunately, in the event it was not possible to organize the first seminar.) A twenty- to thirty-minute presentation, normally a paper, introduced each ninety-minute seminar followed by discussion. These much-appreciated seminars attracted preachers from other churches and denominations; the attendance varied from four to fifteen. They gave participants more confidence to grapple with issues that greatly concerned them, pointed to ways to study them further and indicated ways in which to tackle them in preaching.

*A Reflective Note on Phase Four*

During this phase there was sustained in-depth treatment of key issues over a long period. Some of the work was hard and it stretched our minds, but we were well rewarded. Quite often, especially during the excellent reporting back sessions of the projects, I had exciting mental pictures of many groups beavering away at a range of inter-related themes and sharing their findings with each other. Towards the end of this phase the preachers' meeting assumed responsibility for the facilitation of the programme.

## Phase Five: Further Preaching Projects, October 2007–November 2009

This new phase was inaugurated by reviewing the topics that had been put into abeyance and those on which little progress had been made in order to decide what to do next. The outcome was the following preaching projects. (Detailed reports of the sessions of each of these projects are on the website.)

*Project 1: Needs of Congregations.*

In four meetings over a period of seven months a group of eight preachers studied the worship needs of the congregations that had been identified through the Perspectives on Local Congregations project during Phase Three, and determined their implications for them as preachers.

*Project 2: Hymns And Worship Songs.*

In four meetings over a period of four months, the nine members of this group determined the criteria for the selection of hymns for public worship. Then they made a carefully considered response to a consultative questionnaire sent out by a national committee working on a new hymnbook for the Methodist church.

*Project 3: Helping Preachers.*

In six meetings over a period of seven months, seven preachers helped each other to improve their ability to preach and conduct worship by considering the interactions taking place in public prayer, different modes of prayer and by discussing prayers they had used in services and worship. They also considered sermon composition, illustrations, density, core content and structure by examining the manuscripts from which two of them had preached.

### Project 4: Preaching On St John's Gospel

This unplanned project emerged spontaneously through the initiative of a newly accredited local preacher. Feeling the need for help with St John's Gospel, she invited others to study with her ways of making the lectionary readings relevant for congregations in the twenty-first century. It first met in November 2009, and, at the time of writing, continues to meet and produce excellent notes. It was significant that even a new preacher could take a unilateral initiative of this kind, showing that the method has become deeply embedded in the culture of the preachers.

### Phase Six: Interpersonal Support

It became clear that some of the preachers' needs emerging in the 'helping preachers' project in Phase Three would be best met through consultancy or coaching. This was welcome, experiential confirmation of the conclusions I had already reached from researching the programme for this book. But, as this development seemed too cosy for comfort, I decided to check out with the preachers what they felt about the need to complement group work with interpersonal support and any action they would like to take. A seminar was arranged at which to do this. (A record of the meeting is on the website.) Sixteen preachers discussed the various forms of interpersonal support described in Chapter 9. They said they needed to be clear about the *nature* of our ministry and our unmet needs before they could determine the support required. This led to intense discussion about the *evaluation of preaching* (not to be confused with the evaluation of preachers) and *feedback* (seen as a means of evaluation). They felt reliable data for the evaluation of preaching is not readily available and they had theological reservations about whether they could or should attempt to evaluate their preaching. Some felt it treated preaching as 'performing', which, they said, it is certainly not. Others wondered whether they were in danger of being in denial to potentially helpful critical comments, and in any case, human beings are 'hard-wired' to evaluate; preachers cannot avoid telling themselves or feeling or knowing that they are doing well or badly! (See Chapter 4.) Addressing directly the forms of interpersonal support, the preachers:

- underlined the importance of *self support*
- testified to the general helpfulness of *peer-support*
- felt that accessibility to *consultancy* help when required is a desirable supportive resource

- saw that *co-consultancy groups* would provide useful opportunities for open sharing between preachers in a confidential setting
- were not keen on *coaching*
- had found different forms of *appraisal* in their professional lives variously useful, perfunctory and threatening!

Effective interpersonal support, they argued, must be flexible, not standardized and it is most likely to be fruitful when preachers seek it of their own volition. One preacher wrote to me after the meeting saying:

> ... I was left at the end of the evening feeling that we must each evaluate what we are doing for how else can we grow? My own view is that we get some help in this from our educational sessions both in the Local Preacher's Meeting and in our annual study days, but I think we also need to meet in a way where we can build up enough confidence and trust in each other to give and accept honest comment. I think this is tricky. It involves laying ourselves open, which is a risk, and it involves us in honest, loving, critical comment on the performance of others, which can be difficult. Of the various tools you described I guess it is the consultancy and co-consultancy that comes closest. I certainly think it needs more than just a single friend or confidant and we will need to get the skills in some way. I suspect that done badly it will be worse than not done at all. Also we were not very keen on the idea of coaching as if we are beyond all that, but I am not sure that is so.

Subsequently the preachers' meeting has considered various suggestions for one-off seminars on self-support, feedback, evaluation in preaching ministry, identifying our needs, being open to challenge; short training and/or induction sessions on consultancy and co-consultancy praxis; and supplementary provision of support services. The preachers would avail themselves personally of interpersonal developmental support, as they need it. But there is only limited interest at this stage in incorporating arrangements for it into the programme. However, at their next meeting (Autumn 2010) the preachers have decided to consider a proposal that a one-off seminar be arranged on self-support and determining unmet needs. And that is the story so far!

c *Subject Matter*

A brief overview of the subject matter tackled indicates the impressive scope of the programme. Over the first ten years it addressed more than thirty main topics, and many other subsidiary ones, which can be grouped under the following heads: the Bible; congregations; hermeneutics; interpersonal support; medical ethics; multi-media training; preachers and preaching; racial and ethnic and gender issues; spirituality; and theology. In addition, a wide array of other topics arose in the discussions of the reading and other groups.

### III The Design and Facilitation of The Programme

Now we turn from the description of the programme to the features of the design and praxis that shaped it. Some of these aspects are explicit and others implicit in its description and in Chapter 10. However, risking the accusation of repetition, we draw them together in this section to give an overview of the facilitative driving forces behind this programme.

#### a *Principles*

The facilitating team was committed to the following guiding principles:

- Wherever possible provide joint training programmes for lay and ordained preachers.
- Training programmes are most effective when:
  - they help preachers, individually and collectively to be more self-determining and effective reflective practitioners
  - they enable preachers to develop and integrate their preaching practice, theory and theology
  - they meet substantive needs, which may or may not be felt by preachers themselves
  - attention is given to processes, methods and to subject matter.

#### b *Approach, Methods and Processes*

The following methods were important in facilitating this programme. Some of them are described more fully in Chapter 10.

> *Open questions*: the team used open, unloaded questions.
> *Verbal and written feed back summaries*: the team made extensive use of verbal summaries and records of discussions or workshops or of several months' or years' work.
> *Introducing ideas*: the team fed in for critical examination by the preachers any relevant information and ideas that occurred to them to be considered alongside the preachers' felt needs.
> *Diagrams, models and charts*: diagrams, pictorial and disclosure models and flow charts helped the team to work with the preachers about things difficult or impossible to describe in words alone. (Some of these are reproduced in this book.)

## An Ongoing Local Development Programme

*Working to constraints*: the team took seriously the constraints upon the amount of time the preachers and the preachers' meeting were able to allocate to training. For some of the preachers, the sessions were at the fag end of a demanding day, so, one of the team's cardinal principles was to make best use of the time the preachers were able to give to the project, enabling them to feel that it was time well spent. This involved imaginative planning and attention to detail in order to give the preachers as much time as possible to make the contribution they alone could make to their learning and development. This was demanding; the team often felt that they were trying to get a quart into a pint pot. But the outcome was the preachers' willingness to allocate more time to the programme, in the knowledge that it would not be squandered.

*Working to the authority of the preachers' meeting*: religiously the team kept faith with the programme being under the aegis of the preachers' meeting. This ensured that it did not become the team's project for an elite group of training enthusiasts, and maximized the involvement and learning of all the preachers.

*Cyclical processes which kept preachers in the picture*: the team worked assiduously through cyclical processes with the preachers: scanning the field of study and interest; selecting the topics to work on in the light of purposes, needs and resources; and working at topics in context. Summaries enabled preachers to take hold of situations; to work to agreed situational pictures rather than from diverse, individual private ones; and induced collective participation and forward planning.

*Specific and general learning processes*: the project was directed throughout towards learning about preaching locally in real time in the Leeds churches in two ways: through the use of specific cases or situations, and drawing out insights for general practice; and through studying subjects generally and determining what was being learnt and how to apply it.

*Learning Styles*: many different learning styles and methods were deliberately used in the project in order to accommodate the range of preferred styles in the group. Some learning was experiential; other learning was achieved through academic input. All of it was interactive. Emphasis was placed throughout on self-reflection and on preachers accepting responsibility for their own learning and engaging in collaborative learning. (Cf. the section on thinking moods and reflective modes in Chapter Four.)

*c A Creative Triangle: Study, Praxis and Fellowship*

The danger of the programme becoming too academic was averted without losing the necessary intellectual content through making it praxis-based within the valued preachers' fellowship (*koinonia*), enhanced by social events. At the centre of this creative triangle of study, praxis and fellowship, and connecting all its angles, were mutual respect, affection and pastoral care. This pattern of experientially based study in fellowship enabled preachers who varied considerably in their intellectual ability and practical and academic orientation to learn together and collaborate in ministry.

IV GENERAL RELEVANCE AND APPLICATION

This chapter is a case study of an effective ongoing programme based in a group of Methodist churches. Many aspects and events have buzzed with intellectual and spiritual excitement, revealed new insights, and given new momentum to preaching. It has also involved hard work, and there have been times of difficulty, struggle, frustration, heartache and hesitation. But overall it has been worthwhile, satisfying and rewarding. Three aspects of its general relevance and wider application are noted briefly. First, it illustrates just what can be achieved locally, and the importance of programmes, which promote development from below. Secondly, the data that are emerging are authentic, recorded and available for further analysis and research, deriving from work done for its own sake by preachers dedicated to improvement. Throughout there was continuous assessment of what was being learnt, and findings were checked out with the preachers and used to develop the programme. Thirdly, critical reflection of our involvement in this project and our wide ecumenical experience convince us that the approach used in this in-service training of Methodist preachers can be equally effective when used appropriately in any denominational or ecumenical group of preachers operating in other contexts, churches and Christian traditions. But a crucial proviso needs to be added here: the approach must not be confused with the outcome. It is the approach and methods that are endlessly replicable to development work with any and every group of preachers rather than the outcome. When this approach is applied appropriately, skilfully and sensitively it produces programmes and projects which fit the groups of preachers like made-to-measure garments fit people. Copying the outward shape of this project and pursuing the subject matter it focused on may indeed be beneficial but only if they are a reasonable fit. However, to opt for a garment made-to-measure for someone else rather than going for a bespoke one is to neglect the heart and soul of the approach, methods and processes presented here and to miss out on the creative energy generated by them.

---

## Part 5

## SUSTAINING PREACHERS IN A FAST CHANGING WORLD

## Chapter 12

# *FOR SUCH A TIME AS THIS: CONTINUITY AND CHANGE IN PREACHING*

In the previous sections of this book we have explored the nature of preaching: its working dynamics, its essential tasks and the network of support that preachers need if they are to sustain an effective preaching ministry over many years. In our last two chapters we look outwards, forwards, and upwards, (or whatever metaphor best indicates attention to God.)

In his monumental *A History of Christianity*[1] Diarmaid MacCulloch, Professor of the History of the Church at Oxford, begins his survey by observing that all the world faiths which have experienced long-term success have shown what he calls 'a remarkable capacity to mutate'. MacCulloch wryly observes that many Christians do not like to be told of Christianity's capacity to develop, but he insists that that has been the reality from the beginning. At the end of a survey which does not gloss over the darkest and ugliest features of Christian history, as well as its glories, he has this to say:

> Most of Christianity's problems at the beginning of the twenty-first century are the problems of success; in 2009 it has more than two billion adherents, almost four times its numbers in 1900 ...[2]

This is not to overlook the sharp decline in church attendance experienced in many parts of Europe and of North America, but MacCulloch's comments put that decline in global perspective. He observes that Christian history itself warns against overconfidence, and suggests that the most interesting conundrum for the faith is now posed by a society in which polite indifference has replaced the

---

[1] D. MacCulloch, *A History of Christianity*, (London: Allen Lane, 2009), p. 9.
[2] MacCulloch, *A History*, p. 1016.

battles of earlier centuries. That observation is more true of some countries than of others. But it is possible that MacCulloch's accompanying question may become increasingly pertinent as the twentieth century wears on:

> Can the many faces of Christianity find a message which will remake religion for a society which has decided to do without it?

The author ends with a striking, if somewhat tentative prediction:

> It would be very surprising if this religion, so youthful, yet so varied in its historical experience, had now revealed all its secrets[3].

Professor MacCulloch's language may strike some readers of this book as a little strange, even unsettling. But we quote his work here in order to set the scene for an exploration of a pattern in Christianity which every preacher must work with: the pattern of continuity and change. This book is itself a testimony to that pattern, because our argument that preaching has *not* had its day (Chapter 1, section II), must not be heard as a claim that preaching should continue to be what it has always been. So it will be useful to explore a little more the tension in Christian faith between continuity and change. Two questions may help us:

'How far *must* Christianity change, in order to *remain* Christianity?'

and

'How far *can* Christianity change without *ceasing to be* Christianity?'

The first question needs to be faced by the defenders of 'No change', the second by the proponents of 'All change'. Of course, few of us are likely to adopt such absolutist positions, but if we adapt these questions for our particular purpose, they will help us take the discussion further:

'How far *must* Christian preaching change, in order to *remain* Christian preaching?'

and

'How far *can* Christian preaching change without *ceasing to be* Christian preaching?'

These questions will be our chief concern throughout this chapter.

[3] *Ibid.*

## I  Changing Preaching in a Changing World

Over many years, I have heard preachers argue in two particular ways for continuity and no change in preaching the gospel: they have quoted a verse from Hebrews, 'Jesus Christ is the same yesterday, today and forever' (Heb. 13.8), or they have appealed to the view that human nature is just the same. A still-popular hymn reinforces this view: 'Tell me the old, old story …'.

This is, of course, a vital part of the pattern we are discussing here, continuity and change. But it is only a part. In this section we are concerned with its counterpart: how preaching *must* change, in order to remain Christian.

Christianity is an incarnational faith: God has graced human life and the world with his presence in the person and life of Jesus. So an Incarnation – not a set of values, not a mythology or ideology, nor even, in the first place, a creed – lies at the heart of Christian faith. So faithful, authentic Christian faith will always be incarnated: embodied in, and responsive to, every age and place.

This in turn affects our understanding of the Christian tradition: it is dynamic, not static. (A river is a good image to use.) Dan Hardy, distinguished Anglican theologian, argues that what we call 'tradition' is … 'a concentration of a wider historical diversity'. But, crucially, Hardy went on to say, 'the concentration was not arrived at by excluding this diversity, but by engaging with it to find its deeper meaning in a deepening of Christian faith. … throughout the history of the Christian tradition, this "external" diversity has always been woven into deeper expressions of Christian faith, which in turn found expression in a new simplicity'[4].

The difference between being simplistic and simple is a vital one for preachers. Simplistic preaching, by definition, over-simplifies by failing to go deep and engage where necessary with complexity and difficulty. True simplicity lies on the far side, as it were, of complexity. Students beginning theological training might feel sometimes that simplicity was something they abandoned on the first day of the first term. But their inward journey is rather like a journey I once made up the slopes of Mount Bintumani in Sierra Leone. For hour after hour we could see little but tall trees and thick undergrowth, with little sunlight on anything. But when we emerged from the rain forest near the top, the view was breathtakingly simple and beautiful.

---

[4] D. Hardy, 'A Magnificent Complexity' in *Essentials of Christian Community* (eds David F. Ford and Dennis L. Stamps, (Edinburgh: T. & T. Clark, 1996), p. 319.

So when we start to dig, asking difficult questions of the Bible, the faith and contemporary challenges to the faith, all the time we are working towards a deeper simplicity, the heart of which is the God in whom 'we live and move and have our being' (Acts 17.28). The current Christian scene – not to mention the still wider picture – is bound to seem complex at times: feminism, post-colonial expressions of Christianity, post-modernism itself are just three contemporary strands of 'the external diversity' to which Hardy referred. In what ways will they, or should they, affect the ongoing stream of Christian tradition? Time will tell, or rather, let us say: the Holy Spirit, in the providence of God, will lead us into all truth (Jn 16.13).

There is a similar interaction between complexity and simplicity in the world of science. In a lecture given at the World Methodist Council in 1966, a leading scientist observed that the world around us at first is complex beyond understanding. Yet through patient experimentation and careful thought the scientist arrives at a kind of simplicity. 'And that is how the cycle of scientific research goes on: from complexity to simplicity to complexity – but in each cycle we believe we are penetrating more deeply into the structure of the Universe'[5]. We are back to the Reality in whom 'we live and move and have our being' (the verse from Acts quoted earlier).

It is easy for preachers to imagine that they have to supply answers to all sorts of difficult questions which congregations may be asking. It would be more true to say that their task is to help Christians to live with the questions in faith, love and hope. Michael Mayne, in a Lenten meditation, observing that in the Old Testament God does not give simple answers to Job in his anguish, refers to

> the one thing that changes everything: the claim that God does not give answers. There are no answers. Instead, he gives himself. The most perceptive of the Old Testament writers had written of a God who shares his people's joys and sufferings ...

Here Mayne refers to Hos. 11.3–4, with its reference to God taking his people in his arms. This, says Mayne, was 'inspired guesswork' on the part of the prophet, whereas

> What Christians claim is that in Jesus, rather than providing answers, God enters into the questions – and in so doing transforms them. Enters into them in the only terms we can recognize and understand, in terms of one man's birth, life and painful death. Jesus comes to be the love of God in our midst[6].

---

[5] Professor Russell Hindmarsh, later Vice-President of the Methodist Conference, (1970–1).

[6] I owe this reference to the Rev Val Ogden.

So, paradoxical though it may sound, our very belief in a Creator God, who became incarnate in Christ, is the foundation for expecting change, and weaving it into our ongoing understanding of Christian faith and our preaching ministry.

The very passage of time, of course, leads to change. Preachers' understanding of the faith and of the Bible will hopefully deepen, as the years go by. They will find – or should find – that most of the sermons they preached ten years ago they can no longer preach today in the same way. That doesn't necessarily mean that ten years ago they misled their congregation. Our own partial, conditioned understanding of everything, including the Gospel, ('for now we see in a mirror, dimly ...'. 1 Cor. 13.12) is cause for humility throughout the whole of our lives. Congregations, too, will reflect a pattern of continuity and change. Sometimes preachers will feel that they see more continuity than change, but the people before them will have been getting on with the business of living and facing new challenges to their faith. Most obviously, the world itself is changing at what seems an accelerating rate, and faithful preaching is bound to engage with the world as it is, and not as it was, or as we should like it to be. (We return to this theme in section III.)

So change is built in to preaching by the very nature of Christian faith and tradition. We cannot continue to read the Bible as if the last 300 years of scholarship had never been, any more than Christians can or should still believe that God made the world in seven days, though creationist Christians continue to argue this. Theories of evolution are of course not a substitute for, or an alternative to believing in the doctrine of creation; Christians continue to believe in God 'maker of heaven and earth', while revising their understanding of creation.

The pattern of continuity and change extends to our use of the Bible. We noted in Chapter 6 that we interpret the Bible in a way different from the Christians of earlier centuries, (but without arrogantly dismissing their insights as of no account). Two people in particular have enriched our understanding of hermeneutics. Friedrich Schleiermacher (1768–1834) was not only a distinguished theologian, but also served as the Lutheran pastor of Trinity Church, Berlin, preaching there every Sunday. Schleiermacher defined hermeneutics, not as rules of interpretation, but as 'the art of understanding', developing the concept of the 'hermeneutical circle', a concept we noted in Chapter 6. Hans-Georg Gadamer (1900–2002), introduced the concept of conversing with the text[7]. Thus interpretation is a two-way process: the text, if we are open to it, will interpret us to ourselves, helping us, for example, to see ourselves, life and our neighbour in a new light.

There are two especially important points for preachers to work with. First, the meaning of any text or passage in the Bible is not something to dig for, like treasure in the ground. Its meaning shifts and changes, depending on who is reading it, and in what circumstances. Its meaning, indeed, is likely to be inexhaustible, because through the Bible, God's own Word comes to us. As John Robinson, one of the Pilgrim Fathers, famously said, 'The Lord hath yet more light and truth to break forth from his Word'. But, as we noted in Chapter 7, the Bible can't simply mean whatever we want it to mean, or think it means.

A second point to emerge from contemporary hermeneutics is the effect of our conversation with the text (the hermeneutical spiral) upon us, the readers. The text is not something external to us, and all we have to do is to apply it. The conversation is two-way: we have our questions to put to the text, but the text will also, if we are attending properly to it, have some questions to put to us, or some new insights to enrich our understanding of both the text and the Gospel. A biblical text is not so much something to apply, like an external remedy, but something to be open to, to immerse ourselves in – like a revelation, an encounter with Christ himself.

Two misunderstandings need to be set aside. First, we are not playing academic games. The objective of the discipline of hermeneutics is to make the most of the text in a way which is life-enhancing and life-transforming, because it opens up the word of God for us today. Second, our appropriation of the insights of Schleiermacher, Gadamer and others does not mean that the work of all who came before them is old hat. It is true that scholars do not accept unreservedly the allegorical interpretations of early figures such as Origen and Augustine. But even if Augustine's identification of the inn as the Church in the parable of the Good Samaritan seems to us now rather far-fetched, his identification of the Good Samaritan with Christ himself is both more appealing and more convincing.

So ways of interpreting the Bible have rightly changed, and will continue to do so. Other developments will – or should – affect

---

[7] Anthony C. Thistleton, *Hermeneutics. An Introduction* (Grand Rapids, Michigan: Eerdmans 2009), pp. 153–161, and p. 222.

preaching. We are more aware, thanks to recent educational research, of people's different learning needs and listening styles. Hustler, in his book on the changing shape of the sermon, (on this see also Chapter 1), cites the work of an American preacher, Kenton Anderson, who drew on such research. According to Anderson, there are four types of learners, and every congregation is likely to have some of each: there are those who receive information reflectively, and those who receive it actively and experimentally; similarly there are those who process information cognitively (the abstract thinkers), and those who do so more intuitively, (the concrete thinkers). Each person, of course, both receives and processes information; Anderson classifies the four mutations as deductive/cognitive, inductive/cognitive, inductive/affective, and deductive/affective.

These new insights are a further important reason why a preacher will benefit enormously from increasing knowledge of their congregations, and from the feedback which is such an essential part of the preaching circle (Chapter 4). It is possible that one person's preaching will attract one or two of these four types of listeners. But most people cannot and do not change churches for this reason. It will be better if preachers can respond to the differing listening styles before them each Sunday by varying, on different preaching occasions, the style and form of the sermon, or by including within each section of the sermon material which expresses ideas in deductive and inductive and affective and cognitive ways[8].

Just as the form and style of sermons have changed, and will continue to change, so in some countries and cultures has their length. As we implied in Chapter 1, it is doubtful whether television has made people's attention spans quite as short as is often alleged. Some preachers, however, still err on the generous side in the time they allow themselves, and what matters is not the length of a sermon, but its outcomes. At the other extreme, a sermon which is very limited in its length may be somewhat limited in its outcomes; as someone once remarked, 'sermonettes' tend to produce 'Christianettes'.

So change is all around us, and Christians who believe in 'one God, the Father ... and in one Lord Jesus Christ ...' (1 Cor. 8.6) will work with change, believing that it falls within, not outside, the purposes and providence of God. This means that there is no such thing as preaching the gospel in general, or in a general way. An incarnate faith cannot be so abstracted, however hallowed by long

---

[8] Hustler, *Making*, p. 180; cf. pp. 178–81.

usage our language might be, from the flux and particularities of time and circumstance. The New Testament itself illustrates this well. All the preaching of which we have glimpses in the New Testament is contextual preaching. Even when St Paul appears to be summarizing the gospel in a nutshell, it is never the same nutshell: it is the gospel which the Thessalonians or the Corinthians or the Galatians needed to hear. (See, for example, 1 Thess. 1.9–10, Gal. 4.4–6, and 1 Cor. 1.23.) This is why in the final section of this chapter we shall need to revisit the assertion quoted already in this book, 'The gospel has not been preached until it has been heard'. But first we look at the continuities in preaching.

## II Continuity in Preaching

The phrase 'unchanging truths' is misleading, if it is taken to mean that the language in which those truths are expressed should not change. Nevertheless, while that phrase, like the text in Hebrews, 'Jesus Christ the same ... for ever', cannot be quoted as an excuse for no change in preaching, it alerts us to the need for continuity. Paul's words about 'the tradition I myself received ...' (1 Cor. 15.3) is a very early testimony to an apostolic succession which has continued to the present day. The modern ecumenical movement has sought to identify those beliefs and practices which all Christians share, as well as those on which either we agree to differ, or about which we cannot yet find agreement. This apostolic succession is our concern here.

Its heart is the story of Jesus, and all that flows from that story, including the core beliefs and convictions of Christian faith and practice. I once asked a theologian what those core beliefs are. I was quite unsure what her reply would be, since her life's work had involved her deeply in new expressions of and challenges to Christian faith: feminism and dialogue with other world faiths. Her reply was unhesitating: the doctrines of the Incarnation and the Trinity. That very brief answer contains the heart of the matter; it implies the Church, and life – both corporately and individually – *in* the God who is Father, Son and Holy Spirit.

Even here there is room for some Christian diversity – within certain parameters. Christians can hardly differ in the central convictions that Jesus was fully human and fully divine, but they can and do differ in how they understand and express those central truths. For example, some will interpret symbolically miracles like the stilling of the storm; others will treat it as an historical event. The preacher will acknowledge that both views may be held, and help the congregation to a hearing of the gospel based on that story which is illuminating and transforming.

How is a preacher to approach the awesome task of preaching on essential Christian doctrines? The whole question of belief can easily be skewed. By this I mean that the preacher is not concerned in the first place with the congregation's beliefs. There are different kinds of beliefs: some change our lives, some do not. And a belief is not the same thing as faith. The preacher is passionately concerned with enabling the congregation to encounter God in a way which will be illuminating, liberating, transforming. If that happens, belief will begin to find its proper place. As for particular beliefs, preachers should be wary of asking congregations to believe too much.

Should a preacher invite the congregation to believe in the resurrection? The proclamation 'Christ is risen' has echoed down the centuries, and will doubtless continue to do so. There can be no doubt that this constitutes one of the great continuities of Christian faith and preaching. But we must observe how threadbare even preaching on the resurrection can become. The congregation needs to be helped to grasp not just that it is true, but what it means. The preacher must not ask them to believe too much, nor too little. To insist that they must believe in the *physical* resurrection is a step too far. Some Christians endorse this view, but it is only one interpretation of the mysterious, sometimes conflicting testimonies of the New Testament. Unfortunately, a physical resurrection is easily taken to mean a resurrection which really happened. But St Paul's language about a 'spiritual body', and, indeed, his whole discussion of the resurrection (1 Cor.15. 35–58) reminds us that the central proclamation of Christianity is a mystery as well as a life- and world-changing reality. This is why the preacher on Easter Day, must not ask too little of the congregation either. The resurrection of Jesus is not so much about Jesus coming back to life. (That is what Lazarus, through the power of Christ, was enabled to do.) Nor is the resurrection an event which enables us to leave the cross behind; it is God's *imprimatur* on all that had gone before. So Jurgen Moltmann and others have been correct in writing about its political and social significance. It affirms that the Jesus who sought out Zaccheus, healed lepers and fed hungry crowds really was and is God with us and God for us.

The meaning of the resurrection is inexhaustible. Like Scripture itself, its meaning will change, depending on the people called to believe in it and to live it, and their circumstances. The mystery of the resurrection is like the mystery of God: not something to be explained or proven, but a life-transforming reality to which the preacher testifies and invites the congregation to respond.

To turn to another case-study in potential continuities in Christian faith, what of the often quoted remark that human nature doesn't change? The doctrine of original sin, unfortunately named and frequently misunderstood, is nevertheless an insight of Christian faith which we may not leave behind. The concept has been brought into some discredit because it was associated in earlier days with the question of whether babies should be baptized. Original sin is not something we should try to understand by looking in the first place at individuals at all. Rather, it is an acknowledgement that our human life together, whilst by no means wholly sinful, is nevertheless deeply flawed, and that we are accountable to God for what we make of it. But how we express this is extremely important, since generalizations about sin are seldom illuminating or helpful.

James Stewart[9] rightly suggests that generalizations about life and the world are usually misleading. But it is noteworthy that the three tensions which he observes of the world when he was writing (the 1950s) are with us still: the tensions between disillusionment and hope, between escapism and reality, and scepticism and faith. The preacher, rather than generalize, will be specific, but in a way which points the congregation to deeper needs.

If we go deep, we shall not go far wrong. Going deep takes us nearer to human need and nearer to the God who meets those needs. Preaching with this kind of depth will be simple, without being simplistic, and it will stand in continuity with the apostolic succession of previous centuries, including Scripture itself.

### III Contextual Preaching in a Changing Context

To say the same thing in a different context means saying it differently. This is the central challenge of preaching the Incarnate Word in situations which are changing all the time. One of the convictions behind the writing of this book has been the conviction that the contemporary context for preaching is especially challenging. In Chapter 1 (section III) we took a preliminary look at a fast-changing world; in Chapter 6 (section IV) we considered the challenge of

---

[9] Stewart, *Preaching*, pp. 13–51.

preaching on complex controversial issues, and here, as we look to the future, we shall attempt to survey the wider, deeper picture.

Writing from a British perspective, I find that five features of the contemporary scene stand out in their importance for the Christian preacher. First, though not necessarily in importance, the individualism of societies and cultures in the so-called developed world seems to be the product of both that major shift in human consciousness and self-understanding known as the Enlightenment, and also the economic system we call capitalism. For example, human rights and choice are a more individualistic concept than human responsibilities. (That is not to say, of course, that the concept is wrong.) But an intensely individualistic culture inevitably causes social upheaval. Social mobility and marital breakdown weakens and strains family ties. Cars, televisions and computers, among other things, make for less human interaction in many communities. There is much more that could be said, but from the perspective of Christian faith we need to acknowledge how much such individualism is impoverishing and fragmenting human relationships and communities.

A second feature, arising from the first, deserves our attention: the indifference to Christian faith remarked upon by Professor MacCulloch, and a widespread agnosticism or disbelief in God. Even in the Church we should not underestimate what one theologian has called 'the erosion of Christian imagination'[10]. How far this erosion is affecting belief is difficult to gauge.

Preachers cannot ignore what sometimes seems to be the rising tide of unbelief, which is bound to affect the churches. In an age of globalization we should be wise to anticipate its spread, although it may be that global threats such as climate change, faced by humanity as a whole, will bring a new realization that human life does not consist in how much we possess (Lk. 12.15). But in the foreseeable future, questions and doubts, suspicion and indifference towards the Christian faith are widespread in the so-called 'developed' world.

The decline of belief in God can hardly be unrelated to the individualism briefly discussed earlier. If the fragmentation of human life – familial, social and personal – means that people experience and exercise love with growing infrequency, it is hardly surprising that we find it harder to believe in the God who *is* love. This is one

---

[10] D. Ford, 'Coping With Being Overwhelmed', a lecture given to Church leaders in the north of England in March 1997, and published in autumn 1997 in *Transmission*, the magazine of the Bible Society.

reason why the renewal of the Church and the renewal of preaching – the subject of our final chapter – belong together.

A third feature of our so-called post-modern world is closely related to the individualism and widespread unbelief of our time. Though analyses of post-modernism differ, nearly all are agreed that a far-reaching relativism is one of its leading characteristics: there are no absolutes, all is relative. In the post-modern world, you have your beliefs, I have mine. In such a context, preachers need to distinguish clearly between two things: on the one hand, the relativity of all our experiences of God and our language about God, including all the expressions of the Christian faith there have ever been, and even the language and imagery of the Bible, and on the other hand – quite simply – God[11].

Two other features of our contemporary world cry out for mention. The world's capacity for self-destruction is increasing. The nuclear threat has been with us now for more than half a century, and, alarmingly, we seem to have grown used to it. But nuclear proliferation is increasing the danger of self-destruction all the time, and now climate change threatens the future of human beings in a new way. That brings us to the last of the world's contemporary features singled out for mention here. Climate change is already exacerbating the obscene injustices of the world between rich and poor. Preachers cannot read what the Old Testament says about righteousness and justice, or the New Testament's emphasis on the Kingdom of God and God's righteousness, without those profoundly affecting their preaching today. And this without making congregations feel simply powerless and guilty.

Change, as we have seen, is built into the very nature of Christian faith. But so too are its abiding continuities, however differently they may have to be expressed. Here we are recognizing that individualism and social fragmentation, unbelief, relativism and the possibility of human self-destruction are part of the context in which the Gospel must be preached today. Accordingly, we need to note a worrying feature of the contemporary Church, before drawing some conclusions to our discussion of continuity and change.

The Church, or a church, in any century can slide from being a church into a sect. By sect I mean here a community which has so separated itself from the wider world – whether through internal

---

[11] Scripture, however, remains the measuring-rod ('canon') against which we constantly assess continuity and change in Christianity.

or external pressures – that its language has become an in-house language which no longer communicates meaningfully to that wider world. When this happens, such a church is in grave danger of forfeiting its apostolic and catholic character. (On this see Chapter 12.) So while there is much enthusiasm in some countries today for what are called fresh expressions of Church, the world at large also needs fresh expressions of the gospel for such a time as this.

*Conclusion: 'The Gospel Has Not Been Preached Until It has Been Heard'*

These words were written by a distinguished American scholar, writing about evangelism[12]. It is a sharp reminder of what we discussed earlier (Chapter 1) that communication is a two-way process: I may *think* I have preached the gospel, saying all the right things (as they seem to me), but if no-one has heard the gospel, I am mistaken. A preacher who pays no attention to change, but only to continuity, and, conversely, a preacher who pays no attention to continuity, but only to change, is unlikely to preach the gospel. The first is likely to be using language and concepts which no longer have any currency with his hearers; the second, by embracing wholesale change, risks losing the heart of the gospel. But a still deeper, more costly approach is needed. No reformulation of traditional Christian faith and belief, however urgent and necessary, is sufficient. We need to return to the fundamental question of what preaching is, and to those vital personal qualities of preachers, without which they are unlikely to preach the Gospel.

Preaching is not just, or even primarily, the imparting of information. In any case, 'there is no lack of information in a Christian land, something else is lacking, and this is a something which the one man cannot directly communicate to the other'. These sombre, searching words of the Danish philosopher Søren Kierkegaard[13] may be less true today of the Europe to which they were originally addressed. But they point us back to preaching as an *event*: that understanding of preaching lay behind Paul's language about the power of the Gospel, and of course what was happening in the ministry of Jesus. In the service of this mysterious, transforming Gospel, preachers will need 'the adaptability of love' which Jesus, Paul and apostolic preachers down the ages have exemplified. There

---

[12] For the reference, see Chapter 2, section II and footnote (5).

[13] Craddock, *Overhearing*, p. 9 and elsewhere. (The quotation from Kierkegaard functions as a basic text for the whole book).

is also, as every preacher knows, a cost involved: a 'weakness voluntarily assumed for the sake of the Gospel' (Chapter 1).

We believe that preaching, in the providence of God, will continue. The Church, in any case, has a long way to go. Writing of 'the cosmic story to which the Bible points', Keith Ward suggests that we cannot know what 'the full number of the Gentiles' (Rom. 11.25–6) can be, but 'it seems clear that it will take thousands of years before the gospel is preached in a clear and compelling way to all nations'[14]. What we cannot know is *how* preaching will continue. But in the short-term, at least, we can work towards, and pray for its renewal – the subject of our final chapter.

---

[14] Ward, *The Word*, p. 149.

# Chapter 13

## THE RENEWAL OF PREACHING

This book has been written for Christians of all traditions, both for preachers who have been engaged in preaching for many years, and also for those who are just beginning. Its completion coincides with the centenary of the Edinburgh Missionary Conference of 1910, often regarded as the beginning of modern ecumenism, or, at least one of its major landmarks. One of the hallmarks of that ecumenism, in spite of setbacks and controversies, has been a growing readiness to acknowledge how much Christians of different traditions have in common. Strangely, in all the dialogues and conversations, formal and informal, of the ecumenical movement, preaching seems to have been largely ignored. What, it might be asked, is there to be said? Two things. First, just as there is One Lord and one Church, so there is one order of preachers. Outwardly, that does not appear to be so. Preachers, ordained and lay alike, are trained and exercise their preaching ministry entirely or largely within their own Church. But preachers of all traditions are united by a common vocation. One preaching order is the natural corollary of one Lord, one Gospel and one Church. This is a vital perspective for preachers, even as they inevitably concentrate on those congregations to whom they are appointed to preach.

But secondly, we have not begun to exploit the rich potential of that simple fact: one order of preachers. True, some Christian traditions more than others have emphasized preaching: Dominicans and Methodists for example. But for the most part the ecumenical movement has concentrated on affirming and celebrating the beliefs we share, as well as discussing the differences which still divide us. Yet here, in the ministry of preaching, is an existing ecumenical venture of a quite different kind: how may we (the 'we' here is ecumenical) preach the Gospel to an unbelieving world, and to a semi-believing church?

So the shared task of preaching across the different denominations and traditions of the Christian faith is the background to our exploration of its renewal, and one of the reasons for the writing of this book. Its title, *Sustaining Preachers and Preaching*, reflects the conviction that preachers and preaching these days, perhaps more than ever, need *sustaining*. Readers will form their own judgement, but we have emphasized two things which have led us to this conclusion/conviction:

1. The demands and pressures of the context in which we find ourselves today: a time of rapid, bewildering change, of spiritual and moral confusion and uncertainty, and of serious threats to human well-being and our environment.
2. The danger of preachers, in such a context, working in an isolation which not only impoverishes their ministry, but may even be unhealthy. This is not meant to imply that such isolation is the fault of the one isolated. Like loneliness, and much else in human life, the roots of isolation may be many and complex. But it is still a contradiction and denial of the solidarity of the Kingdom to which both the Gospel and – at its best — the Church invite us all.

I A Renewed and Renewing Church

In the Introduction to this book, we suggested that there could be no renewal of the Church without the renewal of preaching. Yet this assertion can also be reversed: there will be no renewal of preaching without the renewal of the Church. There is a symbiotic relationship between the two, and one cannot happen without the other. We begin with a fundamental question: where is renewal to come from?

There is a theological conundrum to be faced here. No-one – no Church or Church authority – can make it happen. Such renewal is simply not within our control or remit: the Spirit blows where the Spirit wills, (Jn 3.9). But if we reject a Pelagian approach to preaching which places too much emphasis on human effort, we should also reject its opposite: a quietism which says, in effect, 'There is nothing we can do but wait for the Spirit'. The Bible itself, and Christian tradition down the centuries, point to a middle way. We cannot engineer renewal, but we can want it, prepare for it, pray for it, and work for those conditions which make the Church more open to the possibility of renewal. The Acts of the Apostles provides the classic instance: the first disciples had been together in the upper room praying (Acts 1.14) and preparing for the future (1.18–26).

With this biblical picture in mind, we shall take for granted throughout this chapter two things which seem to be integral to the hinterland of church renewal and the renewal of preaching. The first, in traditional credal language, is 'One Holy Catholic and Apostolic Church'. These four 'notes' of the Church, as they are often called, are both God's gift to the Church and God's call. Unity, for example, is both gift and call: already given, but still to be fully realized. The four notes of the Church also belong inseparably together. It is impossible for the Church – or any local church – to be truly holy if it is not also one. The Church – or a church – cannot be truly catholic if it is not also apostolic. And so on.

This may seem remote from the vocation and task of the preacher. In fact, it is the vital background and living environment of preaching. Even though Christians differ in their understanding of the Church's catholicity and its apostolicity (for example), these four notes of the Church must be the passionate concern of every preacher, not least because they are the benchmarks of the Church's – and any local church's – health and well-being.

In the conviction that the renewal of the Church and of preaching belong together, we turn in the next section to the implications of this book: what kind of preacher and what kind of preaching emerge from the approaches we have advocated here?

## II Towards a New Culture of Preaching

The outcomes of this new approach can be summarized under the following headings.

### a *The Preacher's Approach to Congregations*

In the new culture of preaching we are advocating, preachers will think of their congregations, not as an inert 'audience' whom they wish to move from A to B, or whose attitudes they wish to change. Preachers will avoid jumping to conclusions about the spiritual state of their congregations. What matters supremely is that preachers love and pray for their congregations; a preacher who does neither of these things forfeits the right to preach to them. Rather, a congregation is a conversation-partner, with a dynamic life of its own. Congregations vary enormously, not least in the range of their activities. As we pointed out in Chapter 5, they are not identical with the local church but are, as it were, its public face on Sundays.

### b  The Nature of Preaching

Preaching itself needs to be thought of differently. It may be monologic in style, but if preachers have done their work, engaging in the dialogues outlined in Chapter 2, then a sermon, whatever its form, will be dialogic in character, that is, it will encourage people to think and talk. But that is not all. Preaching is an *event*. A sermon becomes a sermon, not when the preacher has finished writing it, but when he/she preaches it. The delivery of the sermon may also need to be rethought, (Chapter 8); it must be as good as it can possibly be. Many preachers pay insufficient attention to practicalities like the quality of the sound-system in the church, or neglect the opportunity of some coaching (one of the many forms of support outlined in Chapter 9) to help them use their voices more effectively.

Because preaching is, fundamentally, an event, we also need to rethink the kind of change which we hope and pray it will bring about. We have argued (Chapter 6) that the preacher's task is not to try to change the minds of congregations about, let us say, a contemporary political issue, or to persuade them that only his/her understanding of the stilling of the storm is the correct one. Instead, preachers are seeking to bring their congregations, with themselves, into the presence of God and to hear afresh the Word of God. If that happens, change will occur: in the Pauline terms we have used before, faith will be increased, hope renewed, and love re-plenished. This is not to say that the change realized through preaching can be described narrowly and vaguely as spiritual. St Paul commends the renewing of the entire mind (Rom. 12.1–2), referring to a deeper and wider reality than what we normally mean by 'mind', and that will ultimately affect the whole of a person's life – including political attitudes.

### c  Reflective Preachers

Although we have focused here on the word 'thinking', this process must not be understood too narrowly. Preachers aware of the private and public vocational cycle involved in preaching (Chapter 3) will be more self-aware and reflective in ways which can only enrich their ministry. Similarly, preachers more alert to the ups and downs to be expected both before and after preaching ('The Preaching Circle', Chapter 4) will be better equipped to deal with those ups and downs when they occur.

How the preacher thinks of, and relates to the wider world is also deeply important, and we turn to that in the next section. But before we come to that, we highlight some of the characteristics of preaching undergirded and nurtured by these renewed ways of thinking, relating and working. Preachers will nurture and exercise a greater reflectiveness. They will be reflective practitioners (Chapter 9), sensitive, for example, to the potential value and the possible dangers of feedback, (Chapter 4).

### d Relating

In the new culture of preaching we are envisaging, preachers will nurture thankfully the network of relationships which they have joined by their very vocation as preachers. Relationships with members of congregations will be strengthened, not weakened; preachers will grow closer to, not more distant from, the people to whom they preach, even though there is a separateness proper to the ministry of preaching.

Preachers – lay and ordained alike – have another important nexus of relationships in their fellow-preachers. How ironical and tragic if, in this all-important ministry, preachers struggle along on their own. Here is a much-neglected or overlooked area for ecumenical endeavour. There is only one order of preachers, and the common vocation and ministry of preachers transcends denominational and confessional divisions. What they share far exceeds their differences.

Within this nexus of relationships with congregations and with those who share their vocation, preachers will be better resourced and will enjoy a greater collegiality. We hope it will become the norm for a preacher to cultivate and benefit from the many kinds of self-support and inter-personal support which are available, or which are easily created (Chapter 9). Many Christians – not least those who are ordained – underestimate what their fellow-Christians can contribute to their spiritual growth. Relationships are central to Christianity and the Christian life, and no-one, including preachers, is immune from the oldest heresy in the book, that of imagining that our relationship with God can somehow be detached from our relationship with other people, whether in the Church or not.

### e A Proper Professionalism

The word 'professional', in some countries today, is a word carrying a good deal of political and emotional baggage. Professional standards are sometimes mocked and eroded, and conversely, activities previously unpaid and voluntary have been, to their impoverishment, professionalized. Chapter 3 argued that the approach of lay and ordained preachers to the ministry of preaching should be vocational and professional. This professional approach will include further training, and Chapter 11 illustrates just what can be done at local level, when a facilitating team attends carefully to the needs expressed by the preachers themselves.

## f  Contextually Rooted

Preaching in this renewed culture will be contextually rooted. It will engage with the congregations' own questions, problems and doubts, for example, as well as with the difficult, complex issues which the contemporary world presents in abundance for Christian faith and living (discussed in Chapters 6 and 11). Preaching at its best has always been contextual. But it is all too easy for preachers under pressure to neglect a sustained, prayerful attention to what is going on in people's lives. It is also easy, as we argued in Chapter 6, to give the wider world short shrift, because church, with its many activities and responsibilities, becomes so demanding, obtrusive and even all-absorbing. Just as the ministry of preaching draws preachers nearer to, not further away from, their congregations, so it draws them nearer to the heart of the world. And that can often be a painful place for a Christian preacher to be.

## g  Preaching With Depth

The metaphor of depth should not be misconstrued. By 'deep' we do not mean preaching which is so intellectual that it goes over most people's heads. We have argued in this book that depth and simplicity in preaching belong together – as they did in the teaching of Jesus. Our concern is with preaching which 'feeds' people, so renewed preaching will be biblically and theologically grounded. The extraordinary range of the Bible and of Christian theology means that this is no narrow remit. Both the Bible and theology embrace the whole of life.

Preaching with such depth and substance will be possible, however, only if preachers and their preaching are sustained by a deeper, refreshed spirituality and by each other. (Chapters 2 and 3 addressed the vital issue of the preacher's own inner life.)

## h  Listening and Conversing

Finally in this section we return to the theme of listening, but we do in a way which will set the scene for the next section of this chapter. In Chapter 2 we referred to dialogues which might be called 'listening to the heartbeat of Athens', (section II). The concept is taken from the picture of Paul in Athens, engaged in discussions in the forum every day 'with those who happened to be there' (Acts 17.17). Times have changed: modern city centres do not lend themselves easily to such discussions, and preachers in city centres are not usually associated with listening. Many stand on soapboxes and harangue passers-by, not always to the credit of the Christian faith. By contrast, an ordained minister sent by her Church to minister in the city of Liverpool, engaged in a listening exercise at the outset of her ministry.

> Not having a (sc. church) building has some advantages as long as you have some good shoes. ... Sitting under the statue caused me to begin to listen to what was going on around me ... There was a whole tide of people flowing in and out of doorways, trying to avoid bumping into each other in the street. ... While pretending to write things in my diary, I eavesdropped on conversations, and noticed who was around. ...

She went on:

> This rich but confusing encounter pushed me into new questions about myself and this place. If God was ahead of me, as I had hoped, where was He and how could I recognize where His spirit was at work? ... What is good news? I was in the process of unlearning a great many things ... I became aware that I had less to bring and more to learn ...[1].

There are three particular groups of people to whom preachers will listen especially carefully. The first comprises those in distress. In the Bible there are many cries of pain and anguish, notably in the so-called psalms of lament, such as Ps. 22, and also in the synoptic gospels, where the cries of lepers, beggars and others keep on recurring. It is never easy to listen to voices expressing pain, anger and unbelief. But the experience of Christ himself in Gethsemane and on Calvary suggests that here, especially, we may expect to hear 'a word from the Lord'. Even if that is to claim too much, Christian faith insists that such uncomfortable encounters bring us close to the living Christ.

There is another group of people to whom the preacher will listen, or with whom they will engage in dialogue, if the other person is willing, and that is people who are expressly hostile to, or critical of

---

[1] B. Glasson, *Mixed-Up Blessing. A new encounter with being church.* (London: Epworth, 2006), pp. 4–7.

Christian faith. Such opportunities are not easily created, but they can certainly be avoided, or conversations of this kind prematurely ended because they are an uncomfortable experience. Yet the story of the blind man in Jn. 9 suggests that it is through such hostile questioning that we can arrive at a fuller, more mature faith.

That brings us to a third group of people, conversation with whom can be especially fruitful for preachers. We refer here to people who may be described in general terms as very different from ourselves: they are adherents of another faith, or of no faith at all, and/or belong to a different ethnic or cultural background, or their approach to and experience of life are very different from ours.

Why should a preacher value such encounters? The fundamental reason lies in one of the striking characteristics of the God revealed in the Bible: God is a God who crosses boundaries – a theme to which we shall need to return in the next section.

Are we aiming too high in the listening to God advocated here? We think not, but with two provisos: first, provided such listening is rooted in the other kinds of listening we have discussed in the course of this book, and secondly, provided the preacher's own life and practice is grounded in a faithful loyalty to 'the Word made flesh'. But listen we must. Listening for God as we read a newspaper or watch the television news is not easy to do. But it is a discipline, a habit to cultivate. Such faithful listening will help to lift preaching above the moralizing, generalizing clichés into which, otherwise, it is all too likely to fall. Instead, preachers will find themselves engaging more often with the great themes of the Bible and the central themes of the faith. And that will mean not only a word for the Church, but a gospel for the wider world.

## III Preaching in a World of Many Faiths and None

The Introduction to this book recognized that preaching cannot and must not be confined to the Church. The gospel of God's love is for all people, whether they come to church or not. In practice, the vast majority of Christian preaching takes place in church buildings, or when there are no such buildings, in other settings where Christian congregations can meet. But because the gospel is universal, both the content and, where possible, the ministry of preaching reach way beyond the Church. So in this section we look forward, as the Bible does, to a world reconciled and at peace. The discussion proceeds in three stages: first the Christian gospel's affirmation of both unity and diversity, secondly the place of Christian preaching in a world of many faiths, and thirdly the ideal of the Church of the Open Door.

The first stage of our argument is a simple one: the Church only really becomes the Church when it embraces people who are very different from each other. It is a consequence of listening to people different from ourselves, discussed in the previous section. This is the implication of the word 'catholic', one of whose root meanings is 'universal'. The Church realizes its vocation to be catholic in welcoming all kinds of people. The mission of God to the Gentiles is the supreme instance in the Bible of God crossing boundaries, and its prominence in the New Testament can hardly be exaggerated.

The unity and diversity of a congregation are a good sign of its spiritual health. If it is united without being homogeneous, and diverse without being divided, that is a healthy sign – even, perhaps, a sign of the Holy Spirit. Congregations can and do sometimes split into homogeneous cliques, ('I'm for Paul', 'I'm for Apollos' etc., 1 Cor. 1.12), but that impoverishes the church. A better way is for all to seek to accept, to understand and to encourage those members different from themselves (Rom. 14.1–15.7). In that way, everyone will grow: not only in love, but also in their broadening understanding of the faith.

So we come to the second stage of our exploration: the place of Christian preaching in a world of many faiths. Since time immemorial, different faiths and religions have interacted with each other, either coexisting peacefully, or engaging in conflict, or alternating between the two. But the process of globalization has meant that more and more people are coming to have contact with people of different faiths, and as a result to know more about other faiths. The challenging questions this poses for Christian preaching are obvious, and we need to address them here.

A first step lies in recognizing the all-embracing reality of one Creator God. It does not follow from this that 'the Christian God' is real, and all others are not. This would be to speak in an all too human way about the mystery of God. We must not be misled by our own terminology, or the terminology of other world faiths. To think that different words, when we speak of God, denote different realities is to get things the wrong way round. There is indeed only one divine Reality, but whether people are in touch with that Reality depends not so much on using the right language to address that Reality, but on something altogether more spiritual – like humility and repentance. Of course the words we use about God and the words we address to God are important. But as the Bible reminds us again and again, whether or not people are really in touch with the one divine Reality is shown more by the quality of their lives than by the words they use.

If we apply this test – and it is a biblical one – it is immediately clear that all religions have a mixed record. Religions have a way of making people more narrow and less tolerant, as well as more generous and compassionate. This is why Jesus himself was both for and against religion. It is a perplexing, saddening fact of church history and, sometimes church life today, that people who are exposed to Christian preaching Sunday after Sunday do not always seem to live as if they have heard the Gospel. There is a simple test which can be applied to preaching: does it make people more Christlike? The renewal of preaching which fans the flames of intolerant zeal is not desirable at all. But it *is* desirable if it proclaims a Christlike God, and grounds and nurtures people in Christ. There can hardly be criteria for right preaching more biblical than these.

A further step in defining the place of Christian preaching in a world of many faiths is to recognize the difference between evangelism and proselytizing. Evangelism we take to be a Gospel-centred mission which enables people of many different kinds to become disciples of Jesus. Christian proselytizing is a more Church-centred activity, in which we promote our cause – i.e. 'our' church – and regard other causes and religions as threats and rivals.

There is a simple test we can apply: does our faith in Christ draw us to the finest exemplars of other faiths, as (we may hope) their faith draws them to those people who best exemplify Christian faith? The life of C. F. Andrews provides a good illustration of the process. Andrews went as an ordained Anglican missionary to Delhi in 1904, and was quickly involved in dialogues with scholars of other faiths. Although he became estranged from his own Church, and even repudiated his priestly orders, he remained deeply Christian, and after nearly thirty years in India, wrote:

> Christ has become not less central, but more central; not less divine to me, but more so, because more universally human. I can see Him as the pattern of all that is best in Asia as well as in Europe.

Gandhi called Andrews 'love incarnate', and the Hindu scholar and poet, Rabindranath Tagore, wrote of him that 'nowhere had he seen "such a triumph of Christianity"'[2].

---

[2] Graham A. Patrick, *The Miners' Bishop: Brook Foss Westcott* (London: Epworth, 2004), pp. 165–6.

For Christians, Christ will be as central as that all-encompassing Reality we call God. But we dare not be so arrogant – especially when we encounter transparently holy people of other faiths – to assume that people who do not name Christ therefore do not know him. Bishop Westcott, one of the greatest biblical scholars of the nineteenth century, after describing the eternal Word as the 'spiritual sun' which enlightens everyone, goes on to say this of John 14.6: (No one comes to the Father but by me):

> It is only through Christ that we can ... apprehend God as the Father, and so approach the Father ... It does not follow that everyone who is guided by Christ is directly conscious of his guidance[3].

To return to the testimony of C. F. Andrews, his words about Christ are especially significant for our discussion:

> Christ [is] ... *not* less divine to me, but more so, *because* more universally human.

This is the vision which Christian preachers need in a world of many faiths. If we think of another faith as a rival or a threat, we need to pause. Of course, some Christians in some parts of the world are persecuted, even killed by the zealous adherents of other faiths. But there are forms of Christianity which make people zealous, intolerant and narrow, rather than generous, peaceable and compassionate. The task of the Christian preacher is clear: to respond courteously, humbly and generously to people of other faiths, and to remember the vital difference between evangelism and proselytizing. 'We shall never gain the non-Christian world until we treat its religions with justice, courtesy and love.' These are the words of a nineteenth century Christian who pioneered dialogue with Hinduism. Kenneth Cracknell, who quotes them in his book *Justice, Courtesy And Love: Theologians And Missionaries Encountering World Religions, 1846 to 1914* comments: 'No higher ideal could be set before Christians or anyone else...'[4].

Even in evangelism, preachers must not try too hard or expect quick results. It may be that, in God's own good time, new kinds of Christians will be formed out of the inter-faith dialogues which must increasingly take place, adding to the already rich diversity of the Church. In the meantime, there is much for Christians to make

---

[3] Patrick, *The Miners' Bishop*, p. 169.

[4] K. Cracknell, *Justice, Courtesy and Love: Theologians and Missionaries Encountering World Religions 1846–1914* (London: Epworth, 1995), p. 119.

amends for, including preaching which has had more religious zeal than Christlike love.

Finally in this section we come to the ideal of the Church of the Open Door. Such a church is always likely to attract an even greater diversity of people. One of the most striking cameos of an early church community is provided by St Paul when he envisages 'an unbeliever or outsider' coming into the middle of a Christian assembly, (1 Cor. 14.24–5). Domestic architecture of the first century and the Mediterranean climate helped to make that possible. In many countries today Sunday by Sunday churches make clear that everyone is welcome to their services of *public* worship. In Britain, some churches in recent years have tried to make their premises, and especially the entrance area, more attractive and accessible. So the presence of a newcomer, Christian or not, is an ever-present possibility.

The presence of people who do not yet share the faith is something devoutly to be prayed for, and therefore expected, and warmly welcomed. Indeed, our experience is that already in some churches there is a bewildering diversity of belief and range of views of the Bible (see Chapters 1, 6 and 11). The more the better. The issue is not whether these newcomers will fit in, and support the church in the way that 'we' have always done. More searchingly and creatively, these very different people will change and enrich the church they have begun to attend. The Church only fulfils its vocation when it embraces people who are different.

Again, the implications for preaching and its renewal are profound and far-reaching. Writing of the parable of the Labourers in the Vineyard (Mt. 20. 1–16), a New Testament scholar had this to say:

> The ... parable will not, probably, really spring to life again until we find ourselves once more in a situation of religious re-awakening. Any such awakening will bring into the Church those from outside ... many disreputable and undeserving. To them the truths of the Gospel will shine with a brilliance that we inside the churches have dulled with familiarity[5].

There is a chicken-and-egg situation here: will our preaching be renewed without 'the Gentiles' – that is, without the influx of people different from ourselves who will transform and deepen our understanding of the faith, the Bible, the Gospel? At the same time, the Church, whatever its situation, cannot simply wait on events.

---

[5] C. L. Mitton, 'Expounding the Parables : The Workers in the Vineyard', *The Expository Times*, 77 (1965–66), p. 910.

Preachers, too, need to examine their approach. It is deeply mistaken to imagine, in any situation, that they are preaching to the converted, or, for that matter, preaching to the unconverted. People's hearts and lives are not so neatly categorized. Admittedly, it is a challenging exercise to prepare a sermon which will be comprehensible and helpful to the seasoned churchgoer and the newcomer alike. But the attempt needs to be made.

Is this possible? Not always, perhaps. But a sermon on one of the great themes of the faith is likely to reach parts which many another sermon will not. A pep talk to the regulars is unlikely to do much for a newcomer, but a sermon on Christ the bread of life may. This brings us to a final theme in our exploration of the renewal of preaching.

## IV Hunger for the Gospel?

In our first chapter (section II) we asked the question 'Has preaching had its day?' We suggested that it was a uniquely personal form of communication ('truth through personality'), reflecting and even embodying the gospel of the incarnate and crucified Christ. It must therefore continue to have a central place in the life of the Church. But now we return to this question in order to consider it from a wider, global perspective. In the over-used language of our consumer societies, will there in the future be a renewed demand for the gospel? In many Christian circles today it is rare to hear talk of people being hungry for the Word of God. It is not easy to know whether people are or not. It would be unwise to jump to conclusions, and we must say the same of the wider world beyond the Church. But the question of humankind's spiritual hunger, rather than its religious hunger, is central to the future renewal of preaching.

Henri de Lubac was one of the great Roman Catholic theologians of the twentieth century. His ideas exercised a far-reaching influence at the Second Vatican Council of the 1960s. In a collection of his writings entitled *The Discovery of God*, de Lubac, after discussing the question of proof for the reality of God, goes on:

> ... it is never the proof which is lacking. What is lacking is a taste for God. The most distressing diagnosis that can be made of the present age, and the most alarming, is that, to all appearances at least, it has lost the taste for God[6].

More challenging still are his comments, drawing on Luther, on the human appetite for God. Unlike our appetite for food, which

---

[6] H. De Lubac, *The Discovery of God*, (Edinburgh : T. & T. Clark, 1996) p. 83.

becomes more insistent the more it is denied, our appetite for God, when it is not acknowledged or satisfied, grows fainter and fainter.

Is it possible that in the twenty-first century the Church in many places faces a situation in which, so far from preaching being renewed, the appetite for the Word of God fades away altogether? Could that ever happen? We should be wise not to jump to blandly optimistic answers. In a telling contrast with Psalm 139, (Where can I go from your spirit? v. 7), the prophet Amos envisages a time when people will hunger again for the Word of God but will not find it (Amos 8.11–12). Yet, dire though this warning is, the Bible also gives a picture of a God who does not easily give up even if we do. Some words of St Augustine give us hope that the human taste for God is not quickly or easily extinguished:

> Thou hast made us for Thyself, and our hearts are restless till they find their rest in Thee.

Even the restlessness of the world's growing number of consumerist societies may be testimony to the truth of Augustine's words, and to the words of the Deuteronomist, quoted by Jesus in the wilderness:

> One does not live by bread alone' ... (Mt. 4.4).

So should a preacher expect to be faced by people who are hungry – or not? The reality is likely to be complex. In many congregations there will be people who are hungry for a life-giving word, and know it, as well as people who are hungry but don't know it, looking for something, but they are not quite sure what. There may also be people whose taste for God has been dangerously blunted by familiarity with religion and the Church. But it is possible, for all kinds of reasons, that the twenty-first century will see, in many parts of the world, a renewed hunger for the Word of God .

So our quest for the renewal of preaching and of the Church brings us to the only adequate foundation and resource for both – namely the eternal God, memorably described to me by a colleague as 'the Church's ultimate non-declining resource'.

As our discussion of the renewal of preaching and of the Church concludes, two points seem to be worth making. Our perceptions of God are not exempt from change, and Christian preachers must speak of the mystery of God with due awe and even reticence. We simply cannot assume that what we understand by the word 'God' will be shared by all members of our congregations. The Christian world, as we have noted before, is still coming to terms, more than 150 years after its publication, with Charles Darwin's *Origin of the Species*.

The effect of this controversy, like so many others of the modern and post-modern eras, has prompted many Christians to rethink the very nature of God, God's relationship with the world, and God's presence within it. During the first decade of this century, God was, so to speak, in the news a great deal. The reasons for this were many, notably the connection between religion and terrorism, and the tragic number of religious conflicts across the world. Such conflicts have been a conspicuous feature of human history for many centuries. But in this century, as in the preceding one, God has been in the dock more than perhaps ever before[7]. So truly Christian preaching, so far from having had its day, is urgently needed if human hearts need to find, as St Augustine recognized, their true rest, and a fractured world needs to find the peace towards which the gospel of Christ invites us all.

The theologian John Macquarrie somewhere suggests that God is more a verb than a noun. Of course, God does not fit into any neat grammatical definition, but that intriguing remark captures an important truth about the mystery of God. The Bible's fondness for referring to God as 'the living God' points us in the same direction. It brings us back to the heart of preaching: it is an event in which people encounter God. But Christian preachers can hardly speak of God without also speaking of Jesus. The story of Jesus brings us to the heart of the Christian proclamation and of the Christian preacher's own spirituality. 'We preach Christ crucified' (1 Cor. 1.23). But as St Paul well knew, the preacher not only proclaims the cross, but seeks to live it. How else could such a proclamation ring true? Preachers, like all Christians, seek to make the cross of Christ their own, interiorly and externally, in whatever ways their life and circumstances require. The cross – and only the cross – is the way to resurrection and to the rediscovery of hope for the Church and the wider world. The cross and resurrection of Christ, lived and proclaimed, are also the road to the renewal of preaching and the renewal of the Church.

*Conclusion*

We return to where this chapter began: one Lord, one Church, one order of preachers. The Edinburgh Conference of 1910 was a landmark in ecumenism. In this still-young century, perhaps we may hope for another kind of renewal: the renewal of preaching. The missiological task before the Church is enormous and urgent. An

---

[7] God in the Dock – 1492 to the Present' is the title, borrowed from C. S. Lewis, of the final part of MacCulloch's *History* (pp. 769–1016).

effective ecumenical preaching force has unique and vital contributions to make to the task. Why should there not be a new ecumenical movement of preachers, committed to resourcing and sustaining their costly, irreplaceable ministry? A struggling Church and a broken world together need the Living Word.

# APPENDIX I: COMMITMENT, CHALLENGE AND FAITH

These are revised notes from which George Lovell preached a sermon at Lidgett Park Methodist Church in 2005. The original notes were used in Project Two in the discussion on 'educative and preparative preaching' (see Chapter 11). It is an example of 'process preaching' (Chapter 5) and the kind of sermon that can be helpful to people who differ significantly in belief and faith (see Chapters 1 and 11 on 'preaching to diversity').

---

### CHALLENGES TO FAITH

Faith and trust are complex aspects of human and spiritual life. They come and go, often unpredictably or inexplicably. During the week we buried a dear friend. While knowing she had cancer she had nursed her daughter who died of the same condition and left two small grandchildren in New Zealand. Through it all her faith had deepened. Similar experiences have destroyed people's faith and sometimes made them bitter. Faith often seems to be vulnerable and at times a fickle factor in human and spiritual life, seemingly beyond our control. It is a gift to be received and at times sadly to be lost.

Some of the things that can cause us to re-examine our faith are exciting but also ethically and theologically divisive. For instance, stem cell research promises sensational new cures but is controversial. There are many things that Christians can find challenging: radical reinterpretations of Christianity and its biblical basis; arguments about the moral and legal issues related to the Iraq war; natural disasters such as earthquakes; evil human actions. Such disturbing events can raise difficult questions about the existence and character of a God of love. Recently, as I have grappled with the issues with varying degrees of success, I have been reviewing my approach to living and working with these challenges. Basically it is open and critical while holding to the integrity of my experience of the Christian faith. This sermon is about ways of tackling tricky questions on the assumption that making the processes transparent and accessible helps us to engage in the dialogues and tensions between faith and doubt, belief and unbelief and to respond to God who is a God of truth and to Jesus who is a medium of truth.

### APPROACHES TO HANDLING CHALLENGES TO FAITH

Now to consider some of the things that hinder us from facing challenges to our faith and some of those that help us to engage creatively with them.

Being defensive is one of the things to avoid. Taking refuge in orthodoxy or fundamentalism and becoming conservative does not help because it involves living in one part only of the real world. When taken to extremes, defensiveness can produce a phenomenon known as 'groupthink'. This extremely dangerous process occurs when groups turn in on themselves and become highly cohesive, develop a sense of invulnerability, pressurize dissenters to conform, ignore and discredit any contrary thinking, on the basis of their belief in the inherent morality of the group. Research suggests that this process blinded the Americans to intelligence about the vulnerability of Pearl Harbour and possibly the British to warnings about the Iraq war. Sadly, signs of it are to be seen in Christianity and other faiths.

### ENGAGING IN CREATIVE PROCESSES

Aspects of the approach I adopt are something like this. Those things to which I am committed, and which I have found to be reliable, form the base from which I explore challenges and doubts: to change the metaphor, they anchor me in a particular religious and spiritual place. The things which give me security are variously conceptual and relational: my Christian faith; my relationship with God through Christ; those people I love and trust, with whom I can engage when we agree and disagree; the means of grace and Christian fellowship; study. At best, these give me the stability, poise and confidence to explore things about which I am suspicious or apprehensive because I am not sure where they will take me. Such explorations can lead to affirming and deepening my faith and beliefs or to questioning and modifying them.

Professor Russell Hindmarsh, a brilliant physicist, described how in his scientific work he experienced conceptual cycles: everything seemed complex and he couldn't see how they fitted together. Then he would discover what he called 'simplicities' – insights or concepts or hypotheses – that enabled him to work on the complexities. But then, he found, things took new forms of disorder and chaos until other simplicities emerged. He went on to say that he had similar experiences in his spiritual life. High dividends accrue from establishing simplicities and reshaping them as new complexities unfold. They are trustworthy instruments. A simplicity that unlocked ethical complexities for Albert Schweitzer, for instance, was reverence for life. Much of my ministry has been based on a similar simplicity, reverence for human freedom. Jesus was a master of simplicities. The Beatitudes contain some of them: 'Blessed are the gentle; they shall have the earth for their possession.' – not those who rape it. He immortalized them in his sayings: 'Seek and you shall find.' 'Pay to Caesar what belongs to Caesar, and to God what belongs to God.' And he set them like jewels in parables.

Engaging in creative processes is one of the great joys and privileges of life. As a twenty-year-old apprentice engineer I left an engineering firm in Lancashire to work at the Royal Aircraft Establishment in Hampshire. It was a transition from a working culture constricted by tradition to one committed to experiment, exploration and research. It was an exhilarating experience, which re- shaped my life in ways surpassed only by my subsequent experience of the mind and free spirit of Jesus and living and exploring life with the risen Christ.

## THE RISK FACTOR

There are risks in defensiveness: our faith may atrophy or become inadequate to contemporary Christian living. But there are also risks in the critical exploration of human and spiritual experience. We may lose our faith or find it inadequate and have to rebuild it; we could be converted to another faith and lose religious friends. It is important that these risks are acknowledged and faced. A short time ago, I preached enthusiastically about engaging in interfaith dialogue. After the service a lady said to me that she agreed with the sermon but that I ought to mention the risks, because, when she first got involved in interfaith dialogue, she experienced a devastating crisis of faith. Whatever the outcome, our humanity and integrity as Christians requires us to take the not inconsiderable risks circumspectly, trusting in the foundations of our faith and that our risk-taking God will accompany us. The approach outlined is one of the ways to do so, which can reward us with new insights and a deeper faith.

### WORKING TOGETHER AT THE CHALLENGES AND OPPORTUNITIES

The great value of the suggested way of thinking through things is that all of us can use it to work at our faith concerns in our own way and in our own time. It is important that we be encouraged to do so as far as we are able. Our personal faith development depends upon it. At the same time, it is essential that those who are able to tackle the big questions facing Christianity and its development must do so for their own sake, and on behalf of the whole church and the society in which it is set. It would be unrealistic to suggest that this is an activity in which all Christians should participate equally, even though it must be the responsibility of the whole church. The church has several responsibilities. First, it must encourage and help all of us to work at our own faith development. Secondly, it must allow, commission, resource and support those pioneering new thinking and work. Thirdly, it must evaluate what emerges and become the custodian of that which is important to its ministry and mission in the world: it must see that it is used, just as technology puts to common use the findings of science. Among other things, doing this involves educating its members about new concepts and encouraging them to become involved in informed ways in new forms of ministry and mission as they evolve.

### THE MESSINESS OF DEVELOPMENT

But it does not normally happen in such a tidy way. Kenneth Cracknell\*, tells the stories of some missionaries who in the second part of the nineteenth century and the early part of the twentieth began a dialogue with people of other faiths and to research their religions in order to understand them and deepen their relationships with them. This was an incredible development at a time when it was

---

\* K. Cracknell, *Justice, Courtesy and Love: Theologians and Missionaries Encountering World Religions* (London: Epworth Press,1995)

common practice to be dismissive of other religions. They were criticized by missionary authorities and pressed to revert to traditional forms of missionary work. The issues were debated at the Edinburgh Missionary Conference of 1910. Now, as we approach the centenary of that Conference, we are, thank God, in a new religious world of interfaith dialogue. Hans Küng is in no doubt about its importance:

> No peace among the nations
>
> without peace among the religions
>
> No peace among the religions
>
> without dialogue between the religions
>
> No dialogue between the religions
>
> without investigation of the foundations of the religions.**

In messy ways, therefore, the Church moves forward. Inevitably, there are tensions and conflicts between those with new insights and those who oppose and resist them, and there can be uneasy relationships between traditionalists and those who pioneer new areas of work, ministry and mission. At best the dialectic between opposing groups is creative, if not in the short term, then in the long term; at worst, it is painful and destructive. However, I believe that the Church will be most true to itself, and most effective in its ministry and mission, if it engages in and promotes, in secular and religious organizations, the creative processes to which this sermon testifies.

## Conclusion: Faith and Witness

Exploring challenges to belief in the way described in this sermon is much more than an exercise of the mind or emotional intelligence, although it is all of that: it is a journey in faith taken within the providence of God. I believe that God has made us for faith and for exploration. Our mandate, deeply embedded in God and the scriptures, can be expressed in several texts or profound spiritual simplicities: God is a 'God of truth'. Jesus is the 'way, the truth and the life.' The Holy Spirit 'will guide us into all the truth.' 'You will know the truth and the truth will set you free.'*** So we can engage with confidence and humility, on our own and with all people, whatever

---

** Hans Küng, *Global Responsibility: In Search of New World Ethic* (SCM – Canterbury Press, 1992).

*** Ps. 31.5; Jn 14.6, 16.13, 8.32.

their beliefs might be, in exploring and reflecting on anything and everything, including the nature of God in the light of our beliefs in open and transparent ways. God give us courage to do that. Amen

# APPENDIX II: WHAT JESUS WANTED MOST FOR HIS CHURCH

(A sermon preached by Neil Richardson in Christian Unity Week, January 2010. The Bible readings were Rom. 14.1–12 and Jn 17.20–26).

'Close your eyes and wish', my parents used to say, and my twin sister and I would each grasp one end of the Christmas turkey wishbone, close our eyes, and wish. Suppose all of us here in church this evening said to each other 'Close your eyes and make three wishes for your church', what would you wish for? A financial windfall to pay for repairs? Some younger people? Life-long immunity from all the hymns and songs you most dislike singing?

But before you wish, recall the prayer of Jesus in St John's gospel, and ask yourself what *he* wanted most for his Church. On the evidence of this prayer, there can be no doubt it was – it is – our unity. Three times in all, Jesus prayed for the unity of his Church, more than for any other single thing.

Our unity, according to this prayer, is the acid test of our spiritual health. (Jesus prayed for other things too, but his prayer seems to imply that everything else will be included in the unity he envisages.) We tend to think that growth – or evangelism leading to growth – is *the* sign of a church in glowing health. That's how a business measures success: growth, and more growth: 'wider still and wider shall thy bounds be set'.

Some of us might prefer a more austere measure of our church's health: toeing the party line, whether that's the tradition of the whole Church, or the teaching of the Bible. The problem is: we tend to have different party lines, including different interpretations of the Bible's teaching.

St Paul knew of churches split down the middle. The conscience of some Christians allowed them to eat anything; not so the conscience of others. At this distance in time we might wonder if that wasn't all rather trivial. If we had lived then, we wouldn't have thought so. But

Paul was adamant: this was not a church-dividing issue, any more than the issues which divide us today should be church-dividing issues. 'Accept one another, as Christ accepted you'. That's how Paul begins and ends the argument.

Does anything go, then, in the Church of Christ? No, certainly not: we can't agree to differ on whether God exists, or whether God raised Jesus from the dead. But if I worship God with, and share Holy Communion with, someone who tells me he is a Christian, and who patently seeks to live in love and charity with his neighbour, but who, on some question of Christian conduct or biblical interpretation, conscientiously differs from me, how dare I say 'You're not a proper Christian!'? When, by God's grace, we all get to heaven, then we shall know, (and that is part of Paul's argument). Until then, 'accept one another'.

Time and again, the New Testament makes our unity, differences and all, *the* benchmark of our spiritual health. And if that is so, no wonder that our unity is what Jesus wanted most for us. 'I pray for them that they may all be one, as you Father are in me, and I in you, that they too may be in us'. That seems to mean: draw closer to God, and we will draw closer to each other. And if *that* is true, then the converse must be true: if we're not really united, not really close to each other, then how can we be close to God? The writings in the New Testament which bear the name 'John' tell us again and again that loving God and loving each other go inseparably together.

This is not about uniformity, or just being nice to each other. It's not about take-overs, as if two churches should behave like two ailing building societies: 'Which one is going to survive?' 'Which one is going to take over the other?' This is about relationships, unity, *and love*.

> May they be one – *as we are one*.

As the Church of Jesus, we know what we are called to be: one holy catholic and apostolic Church. But we cannot realize one of those four traditional 'notes' (as they are called) of the Church, without realizing the other three. We can't become holy, or truly apostolic, or fully catholic, without at the same time becoming one.

There was a Christian of the twentieth century whose life story was a parable of ecumenism. When Thomas Merton entered a monastery in Kentucky, in the USA as a young man, he seems to have taken a rather dim view of the world he thought he was leaving behind. But as he grew in the life of faith and of holiness, his attitude changed.

He *lived* the prayer of Jesus, and the closer he drew to God, the closer he drew to God's people.

Is it really surprising that that unity is what Jesus wanted most for his Church? And that that unity is the acid test of our spiritual health?

*And the means of evangelizing the world.* According to the prayer of Jesus, Christian unity will be the means by which the world will be brought to Christ:

> ... may they all be one, ... so that the world may believe.

Like our three wishes for our churches, this is not what most of us would say. 'Lively modern hymns or songs: that is what will bring the punters in!' Or perhaps a skateboarding ramp in the nave for teenagers?! Or good marketing, slick publicity: isn't this the way to promote a business, and to get a message across? Why ever does the prayer of Jesus link our *unity* with the world coming to faith? But it does – like some earlier words of Jesus in this gospel:

> By this will everyone know that you are my disciples, if you have love among yourselves.

And it happens. It happens when we gladly and amicably share premises, like the Catholics and Methodists of Nelson in Lancashire, who came together a few years ago to build the first Catholic-Methodist church in the country. It happens when, in many places, Christians form themselves into teams of street pastors looking out for people – especially young people – needing help on Friday and Saturday evenings in our town- and city-centres.

But the prayer of Jesus takes us deeper – deeper than simply what we may do together: it is not just about mission strategies, and using resources more effectively – important though these are. The evangelization of the world is the consequence of being grounded together in the life of the Father and the Son:

> as you (Father) are in me and I in you, so may they be in us, so that the world may believe.

As Thomas Merton grew in holiness – sharing in the life of the Father and the Son – he involved himself in the healing of the world. For example, his was one of the first voices to sound the alarm about the ecological degradation of the planet. It seems the closer we come to God the more we become concerned with saving the world, rather than saving the Church.

## Appendix II: What Jesus Wanted Most For His Church

But the unity Jesus wants for us is not only a sure sign of our spiritual health and the means of evangelizing the world. It is also an expression of the very glory of God:

> the glory you gave me I gave them, that they may be one, as we are one.

In the mind of the evangelist, there was no doubt where that glory shone most brightly: paradox of all paradoxes, it shone most brightly in a crucifixion: having loved his own, he loved them to the end – to a triumphant conclusion.

I have caught glimpses of this glory: in the generosity, resilience and even joy of Christians in Sierra Leone as they sought to rebuild their Church and their country after a terrible civil war. I saw it in the warm hospitality a church in Liverpool extended to a young man suffering from Tourette's syndrome. 'The glory you gave me, I gave to them …'

*Why* is our unity what Jesus wanted most for his Church? The answer is as searching as it is simple: God is love. We see it most clearly in the darkness of a cross: God broken on the cross of the world, and yet in the darkness of evil and death, God in the mystery of his love – Father, Son and Holy Spirit abides, undivided and undefeated:

> May they be one, as we are One.

The Gospel *is* unity. It is no wonder that that is what Jesus wanted most for his Church.

# *INDEX OF SUBJECTS*

Authority
   of Bible 6, 88–91, 103–4
   of Church 6
   of preacher 5–7

Bible (see also 'Old Testament')
   authority 6, 88–91, 103–4
   bible-reading notes 87
   canon 89–90
   commentaries 113–8
   conflicting views of 88–90
   ignorance of 18, 27
      interpreting 106–08, 111–13, 202–04
   revelation 90–1
   texts and contexts 111–18
   translations 18, 104–5
Brain patterns 70

Christianity
   changing nature of 198–9
   future of 225
   incarnational character of 198, 202, 204
Christian tradition
   diversity of 198, 205–6
   fragmentation of 18
Church
   authority 6
   calling 110
   catholicity 220
   four notes of 214
   missing generation 95–7
   nature 71–2
   renewal of 213–4
   unity and diversity of 220, 234–7
Circularity 183

Communication 8–9
Congregations 71–82, 178, 179–80, 183–5
   challenges 77–9
   characteristics 72–4
   and churches 71
   dialogues with 24–8
   diversity 10, 18–19, 88, 91–4, 105, 188, 220
   missiological functions 75
   nature of 71–7
   objections to Bible 26–7
   profiling them 80–1, 183–5
   secondary 74, 178
   services offered 74–5
   studying them 79–82
   symbolic boundaries 73
Conversations 184

Diagrams see Modelling

Ecumenism 212–3, 226–7
Edinburgh Missionary Conferences 212, 226
Evangelism 221, 234, 236–7

Facilitating
   facilitators 174–5
   local development programmes 157–172, 192–5
   questions 143–5
   structures 167–8
Faith
   challenges to 228–9
   handling challenge 229–32
Feedback
   carefully solicited 64

240                Sustaining Preachers and Preaching

casually solicited 62–4
reflecting guidelines 63
self-feedback 61–2
understanding of 65–6
unsolicited 62
Fellowship (*koinonia*) 194

God
  appetite for 224–5
  encountering 92
  language about 17–8, 225–6
  listening to 30, 217–9
  nature and purpose 2–3, 12–3, 20
  preaching, subject of 9, 21
Gospel
  hunger for 224–6
  of Jesus Christ 14
  *Overhearing* 96–7
  subject of preaching 9, 226
  world-saving 3

Hermeneutics 185–6, 202–3
Hermeneutic circle 107–8, 186, 202–3
Holy Spirit
  and renewal of preaching 213

In-service training 157, 162, 173–95
Interpersonal support 147–56, 190–1
  abilities of preachers 169–70
  appraisal 151
  approach to 138–9
  assessment 151
  audit 151
  catalysts 150
  coaching 150–1
  consultancy 148–150
  enablers 150
  evaluation 151
  co-consultancy 148–50
  facilitative 150
  facilitative structures 143–4, 145
  group support 152
  journalling 145
  learning from 154–5
  learning styles 141–3
  mentoring 151
  modelling 146–7

nature of 136
need for 135–6
needs 141–2
needs met 154
objectivity 139–40
peer support 148
recording 145–6
reflective writing 144–6
rigour of 139–43
self-support 143–7
services xi, 135–6, 137–8
soul friends 148
spiritual direction 152–3
subjectivity 139–40
supervision 152
supporters 170–2
systems 154–6
triple-loop learning 155
uses 155–6
using support systems 169
work reviews 151

Jesus
  difficult sayings of 111
  High-Priest 116–7
  his use of Scripture 110
  ministry of 210
  other world faiths 221–23
  resurrection of 206–7
  story of 205
  subject of preaching 13, 31, 110
  transfiguration of 117–8, 120, 123
Journalling 69, 145

Learning
  experiential 154–5
  styles 141–3
  triple-loop 155
Lectionary 3, 26–7, 103–7
Listening 107–8, 111, 217–9
Local development programme 173–95
  approach 192–3
  design 192–4
  developmental projects 185–90
  effective programmes 179
  establishing needs 142, 161–2,
    177–8

# Index of Subjects

ethnic issues 179–80, 187
facilitators 162–8
felt-needs 178
general relevance 194–5
meeting needs 142, 161–2
overview 176
preachers' abilities 169–70
principles 192
profiling congregations 183–5
programme criteria 179
programmes 158–62, 194–5
self-organizing groups 181–3, 185
study days 175, 176, 182–3
study, praxis and fellowship 194
training needs 142, 160–2

Mentoring 151
Modelling 146–7
  depicting 146–7
Myers Briggs Indicators 140–1

Needs (cf Training needs)
Non-directive approach 163–4, 165–6

Old Testament
  as Hebrew scriptures 109
  importance of 108–9
  in the New Testament 109–10
  preaching from 108–10, 114–5, 120, 122–3

Post-modernity 17–18
Preachers
  and Bible study (see 'Bible' and 'Dialogues')
  appraisal 151
  assessment 151
  busyness of 2, 84–5
  call of 5–6
  coaching 150–1
  co-consultancy 148–50
  colleagues 24, 86–7, 99, 216
    (see also 'dialogues')
  consultancy 148–50
  dialogues
    shared bible study 26–7, 87, 106–7

with congregations 24–8
with other world faiths 217–19
with wider world 219–22
discipline of 3–95
ecumenical order of 212, 227
group support 152
Internet 85, 87
journalling 145
learning needs 203–4
learning styles 141–3
life cycle (see vocational life cycle)
listening to God – see under 'Listening'
love for congregations 7, 16, 97, 214
members of God's 'laity' 23
mentoring 151
needs 141–2
objectivity 139–40
peer support 148
prayers of 7, 29–3–2, 85–6, 214
preparation 22, 85–6
pressures on 2–3, 84–8
professionalism 44–5
professionals 246
private and public 49–52
private work 43–4, 47–52, 178
private work abilities 50
public work 43–4, 47–52, 178
public work abilities 50
recording 145–6
reflective practitioners 68, 215–6
reflective writing 144–6
relationship with congregation 9, 24–6, 97, 121–2, 214–6
resourcing 21, Ch. 9 *passim*
self-support 143–7
spiritual direction 152–3
spirituality of 29–32, 32, 85, 97, 217
soul friends 148
study 38–9, 40
  with others 32–4
subjectivity 139–40
supervision 152
supporters 170–2
support (see Interpersonal support)

triple-loop learning 155
using support systems 169
vocation 36–7
vocational flow 46 cf 55–60
work reviews 151
Preacher's life cycle see Vocational life cycle
Preaching
    adaptability of 95–7, 210
    and diversity 188
    aims of 7–9, 100–1
    authority of 5–7
    biblical 6, 11, 92–3, Ch.7 *passim*, 123, 217, 219
    biblical variety of 11
    challenge 1, 2, 18
    circle see Preaching circle
    communication 8–10
    confidence in 12
    contextual 205, 207–10, 217
    continuity in 205–7
    controversial issues 98–9
    core activity 4, 11, 13, 15, 19–20
    crisis in 2–4
    decline 2–4, 120
    definition
    a discipline 33
    to diversity 188
    ecumenical movement 212–3
    effective 4, 24
    Epistle 110, 115–7
    existential event 11, 59
    faiths, other 219–24
    feedback (see Feedback and Preaching circle)
    future of 4, 10–20, 211, Ch. 12 *passim*, 214–24
    Gospel 110–1, 117–8
    human character of 5, 13–4
    importance of ix
    misconceptions about 4–9
    misunderstanding of 4–7
    nature of vii, 8–9, 11–15, 96–7, 99–101, 200–2, 211–12, 215–19
    new culture of 32, 214–19
    Old Testament 108–10, 115–7
    outcomes of 100–2, 221

preparation 54–58
professionalism 216–17
qualifications for 5–6, 36
    (see also under 'Preachers', 'prayers of' 'love for congregations' etc.)
rationale for viii
renewal of 20–1, Ch. 13 *passim*
self-effacing nature 13, 92, 99, 107, 128–9
service of listeners 121–2
simplistic/simplicity 200–1, 217, 230
state of
strangeness of 4
teaching, and 9
'truth through personality' 11–13
uncertainty about 3
'weakness' of 14, 210–11
vocation 36–37
vocational flow 46, cf 55–60
and worship ix
Preaching circle 53–70, 177 178
    feedback sequence 60–6
    preaching sequence 58–60
    preparation sequence 54–8
    reflection sequence 66–70
Preaching ministry 35
Preaching projects 185–90
Problem solving 168
Process preaching 78–9, Appendix I
Professionalism 44–5

Questions 65, 167

Reader-response criticism 112
Recording 145–6
Redaction –criticism 117
Reflection 68–70, 177 (cf Thinking)
Reflective writing 144–6
Repentance 100
Resurrection 206–7

Self support 143–7 (see Support)
Sermons
    case studies 114–8
    conclusions 129
    context of 133

## Index of Subjects

delivery 131–2, 215
examples 228–37
form of 124–5, 204
illustrations 146–9
introductions 127–8
perceived as monologues 24–6
structure 124
style 125–67, 204
summary of 124
through history 10
title for 124–5
traditional 4, 8, 14–5
world of work 28, 95
writing of 129–31
Simplicities 200–1, 217, 230
Soul friends 148
Spiritual direction 152–3
Sundays 16, 94
Supervision 152
Support (see Interpersonal support)
Symbolic boundaries 73

Talking work 145, 165–6
Thinking moods and modes 66–8
Training needs
   establishing them 142, 160–2, 177–8
   meeting them 142, 161–2
Triple-loop learning 155

Vocation 36, 44–5
Vocational life cycle 35–47
   death and resurrection 42
   inaugural phase 37–9
   latent phase 36–7
   model 43–7
   phases 36–42
   preaching phase 39–41
   professionalism 44–5
   retirement phase 41–2
   transitions 37–9
   use of 46–7
   vocation 44–5

Work reviews 151
World
   advances in science and technology 4
   attitudes to authority 19
   changing nature of 15–19, 95, 102, Ch. 12
   communication, theories of 8–9
   human beings, nature of 3, 12, 207
   language 17
   media 19, 93, 204, 219
   other world faiths 198, 219–24, 231–32
   preaching, subject of 97–9

Writing (see Reflective writing)

# *INDEX OF AUTHORS*

Amos, Claire 114 n.8
Argyle, Michael 145
Aristotle, 35

Batten, M.142, 164
Batten, T.R. 142, 164
Biddle, Loureide T. 181
Biddle, William W. 181
Blakeslee, Thomas R. 143
Bonhoeffer, Dietrich 30 n.7, 31 n.8
Braxton, Brad R. 16
Briggs, Myers 140, 141
Brooks, Phillips 20–1
Browne, R.E.C. (Charles) 90, 100, 126
Brueggemann, Walter 106 n.3
Buzan, Barry 69
Buzan, Terry 69

Cameron, Helen 76
Campbell, Alastair V. 152
Caplan, Gerald 137
Caplan, Killilea 137
Caussade de Jean-Pierre 29, 30 n.6
Chak, Man-Kuen 155
Clutterbuck, D. 150, 151
Cobb, John xi
Cohen, Anthony P. 73
Copley, David 149
Cracknell, Kenneth 222, 231
Craddock, Fred 93, 97, 125, 210 n.13

Davies, Douglas 76
Deeks, David 99
Dollard, John 144
Donovan, Vincent J. 14

Forsyth, Peter T. 27, 31 n.9
Ford, David 208
Fowler, James 35
Francis, Leslie 140, 141
Friedman, Edwin 76
Frieze, Catherine 177

Glasson, Barbara 218
Green, Laurie 53
Green, Robin 75
Grundy, Malcolm 76

Hampton, David 94
Hardy, Daniel W. 200
Hartner, A. and Eschmann, H. P.8 nn.1–2
Harris, Margaret 76
Henriot, Peter 53
Hill, David 26
Hindmarsh, Russell 230
Holland, Joe 53
Honey, Peter 143
Hopewell, J. 76
Hustler, J. 10, 15, 121 n.1, 204

Isaacs, Nathan 35

Jackson, Peter 150
Jacobs, Michael 151
Janis, Irving L. 15
Johnson, Luke T. P.86 n.1

Keck, Leander E. 101
Koestler, Arthur 68
Kohlberg, Lawrence 35
Küng, Hans 232

Leech, Kenneth 153
Lovell, George 47, 60, 63, 64, 67, 140, 145, 147, 149, 150, 153, 155, 160, 161, 168, 169, 180, 183, 184, 228
Lubac de, Henri 224

MacCulloch, Diarmaid 198–9, 226
Mann, Leon 155
McKay, Richard 144
Mitchison, Naomi 30
Mitton, Leslie C. 223
Morgan, Gareth 155
Mumford, Alan 143

New, Charles 149

O'Connor, Margaret 144
Outler, Albert 27

Palmer, Barry 76
Patrick, Graham A. 221, 222
Piaget, Jean 35
Plummer, Ken 144
Progoff, Ira 145

Ramsay, Ian 146
Richardson, Neil G. 96 n.10
Richter, Philip 76
Rico, Gabriele Lusser 143

Riesman, David 138
Robinson, Marilynne 69

Saarinen, Martin F. 35, 36, 76
St Ignatius of Loyola 68
Schon, Donald 68
Schweitzer, Albert 230
Sellner, Edward 148
Shaw, Patricia 184
Smail, David 70, 140 166
Smith, M.K. 152
Snell, Robin 155
Stacey, John 11
Stewart, James S. 129 n.7, 207

Thistleton, Anthony C. 122 n.2, 203
Thurian, Max 153
Tisdale, Leonara Tubbs 73, 76, 81
Traherne, Thomas 12
Tugwell, Simon 132 n.9

Vautrey, Anne 177

Wakefield, Gordon 36
Ward, Francis 76
Ward, Keith 89 n.2, 90 nn.4, 5 and 6, 106 n.4 211
Wenham, Gordon J. 114 n.9
Wilson, John 35

# BIBLICAL REFERENCES

| *Old Testament* | | | *New Testament* | | |
|---|---|---|---|---|---|
| Genesis | 14.18–20 | 116 | Matthew | 1.23 | 109 |
| | 27.32, 41–45 | 114 | | 2.6 | 110 |
| | 32.22–31 | 114–5, 120 | | 4.4 | 225 |
| | 32.30 | 115 | | 5.1 | 118 |
| | 33.1–17 | 114 | | 5.41 | 127 |
| | 33.3, 10–11 | 115 | | 5.44 | 127 |
| | | | | 5–7 | 25 |
| Exodus | 19.20, 25 | 22 | | 7.28–9 | 6 |
| | 34.30 | 118 | | 10.37 | 27 |
| | | | | 15.29–31 | 118 |
| Leviticus 16 | | 116 | | 16.13–28 | 118 |
| | | | | 16.24–25 | 123 |
| 1 Kings 22.48 | | 5 | | 17.1–9 | 117f |
| | | | | 17.4 | 124 |
| Psalm | 22 | 218 | | 18.20 | 26, 113 |
| | 31.5 | 233 | | 20.1–16 | 223 |
| | 137 | 111 | | 28.16–20 | 118 |
| | 139 | 225 | Mark | 1.12–15 | 22 |
| Isaiah | 7.14 | 109 | | 4.30–32 | 111 |
| | 40–55 | 111 | | 6.30–44 | 122 |
| | 55.11 | 42 | | 9.4 | 117 |
| | | | | 9.6 | 118 |
| Ezekiel | 1.1 | 22 | | 10.25 | 111 |
| | 8.1 | 22 | | 13.11 | 130 |
| Hosea | 11.3–4 | 199 | Luke | 4.16–31 | 11 |
| | 12.3–4 | 114 | | 9.1–6 | 22 |
| | | | | 9.28–36 | 22 |
| Amos | 8.11–12 | 225 | | 10.25–37 | 25, 101 |
| | | | | 10.27 | 127 |
| Micah | 5.2 | 110 | | 12.15 | 208 |
| | | | | 13.21–1 | 92 |
| *The Apocrypha* | | | | 14.26 | 27 |
| Ecclesiasticus 50.1–21 | | 116 | | 18.25, 27 | 111 |
| | | | | 18.35–43 | 111 |

|  |  |  |  |  |
|---|---|---|---|---|
|  | 19.1–10 | 112 |  | 15.58 | 42 |
|  | 19.11 | 112 |  |  |  |
|  |  |  | 2 Corinthians |  |  |
| John | 2.4 | 104 |  | 2.13 | 22 |
|  | 3.9 | 213 |  | 3.7–18 | 118 |
|  | 8.32 | 12, 232 |  | 4.5 | 13, 121 |
|  | 9 | 219 |  | 7.6 | 22 |
|  | 10.10 | 7 |  | 12.2 | 129 |
|  | 14.6 | 12, 222, 232 |  | 12.7–10 | 129 |
|  | 16.13 | 119, 232 |  |  |  |
|  |  |  | Galatians | 1.10 | 96 |
| Acts | 1.14 | 214 |  | 1.17 | 22 |
|  | 1.18–26 | 214 |  | 2.16 | 89 |
|  | 2.14–36 | 25 |  | 4.4–6 | 205 |
|  | 9 | 130 |  |  |  |
|  | 17.16, 17 | 25, 218 | Ephesians | 3.20–1 | 88 |
|  | 17.22–31 | 25, 103, 188 |  | 4.29 | 165 |
|  | 17.28 | 201 |  |  |  |
|  | 19.8–10 | 11 | Philippians | 2.5–11 | 107 |
| Romans | 3.8 | 96 | Colossians | 3.18–4.1 | 127 |
|  | 11.32 | 90 |  | 3.18 | 17 n.7 |
|  | 12.5 | 24, 32 |  |  |  |
|  | 14.1–15.7 | 220 | 1 Thessalonians 1.1 |  | 22 |
|  | 1–12 | 234 |  | 1.9–10 | 205 |
|  | 16.7 | 16–17 |  |  |  |
|  |  |  | 1 Timothy | 4.10 | 90 |
| 1 Corinthians |  |  |  |  |  |
|  | 1.12 | 220 | Hebrews | 1.3 | 117 |
|  | 1.17 | 126 |  | 2.10–11 | 116 |
|  | 1.23 | 205, 226 |  | 2.17–18 | 116 |
|  | 2.1–5 | 126 |  | 4.14–10.18 | 116 |
|  | 2.3 | 14 |  | 4.14–16 | 116 |
|  | 4.17 | 22 |  | 5.1–6 | 116 |
|  | 8–10 | 96, 127 |  | 5.5–6 | 116 |
|  | 8.6 | 204 |  | 7.25 | 117 |
|  | 9.6 | 22 |  | 10.20 | 117 |
|  | 9.19–23 | 96, 188 |  | 13.8 | 200 |
|  | 11.5 | 17 n.7 |  |  |  |
|  | 13 | 32 | James | 2.26 | 89 |
|  | 13.12 | 202 |  |  |  |
|  | 14.24–5 | 223 | 1 John | 2.4 | 32 |
|  | 14.34 | 17.n.7 |  | 2.9 | 32 |
|  | 15.3 | 205 |  | 4.20 | 32 |
|  | 15.35–58 | 206 |  |  |  |